CW01261795

Kate Bush

A Visual Biography

Laura Shenton

Photo credits:
P6-7, P46, P48-67, P71-78: Empire Theatre, Liverpool © Alan Perry Concert Photography; P8-9, P30, P32-33, P36-39: Performing 'Wuthering Heights' in 1978 © Pictorial Press Ltd / Alamy Stock Photo; P10: March 1978 © Trinity Mirror / Mirrorpix / Alamy Stock Photo; P16-20, P192: Blandford W10 film studio, Ladbroke Grove, London 1978 © John Henshall / Alamy Stock Photo; P25, P113: 17th May 1979 © Trinity Mirror / Mirrorpix / Alamy Stock Photo; P34, P40: circa 1978: © Pictorial Press Ltd / Alamy Stock Photo; P41: promotional photo 1981 © Guido Harari Pictorial Press Ltd / Alamy Stock Photo; P42-43, P70: 1979 tour © Pictorial Press Ltd / Alamy Stock Photo; P79: Apollo, Manchester © Alan Perry Concert Photography; P80-81 P95: Amsterdam 1979 © Gijsbert Hanekroot / Alamy Stock Photo; P82: 27th September 1979 © Trinity Mirror / Mirrorpix / Alamy Stock Photo; P84: Inn-on-the-Park, London 17th April 1979 © PA Images / Alamy Stock Photo; P86: Melody Maker Poll Awards 1979 © Odile Noël / Alamy Stock Photo; P87-91: 27th September 1979 © Trinity Mirror / Mirrorpix / Alamy Stock Photo; P92-93: 'Sing Children Sing', November 1979 © Pictorial Press Ltd / Alamy Stock Photo; P94: 28th November 1979 © Trinity Mirror / Mirrorpix / Alamy Stock Photo; P96: British Rock and Pop Awards, 11th April 1979 © Trinity Mirror / Mirrorpix / Alamy Stock Photo; P97: Capital Radio Music Awards, 3rd March 1980 © Keystone Pictures USA/ZUMAPRESS; P98-99, P104, P105: British Rock and Pop Awards, 26th February 1980 © Trinity Mirror / Mirrorpix / Alamy Stock Photo; P100, P102: December 1979 © Trinity Mirror / Mirrorpix / Alamy Stock Photo; P103: Virgin Records, Eldon Square, Newcastle, 10th September 1980 © Trinity Mirror / Mirrorpix / Alamy Stock Photo; P107-109: Glasgow, October 1980 © Trinity Mirror / Mirrorpix / Alamy Stock Photo; P110: 18th August 1980 © Trinity Mirror / Mirrorpix / Alamy Stock Photo; P112: Promotional photo 1980 © Pictorial Press Ltd / Alamy Stock Photo; P114: NME Awards 1st October 1980 © Trinity Mirror / Mirrorpix / Alamy Stock Photo; P120-P121: The Prince's Trust Concert, Dominion Theatre, London, 21st July 1982 © Pictorial Press Ltd / Alamy Stock Photo; P122-P123: 23rd October 1983 © Trinity Mirror / Mirrorpix / Alamy Stock Photo; P124-P125: 23rd September 1983 © Trinity Mirror / Mirrorpix / Alamy Stock Photo; P126-129: Peter's Pop Show, 30th November 1985 © ZIK Images, United Archives GmbH / Alamy Stock Photo; P132 & P133: circa 1985 © Pictorial Press Ltd / Alamy Stock Photo; P134-P135: Comic Relief book launch 23rd October 1986 © ColourNews / Alamy Stock Photo; P136-P139: The British Phonographic Industry award ceremony, 9th February 1987 © Trinity Mirror / Mirrorpix / Alamy Stock Photo; P140: Blazers Boutique, 31st July 1988 © Trinity Mirror / Mirrorpix / Alamy Stock Photo; P142, P152; promotional photo 1993 © Pictorial Press Ltd / Alamy Stock Photo; P144: circa 1979 © INTERFOTO / Alamy Stock Photo; P146: circa 1982 © Pictorial Press Ltd / Alamy Stock Photo; P147: Heathrow Airport, 10th March 1979 © PA Images / Alamy Stock Photo; P150: unknown date © Trinity Mirror / Mirrorpix / Alamy Stock Photo; P154 & P155: Park Lane Hotel, Mayfair London, 29th October 2001 © William Conran, PA Images / Alamy Stock Photo; P156: Buckingham Palace, 1st March 2005 © Steve Reigate, PA Images / Alamy Stock Photo.

Kate Bush

A Visual Biography

Laura Shenton

**WP
WYMER
PUBLISHING**
Bedford, England

First published in Great Britain in 2022
by Wymer Publishing
www.wymerpublishing.co.uk
Tel: 01234 326691
Wymer Publishing is a trading name of Wymer (UK) Ltd

Copyright © Laura Shenton/Wymer Publishing.

ISBN: 978-1-912782-07-3

The Author hereby asserts their rights to be identified
as the author of this work in accordance with sections
77 to 78 of the Copyright, Designs & Patents Act 1988.

All rights reserved. No part of this publication may be
reproduced or transmitted in any form or by any means,
electronic or mechanical, including photocopying, or any
information storage and retrieval system, without written
permission from the publisher.

This publication is sold subject to the condition that it shall not,
by way of trade or otherwise, be lent, re-sold, hired out or
otherwise circulated without the publishers prior consent in any
form of binding or cover other than that in which it is published
and without a similar condition including this condition
being imposed on the subsequent purchaser.

Every effort has been made to trace the copyright holders of the
photographs in this book but some were unreachable. We would
be grateful if the photographers concerned would contact us.

Design by Andy Bishop / 1016 Sarpsborg
Printed by Imago Group.

A catalogue record for this book is available from the British Library.

Kate Bush
A Visual Biography

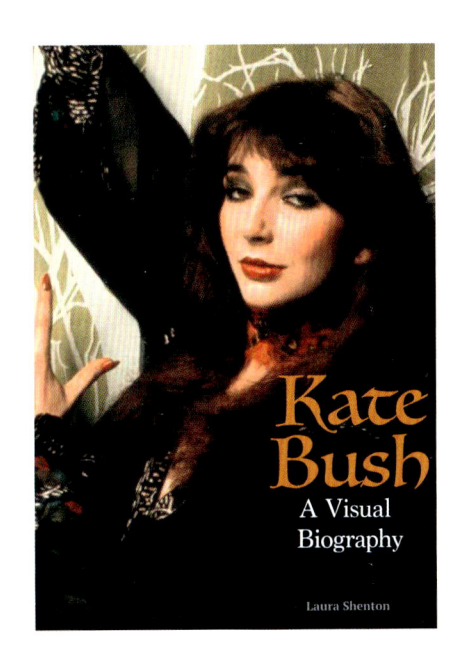

Laura Shenton

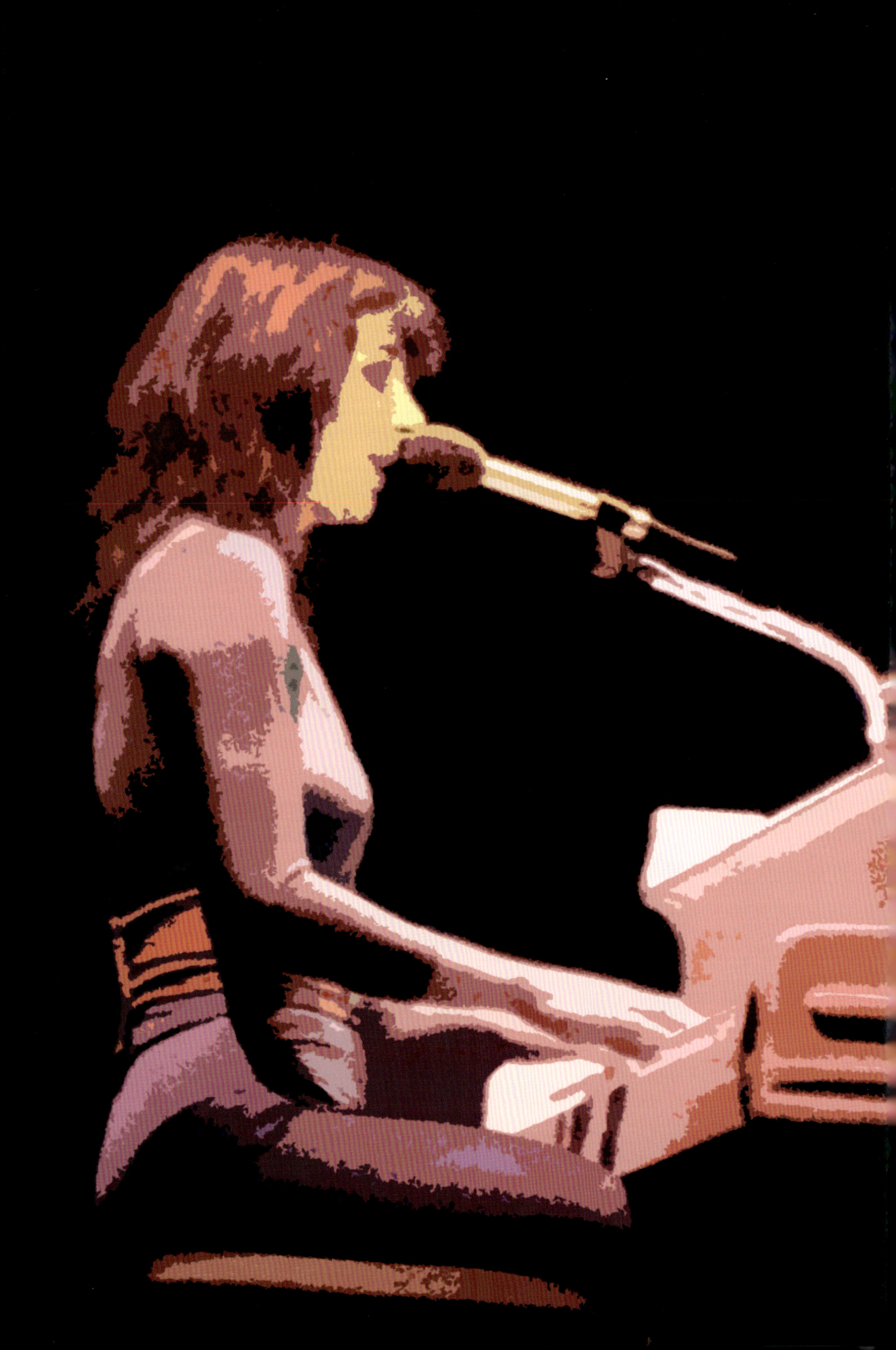

ROLL OF HONOUR

Wymer Publishing duly acknowledges the following people who all put their faith in this publication by pre-ordering it:

Shawn Adams
Kurt Ahrensfeld
Kotaro Aoki
Ritchie Arnold
Terry Barber
Natasha Beavis
John Bell
Ruth Bennett
Mark Berman
Robert Bernardo
Donna Biggs
Damian Boys
Monty Brandenberg
Liz Buckley
Justine Butcher
Aisling Carbin
Steve Carter
Carl Catley
Glenn Caulfield
Kristen Cayton
Xavier Cervantes
Chris Chivers
Debra Clark
Alan Codd
John Cox
Paul Cox
Ray Coyne
Adriano Cristino
Suzanne Davies
Anthony DiMondi
Jayne Eliot
Virginia Esparza
Richard Evans
Pete Farrugia
Bob Fear
Sean Fernald
Nige Fielding

Stefan Fischer
Tracy Formby
Tiffany Gardiner
Stephen Garry
Robin Edward Gow
Ashley Graves
Michael Greenfield
Fran Hamilton
Julia Harrison
Janet Hazeldine
Masashi Ito
Doug Johnson
Thomas Johnson
Lee Jones
Linda Jones
Les Kenward
Neil Killey
Stephanie Landers
Joshua Langton
Michel Lavoie
Lisa Learmonth
Tuomo Leskinen
Martin Lewis
Pamela A Lewis
William Lineberger
Steve Livesley
Yvonne Malcolm
Nicola Marr
Al Martin
Rhona Martin
Gregory Mazure
Alastair McBean
Eric McKay
George McPeek
Jane Mills
Samantha Niblett
Gerry Nolan

Allen Oakley
John O'Connor
Kevin O'Donnell
Ralph O'Flaherty
Ian Oxley
Ken Palmer (a dedicated fan since 1978)
Alison Parry
John Paxman
Heather Pazmino
Mette Pedersen
Tracey Peverill
Bryan Pilkington
Debbie Pugh
Sidari Reddy
Catherine Rose
Lindsey Rossetti
Catherine Rowlands
Paul Rush
Mark Russell
Ben SantaMaria
Gerard Slooven
Sarah Smart
Mark Smith
Erika Spratt
Margitt ter Huurne
Colin Thornton
Martin Todd
David Van Densen
Alberto Vannucchi
Sensei David Walls
Janet Wasek
John Weber
Jonathan Wilford
Harry Williams
Si Wooldridge
Tadahiro Yamamoto
Darren Young

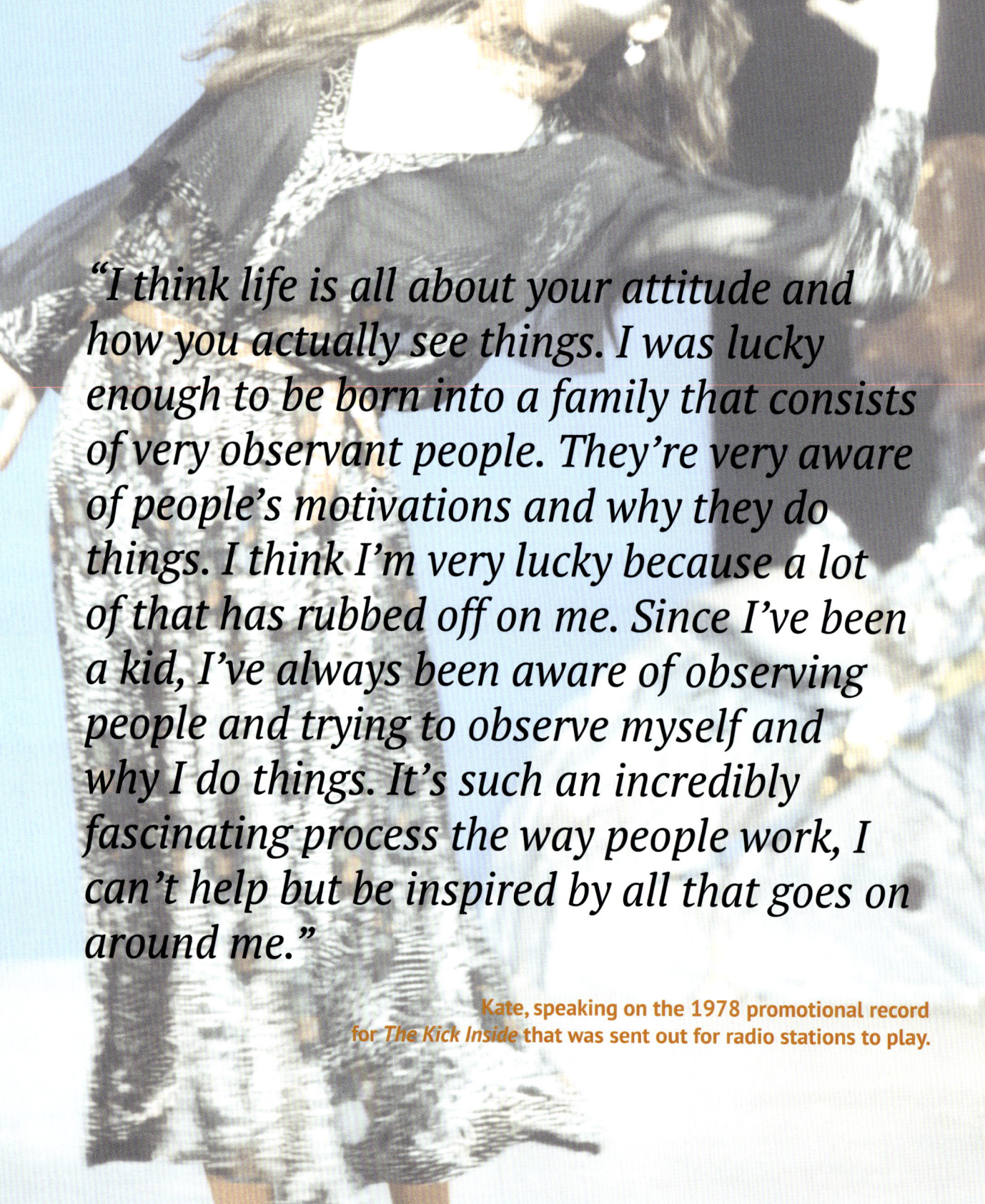

"*I think life is all about your attitude and how you actually see things. I was lucky enough to be born into a family that consists of very observant people. They're very aware of people's motivations and why they do things. I think I'm very lucky because a lot of that has rubbed off on me. Since I've been a kid, I've always been aware of observing people and trying to observe myself and why I do things. It's such an incredibly fascinating process the way people work, I can't help but be inspired by all that goes on around me.*"

Kate, speaking on the 1978 promotional record for *The Kick Inside* that was sent out for radio stations to play.

Performing 'Wuthering Heights' in 1978.

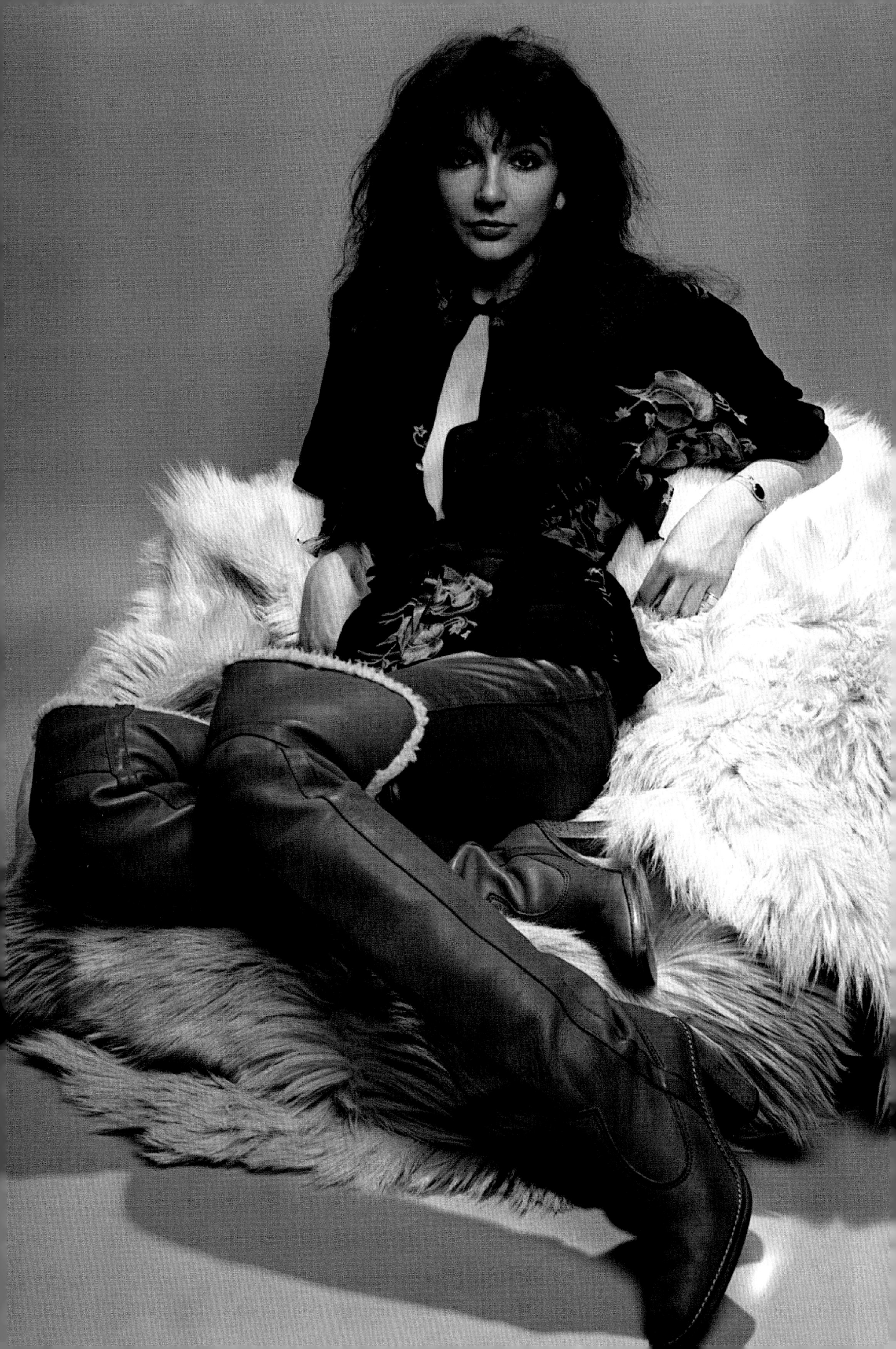

Throughout her career, Kate Bush has successfully delved into many areas of the performing arts as not only a singer, musician and songwriter, but as a dancer and record producer. Born as Catherine Bush on 30th July 1958, she had commercial success at a relatively young age. Just nineteen when she topped the UK singles chart in 1978 with 'Wuthering Heights', she was the first female artist to get to number one with a self-penned song. Following that, her career would see her go on to have twenty-five singles hitting the top forty. Of those, 'The Man With The Child In His Eyes', 'Babooshka', 'Running Up That Hill', 'Don't Give Up' (a duet with her long-time friend Peter Gabriel), and 'King Of The Mountain' were all top ten hits.

Each of Kate's ten studio albums reached the UK top ten. *Never For Ever* (1980), *Hounds Of Love* (1985), and the compilation, *The Whole Story* (1986) all got to number one. Within this, she was not only the first British solo female artist to top the UK album charts, but the first female artist to enter the album chart at number one.

Throughout her musical career, Kate's sound has always been eclectic. She has always embraced various styles, themes and ideas as a point of influence. It has often been the case that as part of this, a vast range of influences have been blended within a single song or indeed, over the course of an album. Critics have described her work as many things: art rock, art pop, pop rock, experimental pop, and avant-pop. Understandably, Kate's music has always been a little tricky to categorise on the basis of how broad her range of influences – and indeed execution of them – have spanned.

Although it is arguably futile to even attempt to compare Kate's unique music and style with her peers, she has been compared to the likes of not only Peter Gabriel, but Roxy Music. *The Guardian* once referred to her as "the queen of art-pop".

Even in her earliest works, when the piano was her primary instrument, she wove together a broad scope of influences. She drew upon classical music, glam rock, and a variety of ethnic and folk styles. This approach has seen her through all of her albums and ever the innovator, when it came to making her third album, *Never For Ever*, she made liberal use of the Fairlight CMI synthesiser. A relatively new technology at the time, it provided her with the scope to sample and manipulate sounds, thus expanding her sonic options.

Kate has a dramatic vocal range. Added to that, she has often included elements of British, Anglo-Irish and most prominently (southern) English accents in her vocal contributions.

March 11, 1978 SOUNDS Page 11
KATE BUSH
HER ALBUM
THE KICK INSIDE
KATE BUSH
THE KICK INSIDE
EMC 3223 also available on cassette
Featuring "WUTHERING HEIGHTS"

Alongside it, in her use of musical instruments from various periods and cultures, her output has differed from what would be more commonly expected of popular music. As part of this, reviewers have often referred to her music as being "surreal". And indeed, her songs do explore melodramatic emotions and musical surrealism which, again, all defies easy categorisation. It has been observed that even Kate's more uplifting songs often contain an undercurrent of melancholy (whilst her more melancholic numbers are not without uplifting moments!).

Lyrically, Kate has often embraced influences from history and literature in her songwriting. This was the case from the very start of her commercial success when in 'Wuthering Heights', she took on the role of the storyteller, embodying the character of Cathy from Emily Brontë's 1847 novel, also called *Wuthering Heights*. Despite the similar namesake of Cathy, Bush has repeatedly spoken against theories that the song is in any way autobiographical.

Kate's lyrics have often expanded into subject areas concerning the obscure, the esoteric, the sensitive, and even, the taboo. For instance, the title track of her debut album, *The Kick Inside*, is based on a traditional English folk song, 'The Ballad Of Lucy Wan', which is about an incestuous pregnancy and resulting suicide. From the same album, in 'Them Heavy People', Bush refers to G. I. Gurdjieff. On *Hounds Of Love*, 'Cloudbusting' was inspired by Peter Reich's 1973 autobiographical book — *A Book Of Dreams* — about his relationship with his father, Wilhelm Reich. The track from *Lionheart*, 'Kashka From Baghdad', is a song about a gay couple. 'Breathing' from *Never For Ever*, explores the impact of nuclear fallout from the perspective of a foetus. Throughout *The Dreaming*, liberal reference is made to war ('Pull Out The Pin' was inspired by a documentary about the Vietnam War, and the subject of struggles for land security is a key theme of the title track).

Bush has also referred to horror films as a source of inspiration for her music, something which has enhanced the sense of the gothic in her work. For instance, at the beginning of 'Hounds Of Love', a sample is featured from the 1957 film, *Night Of The Demon* (the line "It's in the trees! It's coming!" was originally spoken by actor Maurice Denham in a séance scene).

In contrast, other songs of hers have combined horror with comedy in order to put across something of a dark humour. For instance, 'Coffee Homeground' is about murder by poisoning whilst 'There Goes A Tenner' is about a collective of bungling bank robbers — sung in a heightened Mockney accent for maximum effect. The video adds to the humour and indeed, provided scope for expansion on Kate's imaginative approach.

KATE BUSH

Kate Bush: one for the road

KATE BUSH, whose 'Wuthering Heights' single has risen to number 27 in this week's charts, is now rehearsing a show to take out on the road later in the spring. Kate, who comes from Welling in Kent and studied to be a dancer under Lyndsey Kemp as well as singing on the London pub circuit, has already formed a band, but names cannot be released until contracts have been settled.

Her single comes from her debut album, 'The Kick Inside', which has just been released by EMI.

'Ran Tan Waltz' is about an alcoholic mother, whilst 'The Wedding List' is inspired by François Truffaut's 1967 film, *The Bride Wore Black* (of Cornell Woolrich's book about the murder of a groom and the bride's subsequent revenge against the killer). Across several interviews throughout her career, Bush has cited comedy as a substantial influence in her work. As part of this, she has expressed a fondness for a number of particular favourites: Woody Allen, *Monty Python*, *Fawlty Towers*, and *The Young Ones*.

On the innovation front, it wasn't just Kate's use of the Fairlight that put her ahead of the game. She is considered to be the first artist to have used a wireless microphone built specifically for use in music. For her tour in 1979 (named only retrospectively as the Tour Of Life), she combined a compact microphone with a construction made of wire clothes hangers. The result enabled her to be free of needing to use a hand-held microphone, thus providing maximum scope for dance. Just as well really, considering the thought that went into the choreography and the performance thereof. Some say that a rudimentary version of the idea was used in the early-sixties by the Spotnicks but all the same, nobody did it quite like Kate and her design and application of such microphone technology was later embraced by other artists such as Peter Gabriel, Madonna, and Janet Jackson.

Bush had been writing songs from as early in her life as the age of eleven. Her signing to EMI was the result of Pink Floyd guitarist, David Gilmour, helping her to produce a demo tape.

Despite having been given a helping hand to get her career off to a flying start (and not for a lack of talent at all!), it wasn't relatively long before Bush was taking a strongly independent role in her artistic destiny. From *The Dreaming* onwards, she has produced all of her studio albums alone.

In terms of her studio albums, Kate has always been keen to provide quality over quantity. She told BBC Radio Two in 1982; "There seems to be more projects that I do that do take up a lot of time, like maybe a year at a time. But I have to really sit and think, what is the most important thing to me?: To stay in the public's eye or to make sure that the work I do is more interesting and that it gets better. And really the only way to make sure that the work gets better is to concentrate on it. So that's definitely my priority."

Commercially, Bush's approach to the music business has served her well. She has been nominated for thirteen British Phonographic Industry accolades (winning for Best British Female Artist in 1987) and has been nominated for three

Kate performing 'Hammer Horror' during the recording of the video directed by Keef at Blandford W10 film studio, Ladbroke Grove, London in 1978.

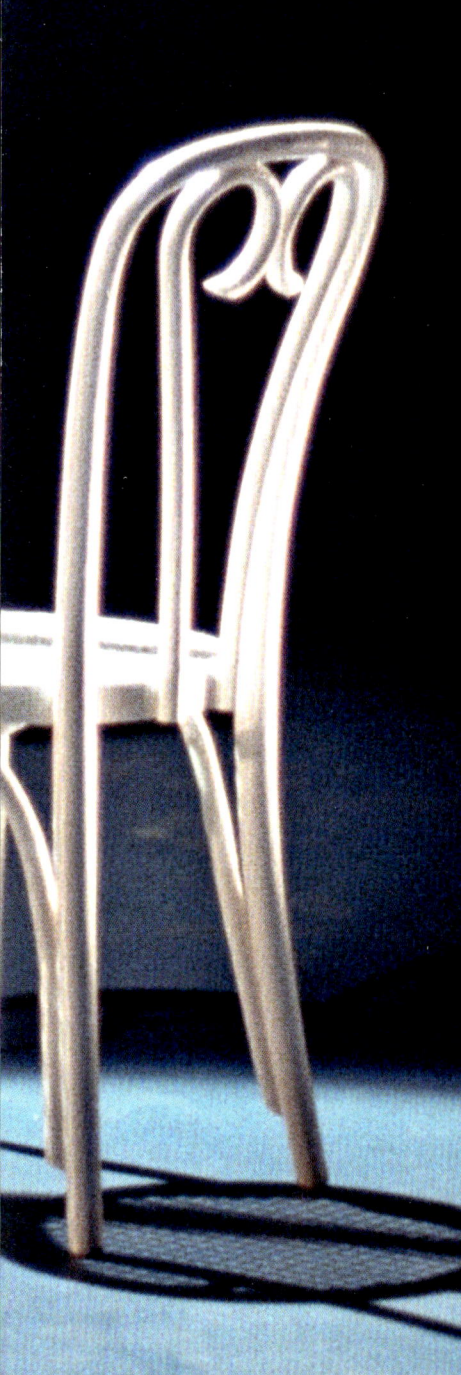

Grammy Awards. In 2002, she was recognised with an Ivor Novello Award for Outstanding Contribution to British Music (importantly, Kate is now a Fellow of the Ivors Academy – the position was awarded to her in 2020). She was appointed a CBE in the 2013 New Year Honours for services to music. On top of all of that, she has been nominated three times for induction into the 2018, 2021 and 2022 Rock And Roll Hall Of Fame (but still hasn't actually been inducted!).

So many achievements from such humble beginnings! Kate was born in Bexleyheath, Kent, to English doctor/general practitioner Robert Bush (1920–2008) and Hannah (1918–1992), née Daly, an Irish staff nurse and daughter of a farmer in County Waterford. Raised as a Roman Catholic, the young Kate grew up in a 350-year-old former farmhouse in the outer London suburb of East Wickham, Welling. The Bush family had moved into the property in the fifties (they still own it to this day and in more recent years, Owen Bush, Kate's nephew, has worked there as a blacksmith).

With Kate, were her older brothers, John and Paddy. Although not to the same commercial scale, of course, the family had a range of artistic talents. Kate's mother was an amateur traditional Irish dancer whilst her father was an amateur pianist. Paddy worked as a musical instrument maker, and John was a poet and photographer. Both brothers were involved in the local folk music scene. The musical influence in the family inspired Kate to teach herself piano. She also played the organ in a barn behind her parents' house and studied the violin, all of which provided a strong foundation for her to begin songwriting from such a young age.

Kate attended St Joseph's Convent Grammar School, a Catholic girls' school in nearby Abbey Wood. It was during this period of her life that her family produced a demo tape featuring over fifty of her compositions. It was turned down by several record labels prior to falling into the hands of David Gilmour, who received it from Ricky Hopper, a mutual friend of Gilmour and the Bush family. Impressed, Gilmour helped the then sixteen-year-old Kate to record a more professional demo tape. A total of three tracks were recorded, all at the expense of Gilmour. The tape was produced by Gilmour's friend Andrew Powell (who would go on to produce Kate's first two albums), and sound engineer Geoff Emerick, who had worked with the Beatles. Upon receiving the better demo, it was EMI executive Terry Slater, who signed Kate with the label.

During the mid-to-late-seventies when all of the latter was happening for Kate, it is argued by some that the British record industry was reaching a point of uncertainty. Much of the record-buying public had tired of the progressive rock that had so often dominated the album charts of the earlier part of the decade. Positively though, the situation provided fertile ground for a new range of creativity to come to the fore. As a result, record companies were open to a range of genres as part of their search for the next big thing.

And indeed, Kate was determinedly ambitious. She told *Melody Maker* in 1978; "Every female you see at a piano is either Lynsey de Paul or Carole King. And most male music – not all of it but the good stuff – really lays it on you. It really puts you against the wall and that's what I like to do. I'd like my music to intrude. Not many females succeed with that."

Upon signing with EMI, Kate was given a large advance from the label. She used the money to enrol in interpretive dance classes taught by Lindsay Kemp (who had previously taught David Bowie, another artist who Kate has often spoken highly of throughout her career). Along with this, she undertook mime training with Adam Darius. Overall, throughout the first two years of her contract with EMI, Kate spent more time on schoolwork than on recording. It was after doing her mock A levels and having gained ten O level qualifications that she left school.

"I had finished taking my O levels at school and was coming up to the stage where you start thinking about A levels and university," she recalled. "And I wasn't really into the idea of going to university, so I thought I should leave school and concentrate on my career, already having signed a contract with the record company."

Still though, prior to getting to work on her debut album, Kate had penned and made demos of almost two-hundred songs, some of which have since been circulated as bootlegs. Throughout the spring of 1977, she fronted the KT Bush Band at public houses in London. The line-up included Del Palmer on bass, Brian Bath on guitar, and Vic King on drums. It was in the summer that she started to record material for her debut album.

For the recording of what would become *The Kick Inside*, Kate was persuaded to use established session musicians instead of the KT Bush Band. She retained some of these even after she had brought her bandmates back on board. Her brother Paddy played the harmonica and mandolin. Stuart Elliott played some of the drums and became her main drummer on subsequent albums. Released when she was just nineteen, some of the songs on *The Kick Inside* had been penned when she was as young as thirteen.

In September 1977, EMI initially stated that they wanted

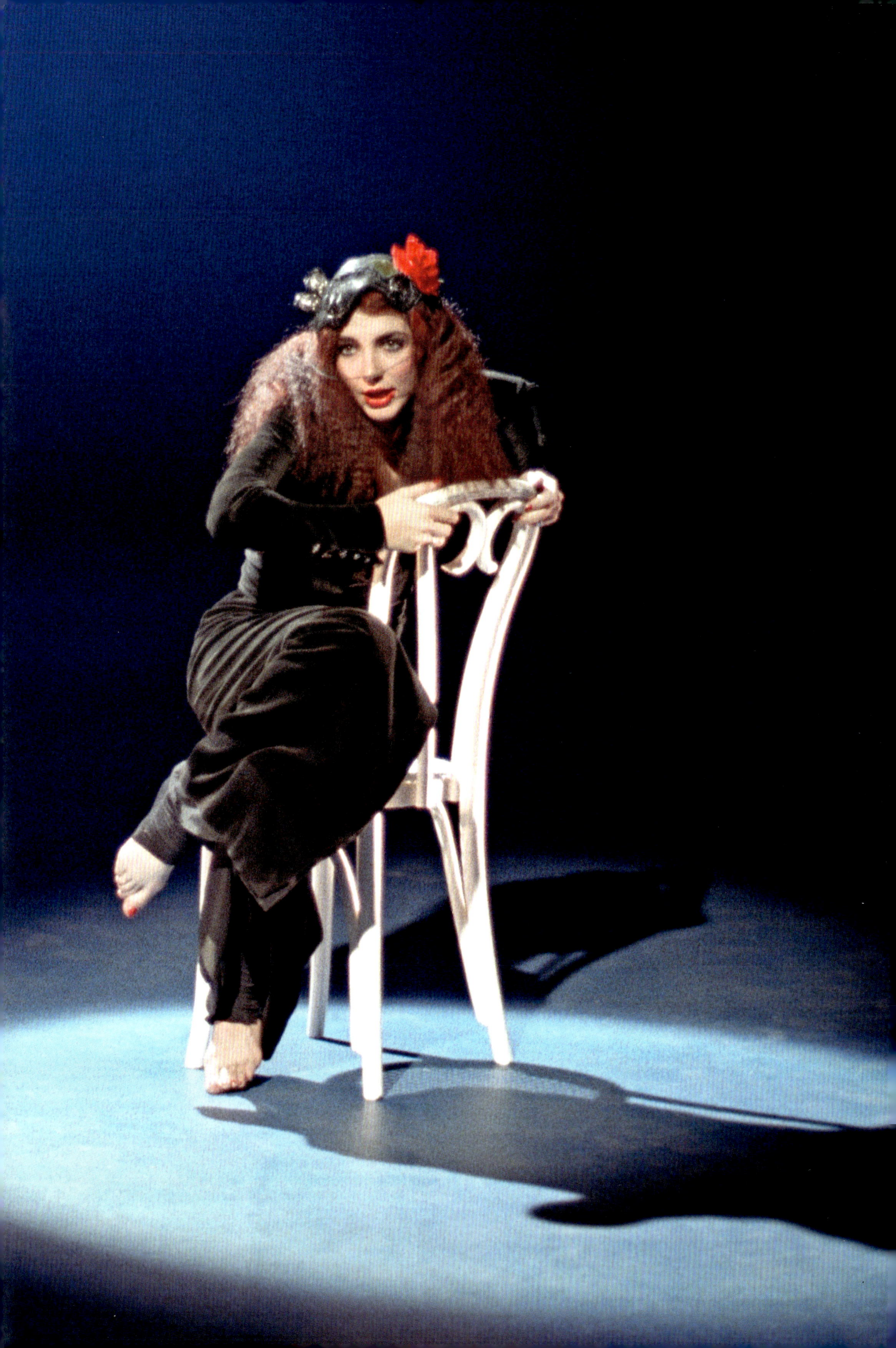

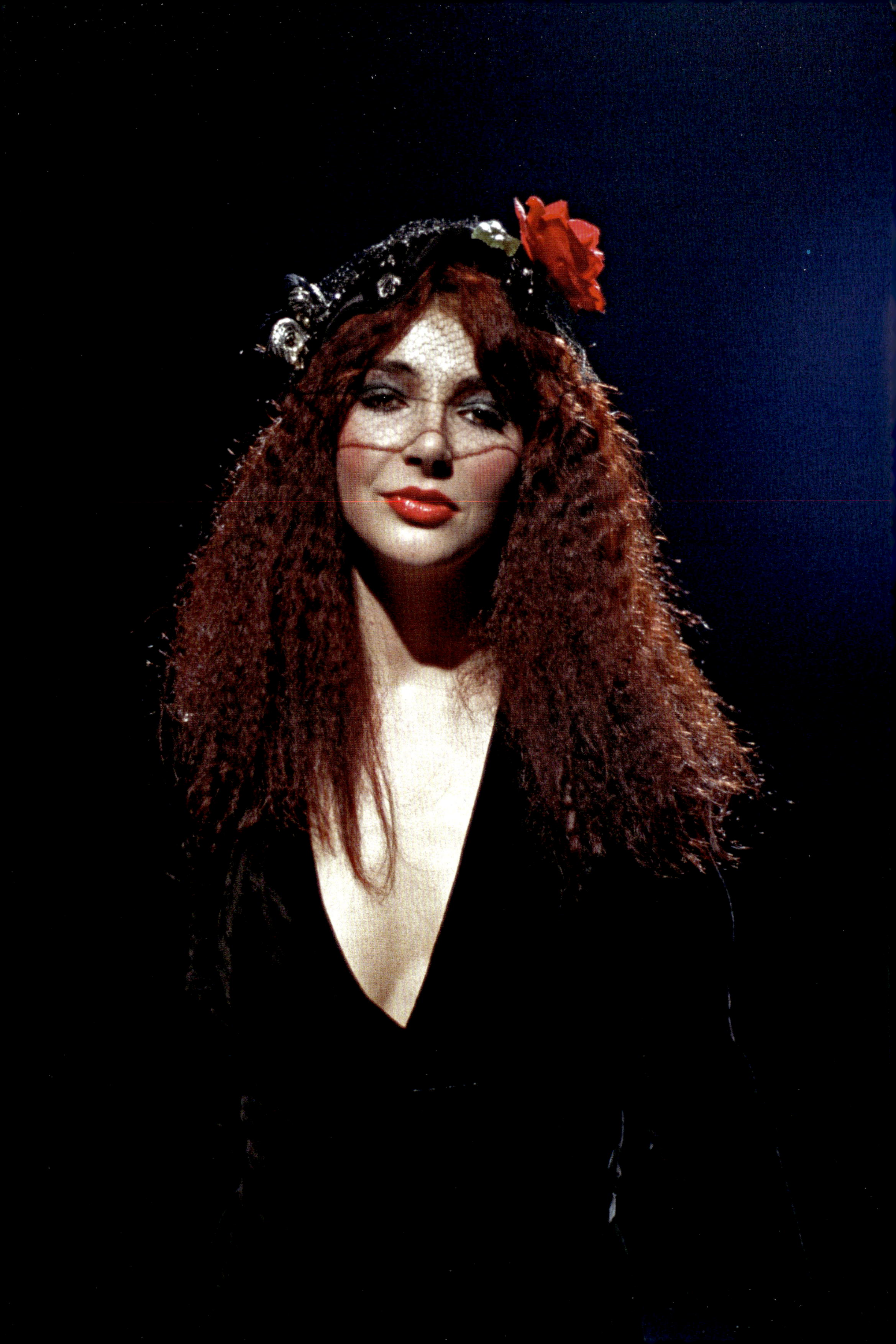

PIX: JIL URMANOVSKY

You don't have to be beautiful...

...to get your face in SOUNDS, a top twenty album and a top five single are usually enough. Fortunately Kate Bush has both, so you can't call us sexist

SOULFUL, SENSITIVE, salubrious. So why all the fuss about Kate Bushs' *age*? Is it the fact that you don't usually get such cohesive intelligence from 19 year old females? Is it that 'child' prodigies are out of our mode? Or is it simply the fact that the journalists are getting older? It wasn't *that* long ago that the charts were brimmed from 1 to 10 with teen-aged stars. It may *seem* that only yesterday she was your average unknown person, but in fact, Kate has been developing her unique talents on rinky-dink second hand pianos since she was the ripe old age of 14. Recently she moved into a three storey flat in Lewisham, which is owned by her general practioner daddy-o, and whose other two storeys are occupied by her two older brothers.

The story is not at all as overnight as it seems to be, it was in fact two years ago that Pink Floyd's Dave Gilmour bopped around to Kates' flat with a Revox — goal in mind to get some of Kates tunes published. She wasn't, at the time, considered a singer but Gilmour, who is genuinely interested in giving undiscovered talent a shot-in-the-arm (with his Unicorn organisation) felt that the bubbling under songs should have the opportunity to be heard. They recorded about 15 songs per tape, and took them around to various record companies. The unanimous opinion, then, was 'non-commerical', and after all ... it's not creative unless it *sells*, 'eh?

How Kate and Gilmour hooked up is rather a vague 'girlfriends'-boyfriends'-girlfriends-friend' sort of rigamaroll, but the fact is that he never did lose interest in her er ... talents, and decided that the only way to reach a record company's goldfined pocket was to produce finished product. Which is exactly what they did. Gilmour put up the money, and Kate went into Air studios complete with a band, and laid down the three tracks she and Dave both felt were best. This is the tape which eventually landed Kate her contract with EMI Records.

Despite the fact that she has been already wrongly built (no pun intended) in the media to be a mere child, she is surprisingly aware of what is going on around her, and is accepting the entire shindig with a pleased air of disbelief.

"They keep telling me the chart numbers, and I just kind of say, 'Wow' (she sweeps her arms) ... it's not really like it's happening. I've always been on the outside, watching albums I like go up the charts, and feeling pleased that they are doing well, but it's hard to relate to the fact that it's now happening to *me* ..."

WUTHERING Heights', Kates' self-penned song, inspired by the book of the same title, is literally catapaulting up the UK charts, and looks as though it will be one of those classic world-wide smasherooneys, though it has yet to be released in most other countries. She recently took her first air-bourne flight to Germany for a television appearance, as the single, apparently, has been chosen as whatever the German equivalent of 'pick-of-the-week' might be.

"It was mind blowing," she said euphorically, in reference to flying, "I *really* want to do more of that ..." Wonder how she'll feel about in in two years time.

She writes songs about love, people, relationships and life ... sincerely and emotionally, but without prostituting her talents by whining about broken hearts.

"If you're writing a song, assuming peope are going to listen, then you have a responsibility to those people. It's important to give them a positive message, something that can advise or help is far more effective than having a wank and being self-pitiful. That's really negative. My friends and brothers have been really helpful to me, providing me with stimulating conversation and ideas I can really sink my teeth into."

For as long as she can remember she has been toying around with the piano, much, I reckoned, to her parent's chargrin. Can *you* imagine living with a nine-year-old who insisted on battering away on said instrument, wailing away at the top of her lungs in accompaniment?

"Well, they weren't very encouraging in the beginning, they thought it was a lot of noise. When I first started, my voice was terrible, but the voice is an instrument to a singer, and the only way to improve it is to practise. I have had no formal vocal training, though there was a guy that I used to see for half-an-hour once a week, and he would advise me on things like breathing properly, which is very important to voice control. 'He'd say things like 'Does that hurt?' Well, then sing more from here (motions to diaphram) than from your throat.' I don't like the idea of 'formal' training, it has far too many rules and conventions that are later hard to break out of ..."

IT IS QUITE obvious from the cover of 'The Kick Inside', her debut album, that Ms. Bush is Orientally influenced, but apparently it was not meant to take on such an oriental feel.

"I think it went a bit over the top, actually. We had the kite, and as there is a song on the album by that name, and as the kite is traditionally oriental, we painted the dragon on. But I think the lettering was just a bit too much. No matter. On the whole I was surprised at the amount of control I actually had with the album production. Though I didn't choose the musicians," (Andrew Powell, producer and arranger did). "I thought they were terrific.

"I was lucky to be able to express myself as much as I did, especially with this being a debut album. Andrew was really into working together, rather than pushing everyone around. I basically chose which tracks went on, put harmonies where I wanted them ... I was there throughout the entire mix. I feel that's very important. Ideally, I would like to learn enough of the technical side of things to be able to produce my own stuff eventually."

Kate has a habit of gesturing constantly with her hands, and often expressing herself with unspellable sounds and grimaces. Though this make tape transcriptions difficult, it does accentuate something which is very much a part of her, 'movement expression'. She has studied under the inimitable Lindsay Kemp, mime artiste, an experience shared with Kate's favourite musician, David Bowie.

"I admire actresses and actors terribly and think it's an amazing craft. But singing and performing your songs should be the same thing. At this point I would rather develope my music and expressing it physically, as opposed to having a script. I think I'm much better off as a wailer ..."

She is, indeed a beautiful woman. Carved ivory, with nary a nick. So obviously there is no way she can avoid becoming the target for sexist minds. Although she does not advocate this reaction, she's not flustered by it. After all, it *is* a compliment.

"As long as it does not interfere with my progress as a singer/songwriter, it doesn't matter. I just wish people would think of that first, I would be foolish to think that people don't look. I suppose in some ways it helps to get more people to listen ..."

THE KICK Inside' suggests a keen interest in mysticism.

"I try to work on myself spiritually, and am always trying to improve my outlook on life. We really abuse all that we've got, assuming that we are so superior as beings, taking the liberties of sticking up cement stuff all over the place. I think there is a lot to astrology, and the effect the moon has upon us all, but I hate the way it's become so trendy now.

"I'm a vegetarian, and now that's trendy as well ... but what annoys me the most is the way people are so automatically cynical about astrology. I mean, like the Greeks put an incredible amount of hard work into carefully planned geometric charts, based purely on mathematics. People just shrug off. It's the same with coincidence, as I said in the song 'Strange Phenonema',"

At first, Kate was opposed to having any sort of management, feeling strongly that less mistakes are made if you deal with situations yourself, directly. But she quickly found out that this sort of idealism does not work, and now has Peter Lyster-Todd handling her business affairs.

"He has worked more on the theatrical side of entertainment than music, I like that. I think most managers are crooks, speedy and non-musical, and that mixing with other music managers is contageous. I think Peter will be amazing ..."

There are tentative plans for a Kate Bush tour in the late spring, but it is only being discussed at this point.

To accompany Kate on the road will be Cuban drummer Sergio Castillo; guitarist Brian Bath; bassist Del Palmer; keyboardist Ben Barson, and brother Paddy Bush on mandolin and backing vocals. Again, primarily friends of friends of friends, and wide-eyed optimism.

JUST AS I'M about to leave a pile of fan mail arrives, and she gapes, amazed, "Cor ... is all this for *me*??? This is amazing!"

Oh, dear, dear, Kate. Do stay above it all. Don't ever fall into your very own lyrics, which could be ironically twisted. From 'Kite':

"I got no limbs, I'm like a feather on the wind.
Well, I'm not sure if I want to be up here at all.
And I'd like to be back on the ground.

DONNA McALLISTER

AN INTERNATIONAL CLASSIC

KATE BUSH

THE ALBUM THE KICK INSIDE

SW-17003

THE SINGLE WUTHERING HEIGHTS

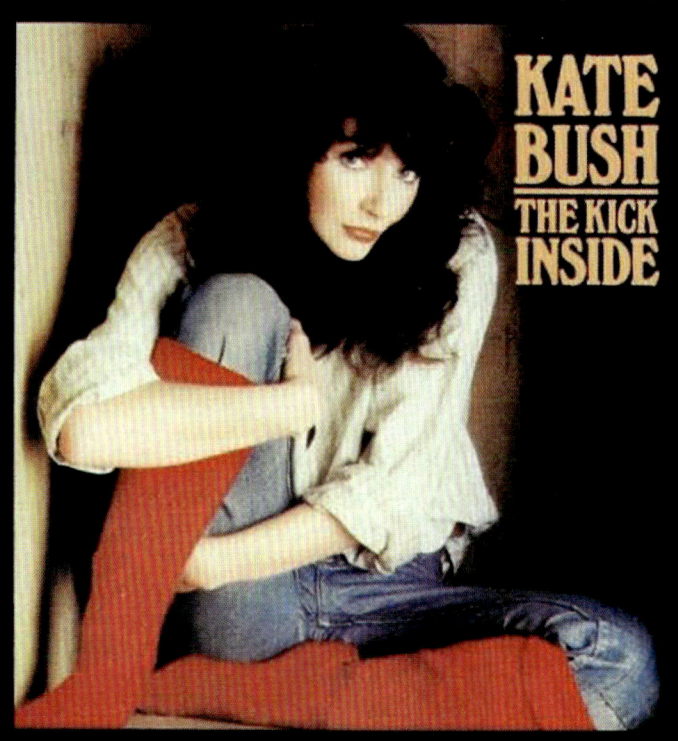

8003

ENGLAND	SINGLE #1 (4 WEEKS) GOLD	LP #3 GOLD
AUSTRALIA	SINGLE #1 GOLD	LP #1 PLATINUM
HOLLAND	SINGLE #3	LP #1 PLATINUM
NEW ZEALAND	SINGLE #1 (5 WEEKS) PLATINUM	LP #2 GOLD
BELGIUM	SINGLE #4	LP #2
DENMARK	SINGLE #4	LP #5
FINLAND	SINGLE #4	LP #3
SWEDEN	SINGLE #13	LP #9

the more rock-oriented track, 'James And The Cold Gun', to be released as the debut single from the album. Already with a reputation for asserting herself in decisions about her work, Kate insisted that the track of choice needed to be 'Wuthering Heights'. She told *Tune In* in December 1978; "For me, 'Wuthering Heights' was the only single and I felt very strongly about it. Eventually they agreed, but it would have been terrible if it had failed after all the effort I had put into it."

In the UK alone, *The Kick Inside* sold over a million copies. 'Wuthering Heights' topped the UK and Australian charts and became an international hit. 'The Man With The Child In His Eyes' made it onto the American Billboard Hot 100 (notably though, it only got to number eighty-five in early 1979). The track went on to win her an Ivor Novello Award in 1979 for Outstanding British Lyric. According to the Guinness World Records, Kate Bush was the first female artist in pop history to have written every track on a million-selling debut album. A flying start for the young Kate.

Regarding how she was yet to really strike a chord with an American audience, Bob Mercer, who had also been part of the decision to sign Kate to EMI, blamed the American radio formats, stating that they were incapable of being able to get Bush's visual presentation of the music across, and that something more was needed in order to engage with listeners across the pond.

It was all happening for Kate Bush's fans in the UK though. EMI chose to capitalise on her appearance by running a somewhat controversial promotion for *The Kick Inside*: a poster of the singer in a tight pink top that emphasised her breasts. In an interview with *New Musical Express* in 1982, Kate went on to criticise the record label's decision: "People weren't even generally aware that I wrote my own songs or played the piano. The media just promoted me as a female body. It's like I've had to prove that I'm an artist in a female body."

The success of *The Kick Inside* was such that EMI were quick to persuade Kate that a follow-up album needed to be made. The resulting album was *Lionheart*, which was recorded between July and September, and released in November 1978.

It wasn't troublesome coming up with material for *Lionheart*; most of the songs on the album had been written by Kate even before *The Kick Inside* was made. Of the ten songs on *Lionheart*, only 'Symphony In Blue', 'Fullhouse' and 'Coffee Homeground' were newly written for the album. However, all of the other songs that had been written long before Kate's rise to fame were reworked prior to the recording of the album. She was quoted in the *Liverpool Echo* in April 1979; "I

Kate Bush
Lionheart
ELECTROLA
KATE BUSH
auf Deutschland-Tournee
28.4. Hamburg Congress Centrum
2.5. Stuttgart Liederhalle
3.5. München Circus Krone
7.5. Duisburg Mercatorhalle
8.5. Mannheim Rosengarten
10.5. Frankfurt Jahrhunderthalle
Take Kate Bush
out tonight.
Kate Bush
Lionheart
'Lionheart' is the latest
cassette from Kate Bush.
Also available on record

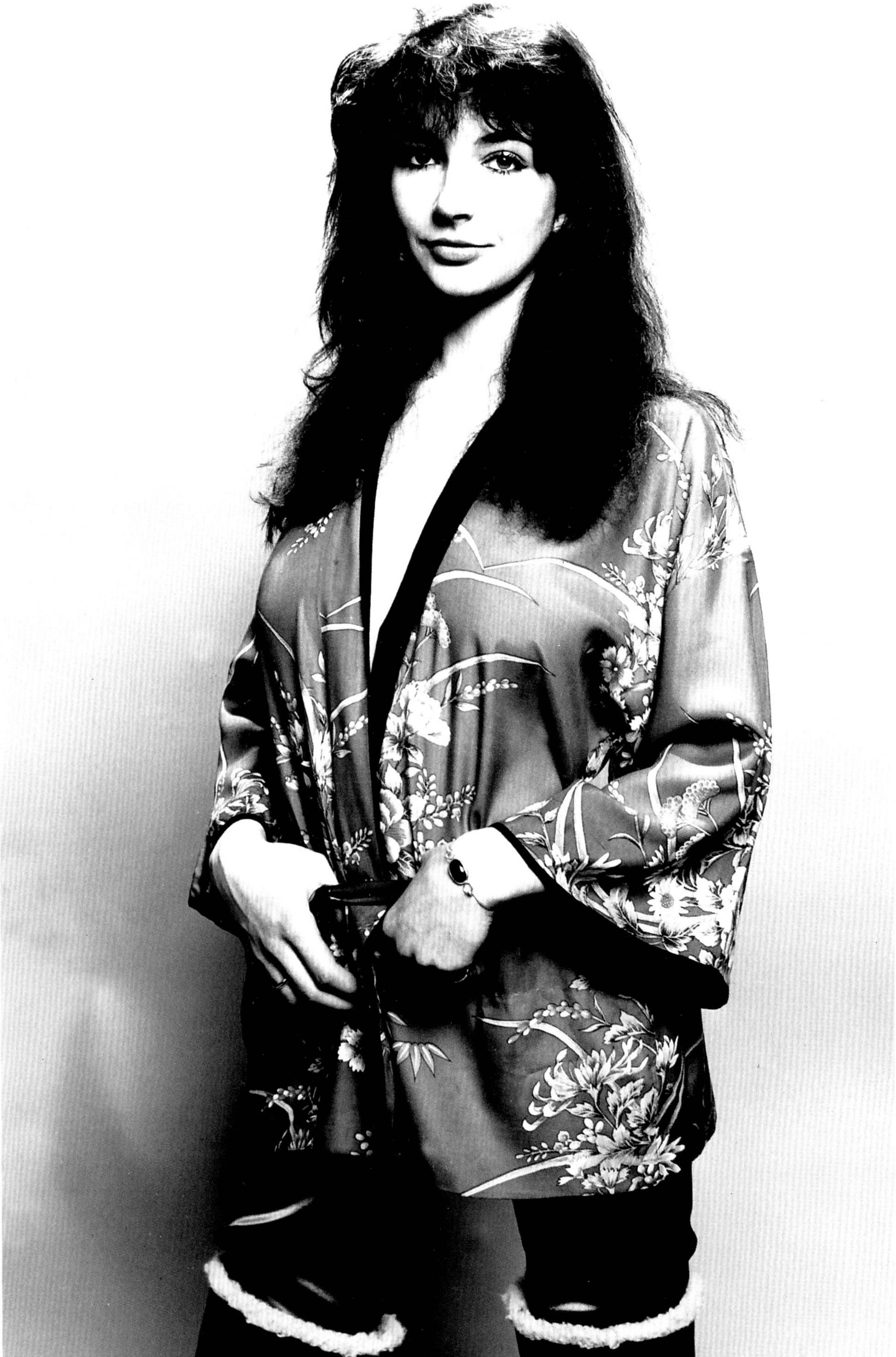

Kate Bush
Lionheart
Symphony In Blue
Wow
In Search Of Peter Pan
Don't Push Your Foot On The Heartbrake
OH ENGLAND MY LIONHEART
Fullhouse
In The Warm Room
Kashka From Baghdad
Coffee Homeground
Hammer Horror

SHE'S HERE
Kate Bush
Lionheart
HER ALBUM
LIONHEART
featuring the hit single 'WOW'
ON TOUR
April
3rd Liverpool Empire
4th/5th Birmingham Hippodrome
6th Oxford New Theatre
7th Southampton Gaumont
9th Bristol Hippodrome
10th/11th Manchester Apollo
12th Sunderland Empire
13th Edinburgh Usher Hall
16th/17th/18th/19th/20th London Palladium
KATE BUSH

September 30, 1978 SOUNDS Page 21

PETE SILVERTON FAILS TO PENETRATE WUTHERING KATE'S IMPREGNABLE NICENESS

KATE BUSH

BUSH WHACKED

KATE BUSH as seen by the EMI publicity department (above) and by Janette Beckman (right)

AN HOUR or so in the company of Kate Bush is rather like being trapped for the duration as an unwitting participant in a very wholesome kids' TV show with definite but unwarranted intellectual aspirations. Blue Peter meets Tomorrow's World maybe. Pleasant, charming even, and certainly *nice* but ultimately insipid to the point of unreality.

Holding court in the two storey suite in Marble Arch's superficially distinguished Montcalm Hotel that EMI hired to present her to the day-long procession of journalists, she showed no signs of tiring by the time I arrived for the last session of the day's schedule. She was friendly, reservedly effusive in her greetings, smiled a lot and displayed an almost continual expression of wide-eyed innocence.

And, just as she was so *nice*, so were her answers to any questions I cared to offer up to her. I came out feeling that she'd talked for that hour or so very sweetly about absolutely nothing, that not once had she opened up even a tiny chink in her *nice* armour. Either she was an absolute professional determined not to reveal anything that would jibe with the image of sweet little Kate Bush that has been so casually but so carefully assembled since she was first unleashed on the nation's ears earlier this year . . . either that, or there really was nothing behind the facade and she really is that *nice*, that vacuous. (*Or maybe you didn't ask the right questions. — Ed.*)

Conversation is lightly sprinkled with five year old hip slang. She talks about 'vibes' refers to 'something I'm into' and frequently mentions her belief in 'coincidences'. She also continually explained her pet 'theories' — she seemed to have more of those than you'd find in a Ph.D. thesis on the nature of light. And, above all she was conscious of promoting the career of Kate Bush. Of course, that's true for virtually every interview — the talk which boosts the single which in turn launches the album — but she seemed more eager to grasp and exploit that route than most. Just about every move in her short public history was explained in terms of how it had served the purpose of promoting her artistic wares. Even the reason for this interview being done now and not in two months time, when her second album, 'Lion Heart' is released.

"I think mostly because the album's coming up and from now till the time the album is out this is the only time I'm going to have to do interviews and the reason why the timing's so tight is 'cos we've run over the time expected (recording the album). I think it's really just to let people know that the album's on its way . . .

"I don't really question it 'cos far as I'm concerned any publicity, any kind of communication that's getting from me to the public is good. I mean it can't be bad if people are hearing about you. Great. That's what it's all about — communicating to your public. And you can only do that directly on such a small level."

Although she insisted that she very much had complete control over her career at all points, I found it interesting that she'd shifted from her original position of saying she needed no manager to finding one, praising his abilities to the skies and then splitting from him and acquiring a new manager in Hilary Walker who sat upstairs and answered the phone throughout the interview.

"Well, that's something that I can't really talk about at the moment. It's something very personal between the two of us (her and her previous manager) that I can't really talk about now because if I do, er . . . um . . . it's gonna be very hard . . . were. . .er. . . um, y'know, we're in *dealings* at the moment that have to be sorted out and we're still friends and everything's fine. It was an agreement between the two of us and it's something that I'd like to talk to you about but if I do at the moment I could well get into trouble".

Forcefully rejecting any question of her taking her previous manager to court, she also talked about another aspect of her career which has had a similar on/off history — the promised live shows. First it was going to be sometime after the album was released, then more definitely this autumn and now Kate Bush on the road is promised for next year.

"Since the single ('Wuthering Heights') took off there was an awful lot of promotion needed in order to keep the momentum of it going in order to get the album through. And not only did it take off in this country but it took off in Holland . . . and other places. All my time is concentrated on getting myself established on some level or other around the world — basically in as many countries as I could. The opportunity to do that is very rare for a new artist."

So the live dates were put off in favour of that kind of direct, business-decision type of promotion.

"Hopefully, we're heading for February to do England. It'll be pretty small places, medium sized theatres so I can get an intimate atmosphere which you don't get in those big gigs.

"I doubt if I'll take a large theatrical show. I do want to combine . . . what's the word? . . . theatre with music but I'm honestly not sure myself yet to what level I can take it. It's something very unexplored for me yet . . . I know what I'd like to do but whether I'm going to be able to do it I don't know because I haven't even started preparing for that yet. We're gonna start in October."

Probably like most people, I'd assumed she'd never done live gigs. In fact, she was the singer in the Kate Bush Band (what else?) for a while last year and she talked about that period as though it were part of a fondly remembered but long lost childhood, her affection for it for once obscuring the hesitance and inarticulacy of her speech.

"We did some pubs in the West End and around my area . . . south east London in the spring of '77. We just sort of did it for about five months . . . had a little band . . . it was great, very good experience. It was all other people's stuff . . . Stones, Beatles, Free. It was the first time I'd every sung anyone else's songs.

"It was at a time I'd just been staying home and writing songs a lot and going dancing (with Lindsay Kemp). And some friends of my brother turned up one day and I was on my way to get a train up to London to go dancing and I popped into see them and they were talking about forming a rock and roll band and they said they needed a singer and so I said 'Ooooo, yeah. I've never done that'. And they said 'Would you like to do that?' and I said 'Yeah, great' and they said 'Right, first rehearsal two days time' and it was absolutely great, terrific'.

Two of the members of that band are still with her and contributed to both 'The Kick Inside' and the new album. There was some indication earlier in the year that she was having to write to order for this second album.

"No, I could never feel that way about my songs. But it all happened fine. A month before I went in (to the studio) I was extremely worried about my material but it was okay because I had about three, four solid weeks in order to concentrate on that and I'd written about four, five new songs in that period. What I've done really is that there are quite a few old songs that I'd written about a year and a half ago that didn't go on the last album that I've rewritten which obviously isn't such a long process and they're exactly the way I would want them and they're on this album."

Predictably, she thinks the new album is better than 'Kick Inside' but, perhaps surprisingly she doesn't feel that she has changed much within herself.

"There is obviously a difference between me today and yesterday. I've got new skin molecules and everything. I'm more confident, a little more confident, sometimes not nearly as confident . . . I doubt the things I'm doing sometimes. I wonder if I really do believe in myself — I think they're very natural fears for someone to have."

But one thing she doesn't seem uncertain about is her sense of responsibility towards her audience.

"I did Ask Aspel the other week and there was one song that I really wanted to sing and I was really worried about singing largely to a child audience and it mentioned words like 'thighs' and I didn't want to sing that to children (sic) audiences. I was worried about the effect it would have on them and I sang a slightly milder song. I think of children and I don't want to sing about sex to them."

In that as in other ways she really does appear to be insufferably nice, the kind of picture of goodness that is boring because its origins seem so fundamentally passive.

"I've very, very, very rarely lost my temper. I've lost my temper once in the last year and that's the first time I've lost it in five or six years. I think losing your temper is a waste of time and a bloody nuisance. If you're uptight about something it's often your own fault so you should keep it to yourself. If someone does something that I'm really not into, if they're doing something to offend me or someone I love then I will assume annoyance to get at them. but I don't really mean it.

"What's the point of losing your temper. It's an irrational, emotional reaction which does no good at all. It just makes people treat you like a hysterical . . . particularly in my position. If I was to jump up now, pull this table up, hit you on the head and take all my clothes off and jump out of the window . . . for the next year I would be called a tantrum maker."

Probably, once they'd given her a decent burial.

Somehow this emotional passivity seemed to fit in with her belief in psychic phenomena.

"It's like astrology. So many people say it's a lot of shit but real astrology, that's something that men spend years with real pure mathematics getting together."

No, she hadn't had her horoscope done — she's a Leo, whatever that signifies — but she had had her tarot cards read.

"They were quite amazing. I had them done in the November before the album came out and it practically predicted my success."

I suggested that maybe EMI should give up advertising and just cast the Tarot, Kate Bush smiled and the interview was over — she had to go straight into the studio.

She said goodbye cheerfully and I thanked her for the time. It was all very *nice*.

take the majority of my ideas for songs from just watching and listening to people. It's people who make life, and that's where my songs come from... I have to work at it and it takes time, because I won't use a song until I'm really happy about it."

Produced by Andrew Powell with Kate's assistance, Lionheart sold well and spawned the hit single, 'Wow', but it didn't reach the commercial heights that The Kick Inside had. It got to number six in the UK. (Notably, 'Hammer Horror', the first single released from the album, fell short of the UK top forty).

Kate went on to express dissatisfaction with her second album, stating that in order for it to be everything that it could have been, it needed more time. With hindsight, she went on to say in later years; "I was lucky to get it together so quickly but the songs seem to me, now, to be somewhat overproduced. I didn't put enough time into them... It was rushed and that was responsible for me taking as much time as possible over albums. Considering how quickly we made it, it's a bloody good album but I'm not really happy with it."

Following the release of Lionheart, and keen to prove her doubters wrong, Kate was required by EMI to undertake heavy promotional work, and as part of that, a tour.

Although the tour of 1979 came to be known as The Tour Of Life, it was originally known as the Lionheart Tour. At the time, it was also officially referred to as the Kate Bush Tour and by some outside sources, the Kate Bush Show. The performances consisted predominantly of songs from both The Kick Inside and Lionheart.

When the tour was announced, most dates sold out so quickly that more dates had to be added in order to meet the high demand. Members of the Kate Bush Club were guaranteed a ticket.

A BBC special was filmed. Titled Kate Bush: On Tour, the documentary showcased the production and staging of the set. It also revealed the extent to which Bush was involved. When it was broadcast on 31st August 1979, it did not show any of the full performances. It did however, feature Kate discussing her involvement in the tour, and incorporated footage of dance and band rehearsals. It also showed footage of the final rehearsals at the Rainbow Theatre and the official opening night in Liverpool. Along with all of this, a screening of the music video for the single, 'Hammer Horror', was included. For German audiences, a documentary following two performances of the tour — titled Kate Bush In Concert — was aired in May 1980.

Fortunately for all of Kate's fans, the concert spawned two physical releases. The On Stage EP (1979) got to number ten

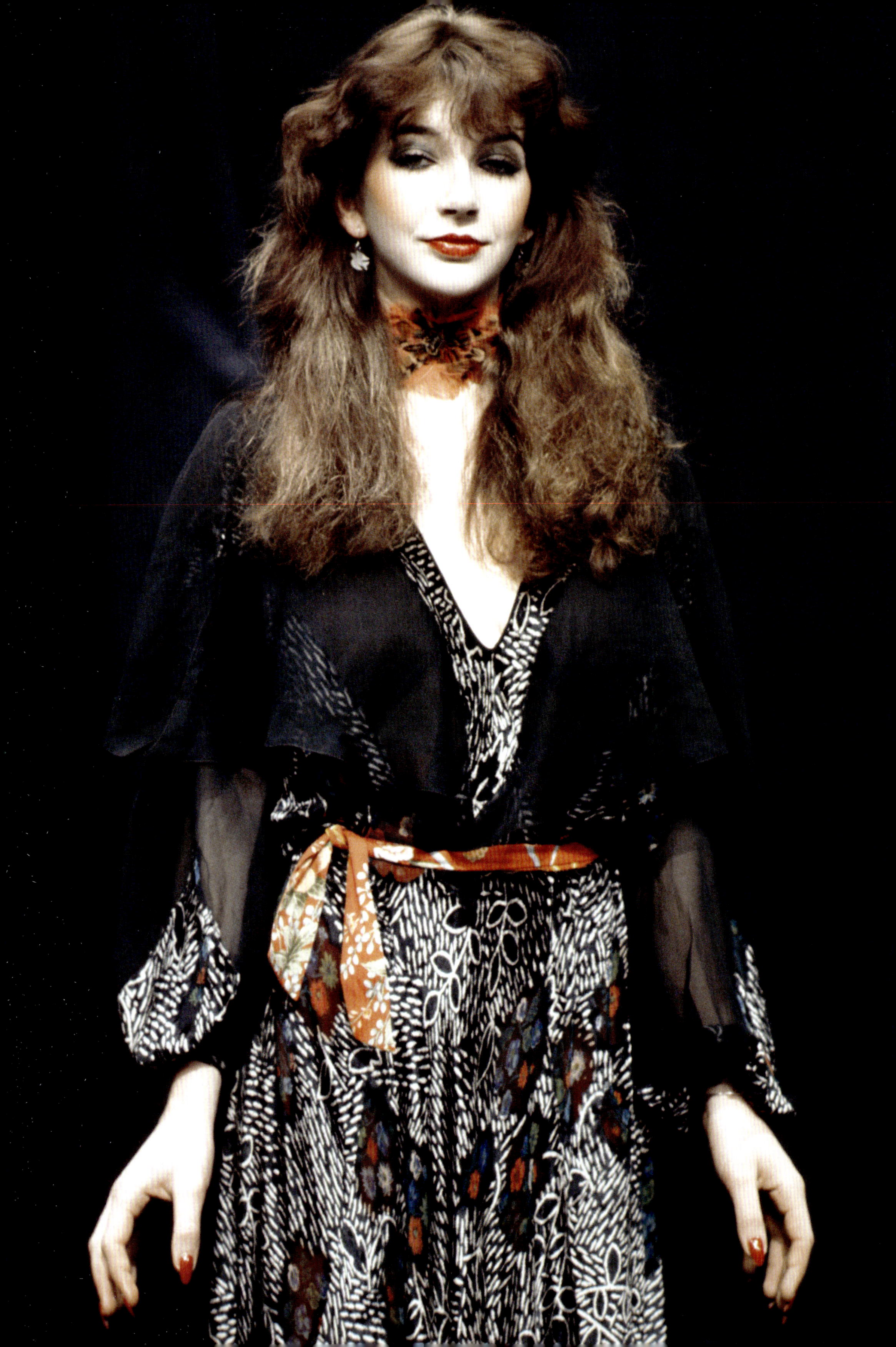

in the UK, where it spent nine weeks on the singles chart. It features live performances of the songs, 'Them Heavy People', 'Don't Push Your Foot On The Heartbrake', 'James And The Cold Gun' and 'L'Amour Looks Something Like You' – as recorded at the Hammersmith Odeon on 13th May 1979. The home video, *Live At Hammersmith Odeon*, directed by Keith "Keef" MacMillan, was released in 1981. It features just twelve songs (also recorded on 13th May 1979). In 1994, *Live At Hammersmith Odeon* was re-issued as a boxset. It included an audio CD of the broadcast as well as the video. Notably, neither the EP nor the home video makes any reference to the name, The Tour Of Life.

Prior to getting to work on production for the tour in December 1978, Kate had turned down an offer to perform as the support act for Fleetwood Mac. From the very start of the tour preparations, she was involved in almost every aspect. This included the show's design, rehearsals, and performances.

The show was co-devised and performed on stage with magician Simon Drake and would go on to be praised for complex lighting, Kate's dancing, and her seventeen costume changes per show.

She choreographed the show with Anthony Van Laast, along with dancers Stewart Avon-Arnold and Gary Hurst. The dance rehearsals commenced at The Place (a dance and performance centre in Duke's Road near Euston) during mornings leading up to the tour, before afternoon vocal and band rehearsals at Wood Wharf Studios in Greenwich. Production rehearsals featuring all personnel and audiovisual technology took place at the Rainbow Theatre, Finsbury Park.

Kate intended for the performances to provide the audience with a theatrical experience and something very much in contrast to the performances of other contemporary rock musicians. The combination of music, dance, poetry, mime, burlesque, magic and theatre all helped to facilitate this.

A large, ribbed screen was a key aspect of the set. Slides and film footage could be projected onto it. There was a central ramp angled down towards the front of the stage. In the shadows, the band were situated either side of it. For 'Room For The Life', Kate performed from a large three-dimensional egg, designed to mirror the womb and the idea of the origins of life. The design was such that it could be rolled on and off stage.

The tour opened on 3rd April 1979 at the Liverpool Empire, following a warm-up gig that had taken place in Poole the day before. It was after the Poole show that the tour's lighting engineer, Bill Duffield, was killed. He fell from a staging

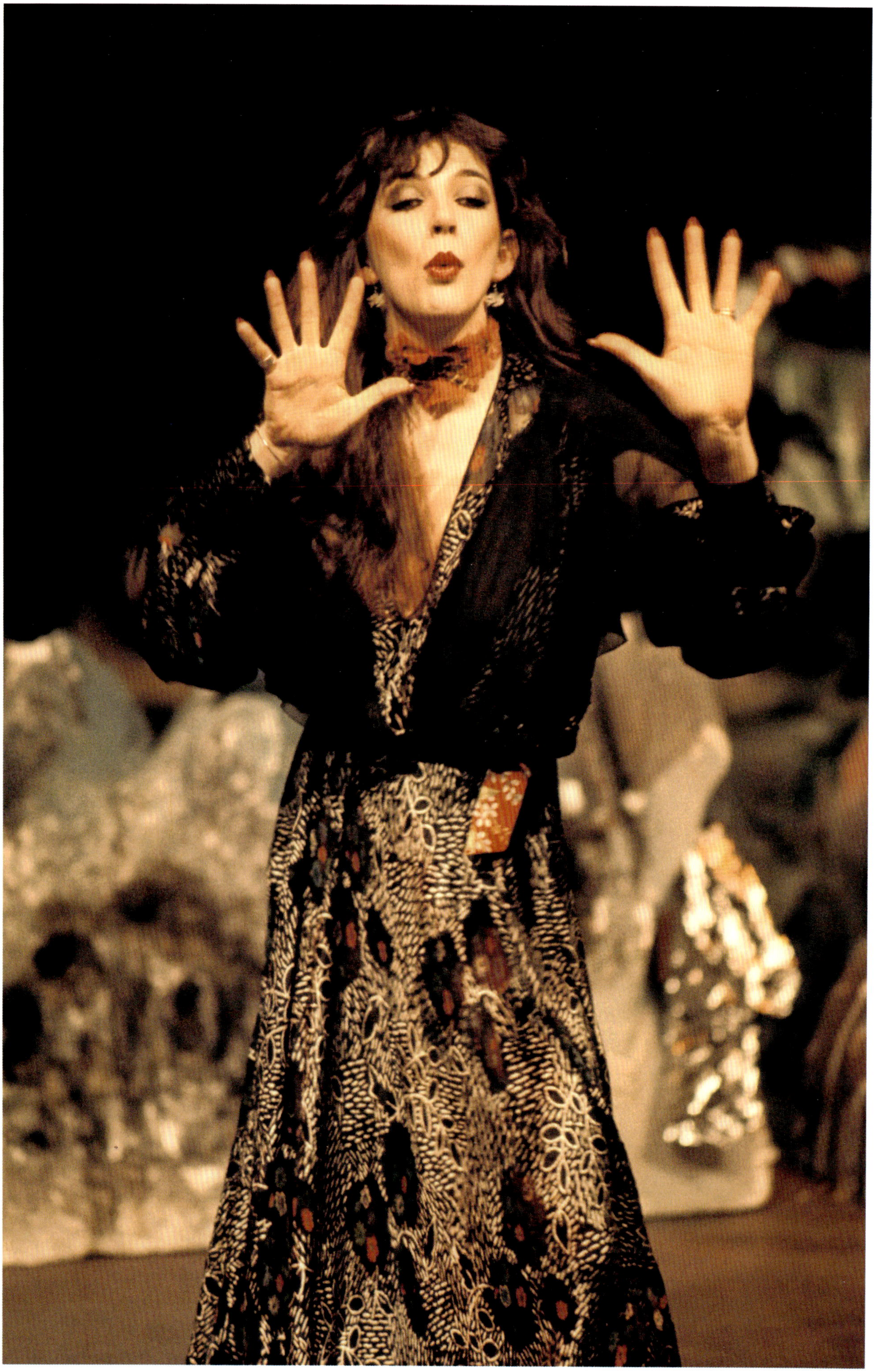

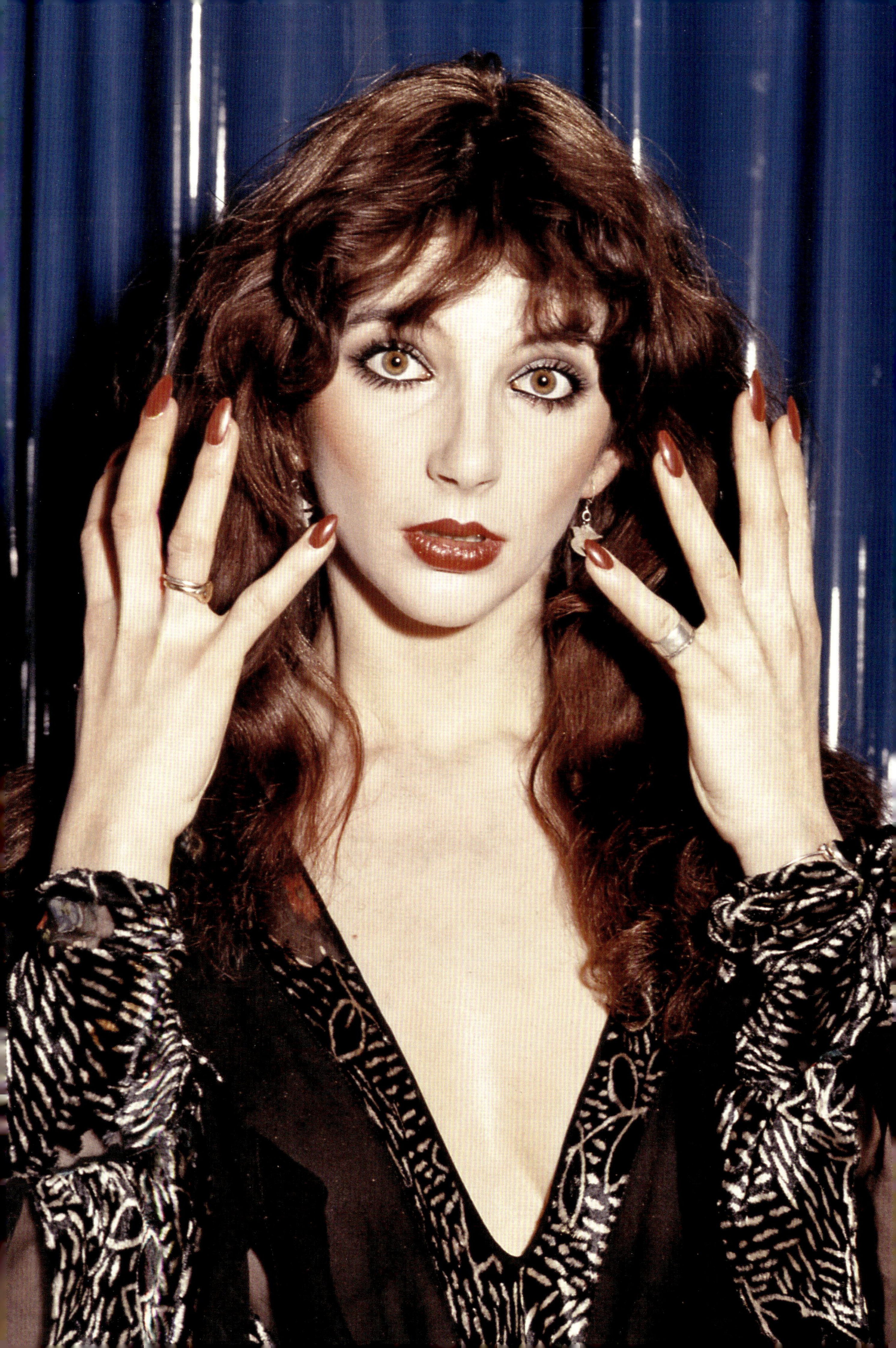

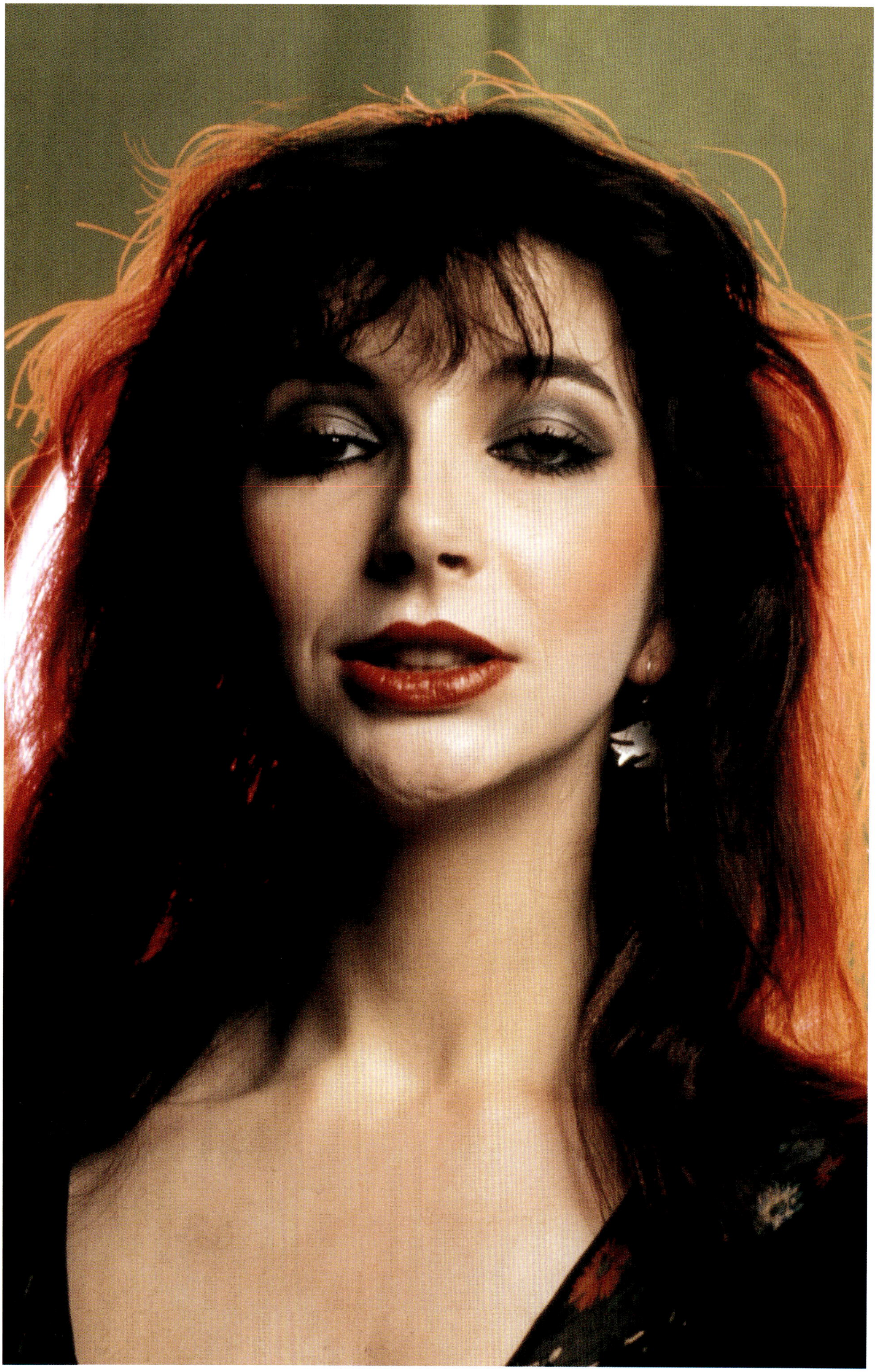

structure at the venue. In response, the first of the final three London dates on 12th May 1979 was performed as a benefit concert for Duffield's family. It included a modified setlist and performances from Peter Gabriel and Steve Harley. Also, on *Never For Ever*, Kate would go on to dedicate a song to him, 'Blow Away (For Bill)'.

The show opened with playback of whale song. Alongside this, Kate's shadow was projected. As she began to dance, the curtain parted to reveal the stage. Wearing a blue leotard, she sang the first song, 'Moving'. During the next number, 'The Saxophone Song', a shadow of the band's saxophone player was projected. Then, the theatre was flooded with the sound of a heartbeat as red lights flickered, all whilst the onstage piano was removed. It was at this point that the large egg-like oval, upholstered with red satin, was rolled out onto the stage. From within it, and as it was rolled around the stage, Kate sang 'Room For The Life'. Dressed in a long coat and trilby hat, she was then joined by her two dancers to perform 'Them Heavy People'. For her performance of 'The Man With The Child In His Eyes', she was back on the piano.

After that, the band played the yet-to-be-released 'Egypt'. During this, Kate came out from the back of the stage sporting an Egyptian-style outfit. An extended introduction to 'L'Amour Looks Something Like You' was played in darkness, biding Kate some time to get changed into a black leotard and red skirt. While centre-stage and next to a tall mirror, the magician emerged to perform with a flying cane. Wearing bat wings and alongside her two dancers dressed as giant violins, Kate performed the song named after said instrument. As the stage darkened, John Carder Bush recited a poem. It culminated in a spoken duet with Kate, who was then illuminated by a spotlight for her performance at the piano of 'The Kick Inside'. To signify the end of the first section of the show, a black veil was placed over her, and then the curtains closed.

The curtains parting to reveal Bush wearing a long black dress marked the beginning of the second section. Sitting on top of the piano, she performed 'In The Warm Room'. She then moved to play the piano to perform 'Fullhouse'. Following this, the band played an extended introduction to 'Strange Phenomena' to enable Kate to change into a magician's top hat and tails. Her dancers were dressed as spacemen to perform with her. The magician then reappeared with his cane. He walked to the back of the stage whilst holding a black cloth, which he then majestically dropped. Behind it was Kate, who was wearing a veil by that point. Recreating the routine from the song's music video, she danced with one of the dancers to

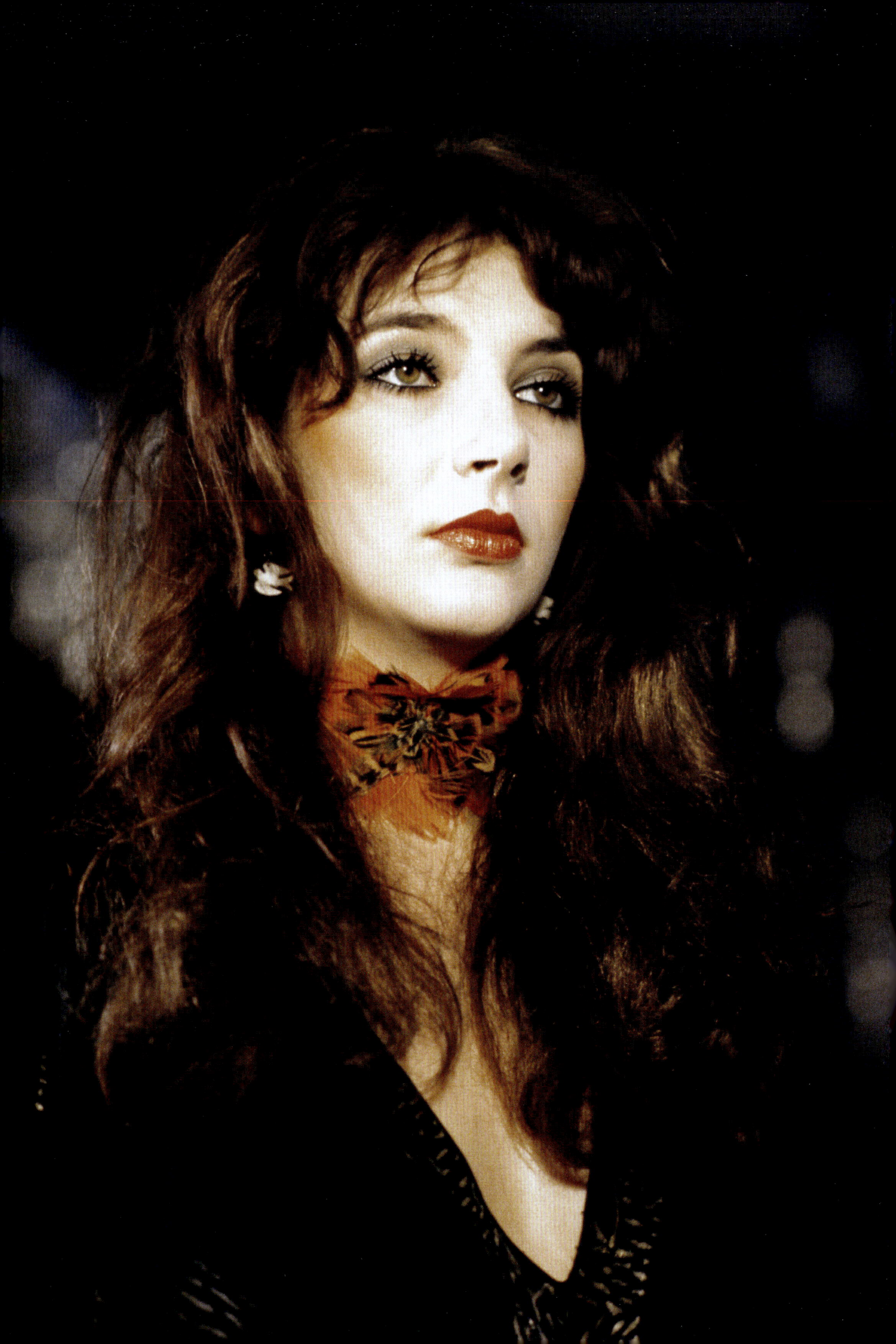

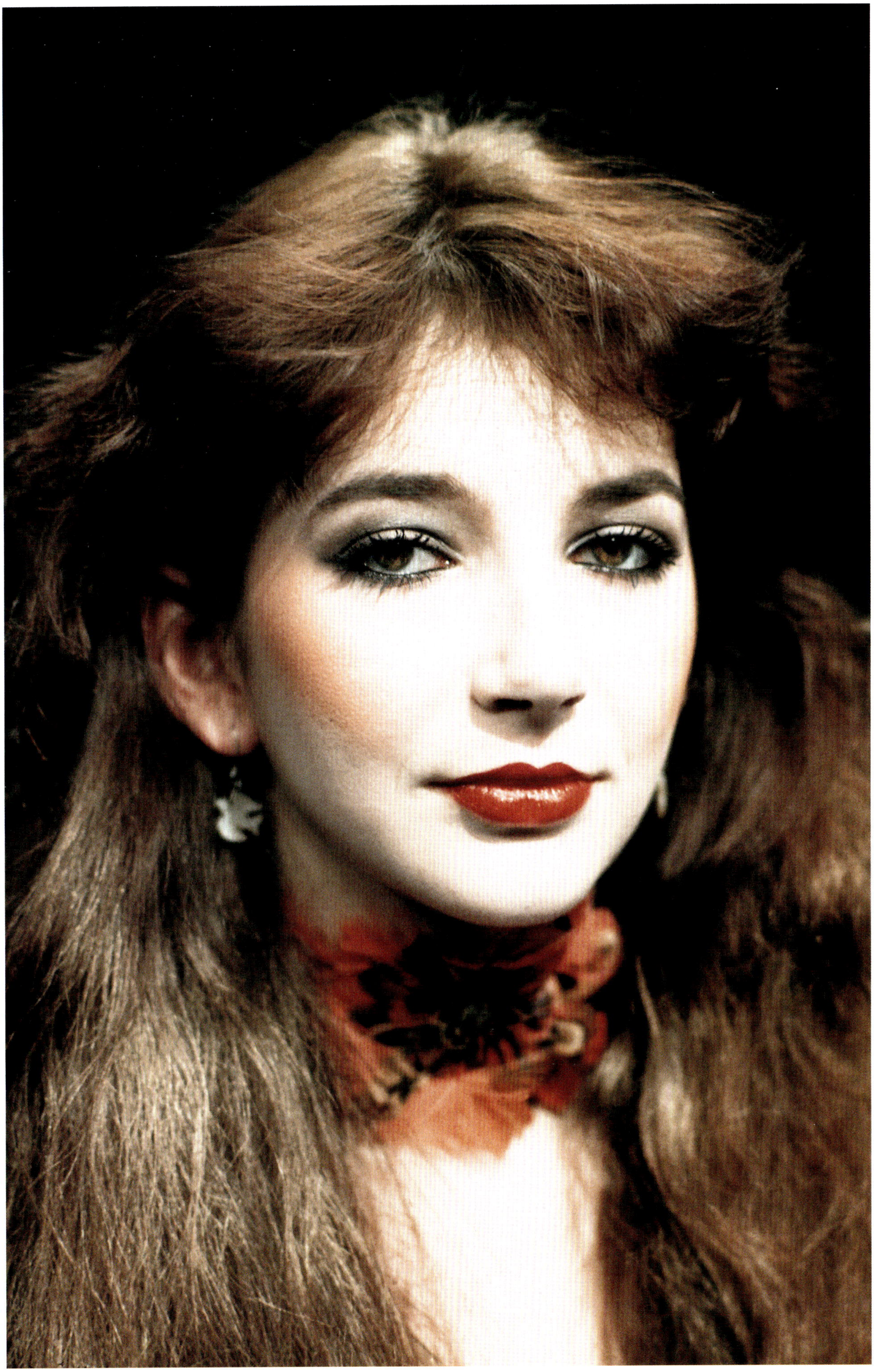

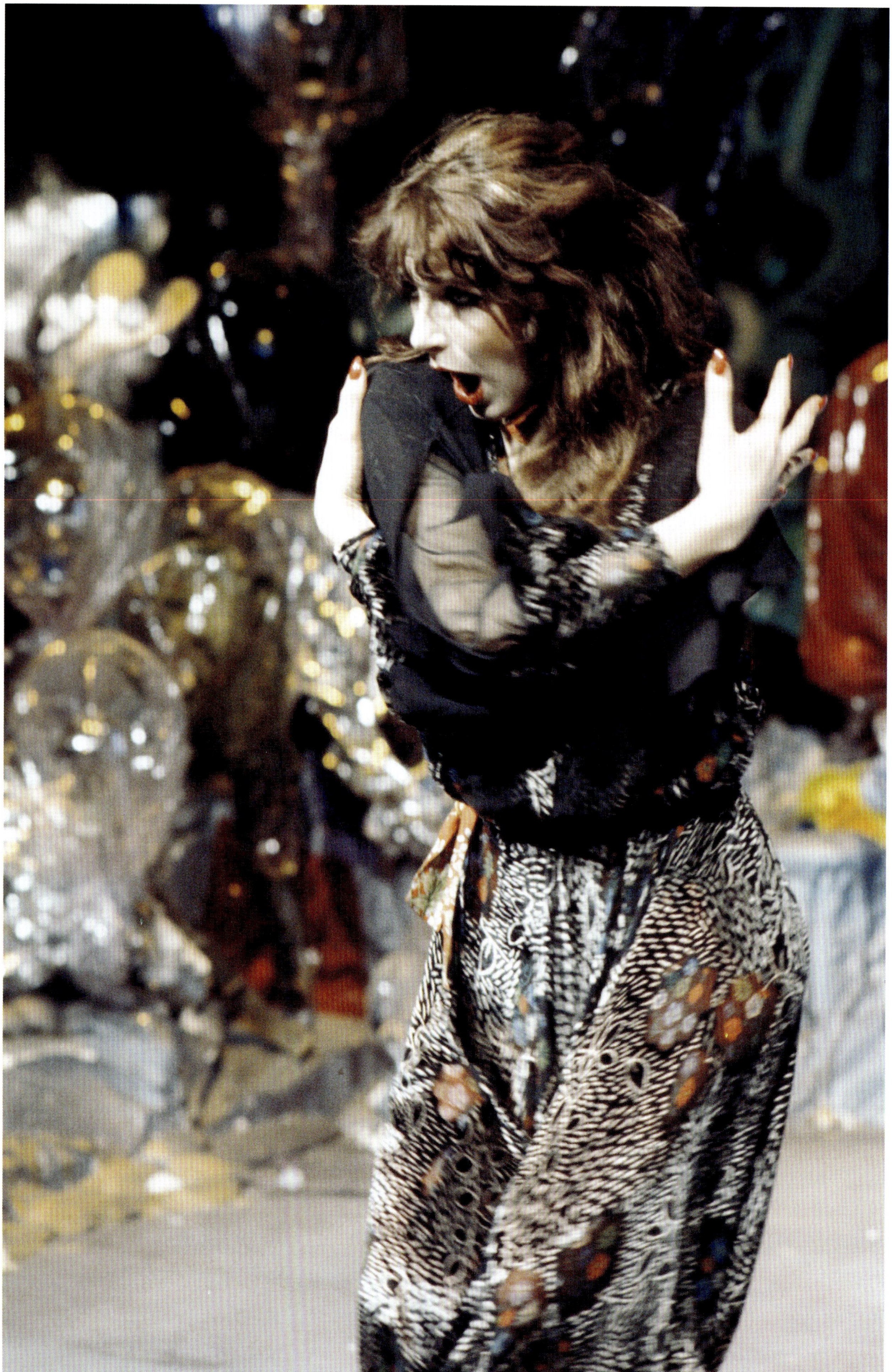

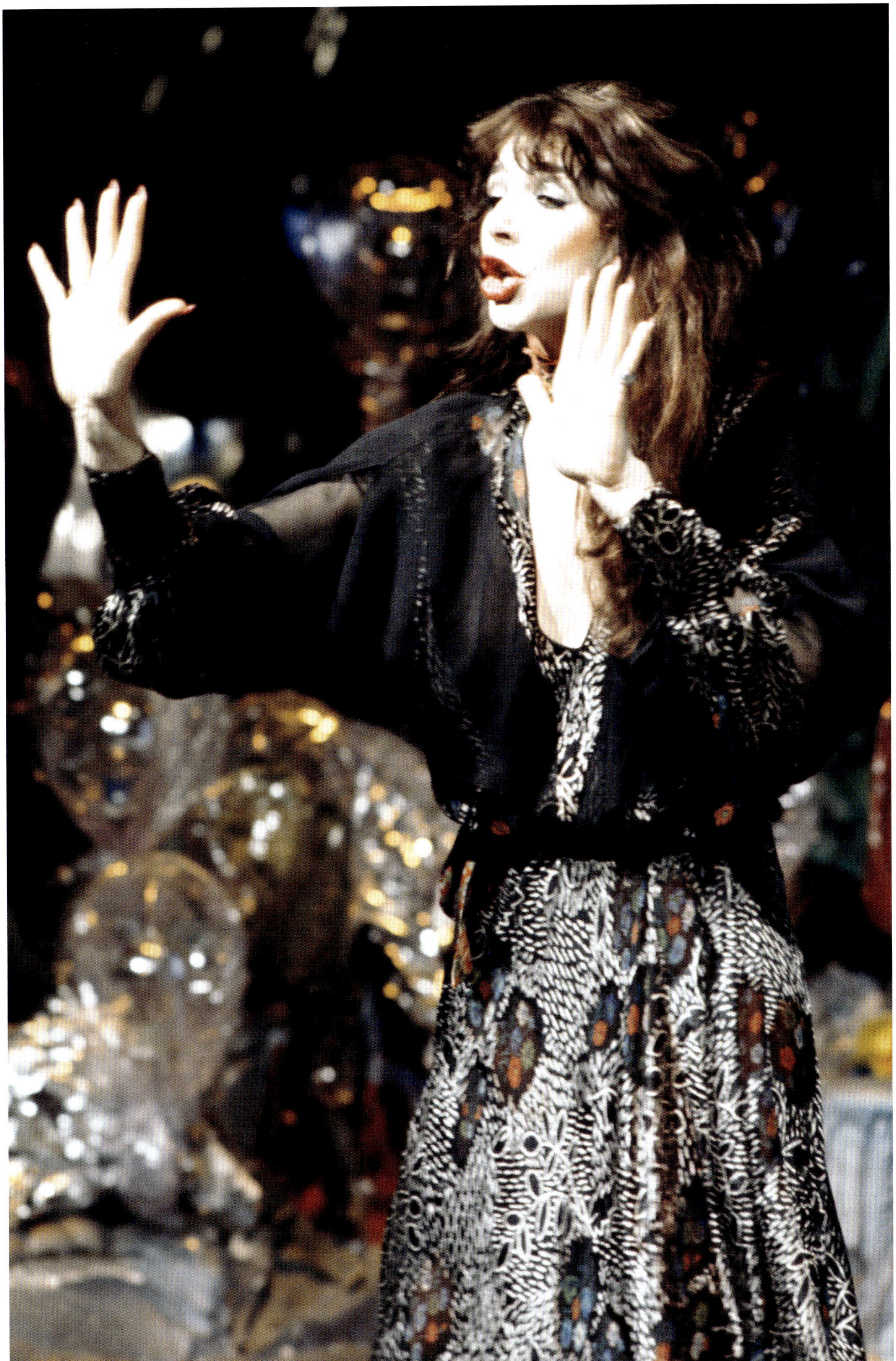

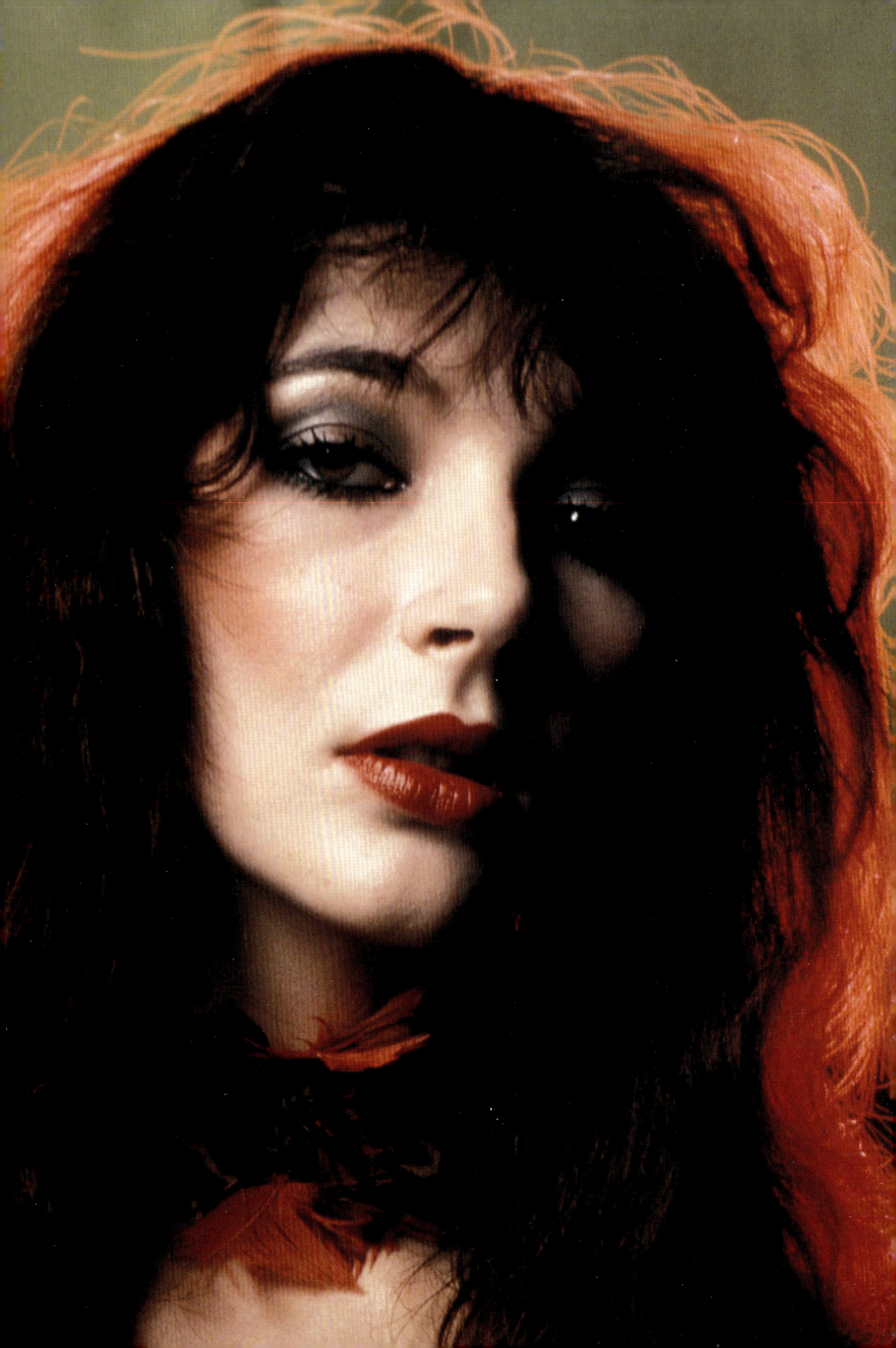

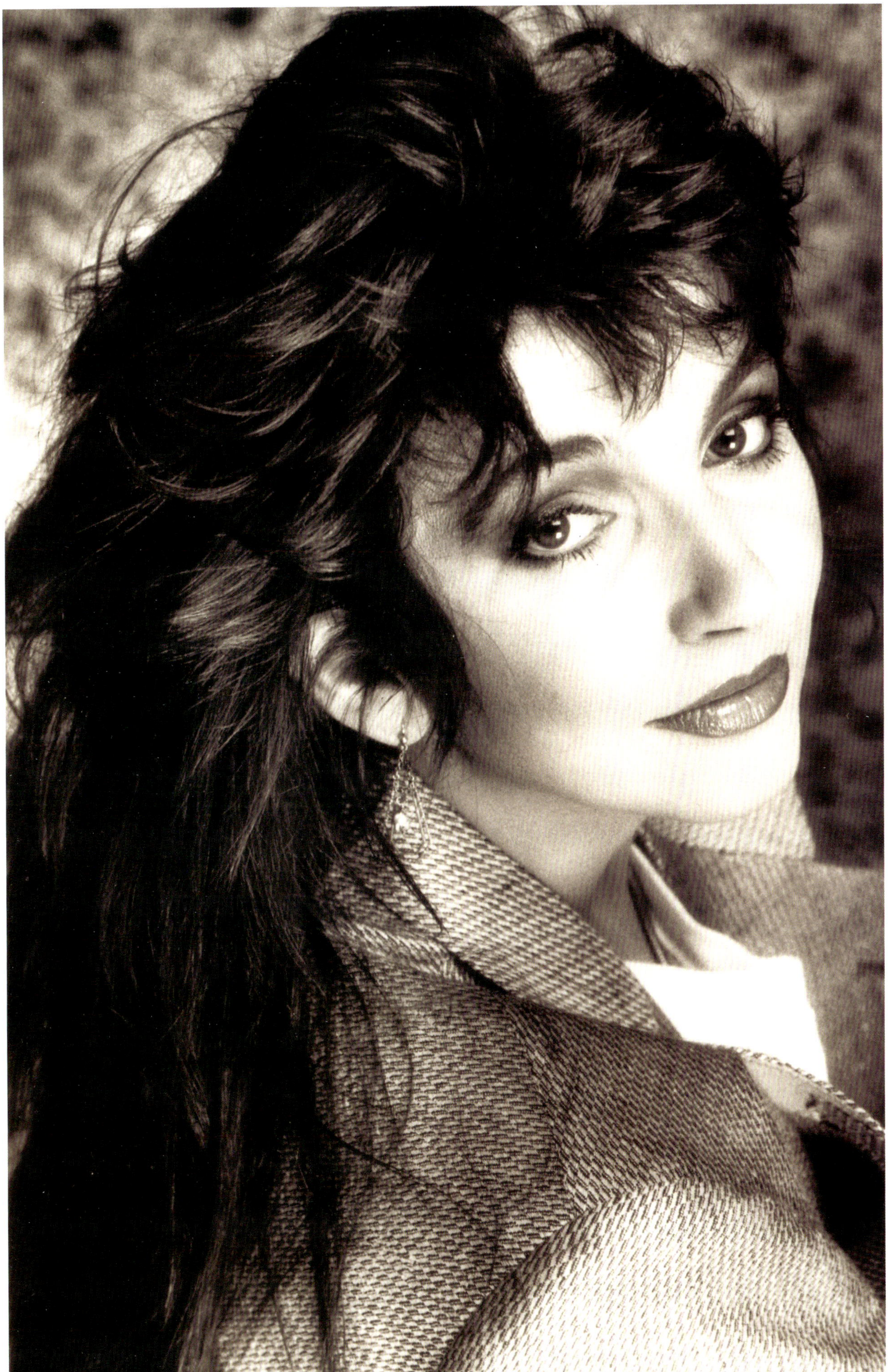

a live rehearsal playback recording of 'Hammer Horror'. Next, a chant commenced. It led into 'Kashka From Baghdad', which Kate performed at the piano. While the stage was fitted with a street theme – including fences which the dancers illuminated with torches – traffic noise was played to the audience. A spotlight was switched on and then Kate sang and danced to 'Don't Push Your Foot On The Heartbrake', the number that brought the second section to a close.

For the third section, the curtain opened to reveal Kate in a purple dress. Positioned at the edge of the ramp that had been lifted to replicate a pier, she performed 'Wow'. As a prisoner cell set was assembled, 'Coffee Homeground' began. It saw Kate singing on a centre-stage chair as corpse props fell out of the walls. Following this was another spoken-word poem from her brother. 'Symphony In Blue' – incorporating elements of 'Gymnopédie No.1' by Erik Satie – then began to play. Dressed in a blue leotard covered by a leather jacket by this point, Kate performed while waving to the audience as images of a cloudy sky were projected. By then covered in party streamers, she refused a floating glass of champagne from the magician and performed 'Feel It' at the piano. As the song came to an end, the sound of thunder was played as Kate once again changed outfits. It saw her emerging with her leotard fitted with wings. After performing 'Kite' in the attire, she was lifted off the stage as the song came to an end. She then appeared in Wild West attire. Brandishing a prop shotgun, she danced and sang 'James And The Cold Gun'. Towards the end of the song, her dancers emerged from the wings. They were shot by Kate, with red ribbons used to communicate the idea of gunfire. The curtains then closed.

For the show's first encore, Kate and her dancers emerged wearing World War Two Spitfire pilot attire. A parachute was spread across the stage and she sat to sing 'Oh England My Lionheart'. Following this, the curtains closed again. After a short time, they re-opened to reveal the stage covered in dry ice fog, illuminated in red with a forest backdrop. As the music for 'Wuthering Heights' started, Kate moved charismatically through the fog, costumed as the ghost of Catherine Earnshaw from Emily Brontë's novel. The dance routine was the same as the one from the song's music video. Kate then retreated to the top of the ramp. She waved to the audience and left the stage as the curtain closed.

****

1979 Tour, Kate performing 'Egypt'.

LIONHEART
Kate Bush Band, U.K. & European Tour 1979.

Who.

Who	What	Who
Management HILARY WALKER 5, HURST LANE, EAST MOLESEY, ALSO SEE SURREY PRODUCTION OFFICE 01-941-3741	'THE BUCK STOPS HERE'?	Tour Manager RICHARD AIMES 11, LINCOLN RD, EAST FINCHLEY, LONDON, N2. 01-883-1060
Record Company E.M.I INTERNATIONAL LTD. MANCHESTER SQ LONDON, W1. 01-486-4488.	TOUR SUPPORT RECORD PROMOTION + SALES @ VENUES.	Press & P.R.
Promoter SEE BOOKING AGENT.		ALSO SEE RECORD COMPANY. Photography
Booking Agents LYNDSEY BROWN. ROCK EXCHANGE, 1, DERBY ST, LONDON, W.1. 01-493-9637	TOUR PLANNING, VENUE LIASON ON TOUR	Merchandising
Production Company PRESENTATION SERVICES 205A, ARCHWAY RD, HIGHGATE, ALSO SEE LONDON, N6. PRODUCTION DESIGNER 01-340-6970	PRODUCTION DESIGN AND ORGANISATION STAGE MANAGEMENT + DIRECTION	Production Designer DAVID JACKSON 205A, ARCHWAY ROAD, HIGHGATE, LONDON, N6 01-340-69
P.A. Suppliers	SOUND EQUIPMENT + SOUND CREW	Sound Engineer
Lighting Suppliers SHOWLITES T.B.C. UNIT 8, LEATHER MARKET, WESTON ST, LONDON S.E.1. 01-403-2877	LIGHTING, CONTROLS + LIGHTING CREW	ALSO SEE P.A. SUPPLIERS. Lighting Consultant JAMES DANN 61, WHEATSHEAF WAY, LINTON, CAMBS. 0223-892783.
Graphic Design	LOGO'S, POSTERS, PROGRAMMES, TICKETS, SECURITY PASSES	CHIEF PROJECTIONIST.
Printing		

When & Where

PRODUCTION SCHEDULE	REHEARSAL SCHEDULE	TOUR SCHEDULE U.K.	TOUR SCHEDULE EUROPE.
January ARTISTIC + SCRIPT MEETINGS 2nd DAVE, KATE, PADDY + DEL @ WICKHAM RD 4TH " 7TH " 10TH " 16TH DAVE, KATE, HILARY, PADDY, DEL NICK, JAMES + LISE @ WICKHAM RD 18TH DAVE, KATE, HILARY, RICHARD, NICK + BAND @ GREENWICH. 22nd KATE + LISE. COSTUMES. 25TH KATE + DAVE. SETS + B.P PRACTICAL + FINANCIAL 5TH DAVE + HILARY @ BRYANSTON CRT. 11TH DAVE, HILARY, RICHARD " 13TH DAVE, JAMES @ ARCHWAY 14TH DAVE, LISE @ " 17TH DAVE, HILARY, KATE, RICHARD, JAY, MR BUSH. 18TH " " - WICKHAM FARM 19TH 20TH 22 23 24 25 26 27 28	**January** BAND @ WOODWHARF STUDIOS ALL MONTH. **February** BAND @ WOODWHARF STUDIOS ALL MONTH 2nd OR 6TH @ SHEPPERTON TO CHECK P.A. + STAGE SIZE. **March.** 5TH/6TH TO 10TH/11TH BRIXTON 12TH TO 23rd @ RAINBOW. T.B.C THERE WILL BE A GET-OUT/PACK/FIT-UP 'REHEARSAL' FOR THE CREW BETWEEN BRIXTON + THE RAINBOW. T.B.C.	**March** 25TH 26TH 27TH 28TH 29TH IRELAND? 30TH IRELAND? 31ST. **April** 1ST 2nd 3RD LIVERPOOL EMPIRE, 4TH BIRMINGHAM HIPPO' 5TH	**April** 15TH EDINBURGH KINGS THEATRE. 16TH 17TH 18TH } RAINBOW OR 19TH } DRURY LANE EUROPE **May**

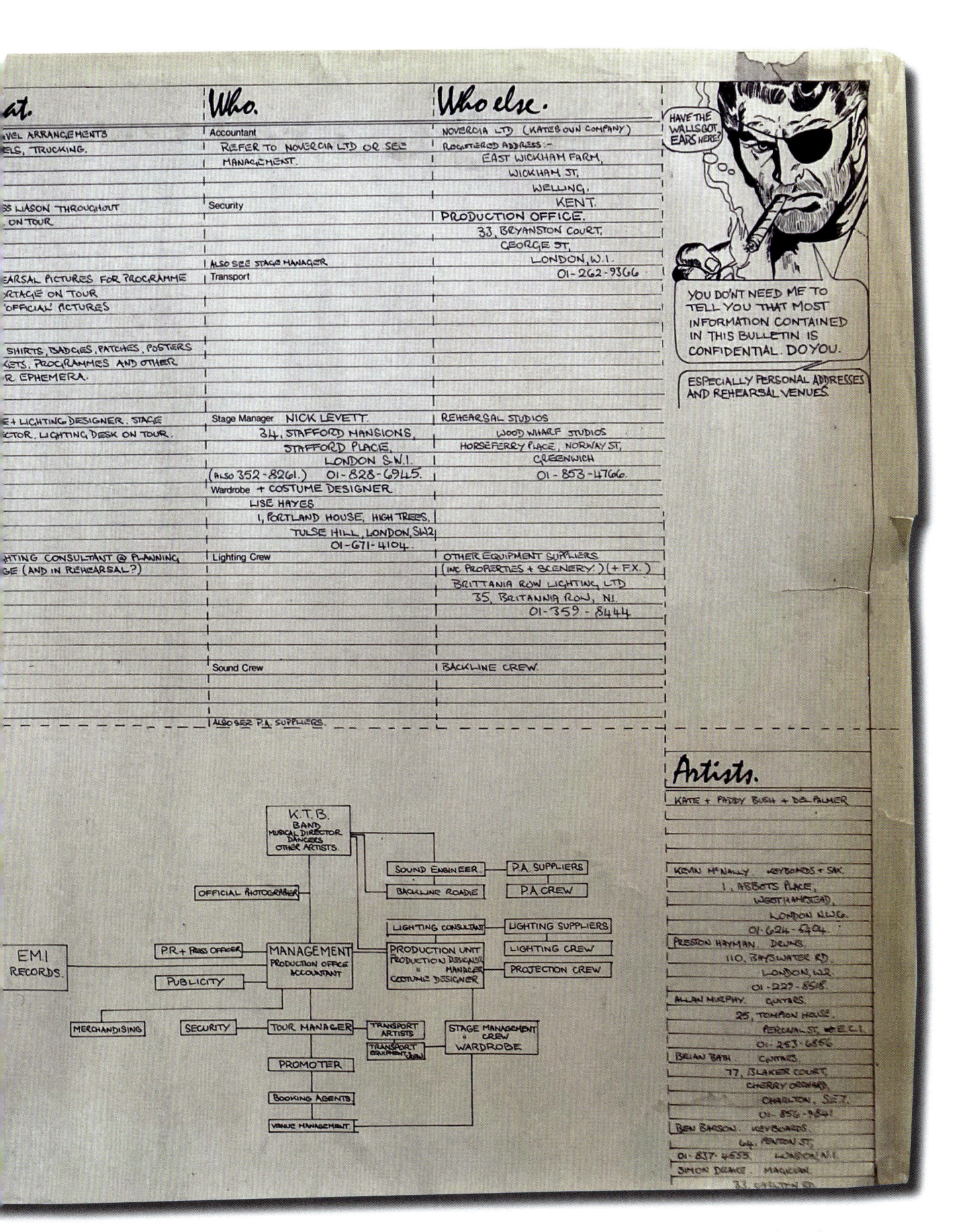

Tour planning was meticulous, as can be seen here from the tour production overview sheet (from the collection of stage and lighting production manager David Jackson).

Opening night,
3rd April 1979,
Liverpool Empire.

© Alan Perry Concert Photography

Breakdown of the tour's setlist:

Moving
The Saxophone Song
Room For The Life
Them Heavy People
The Man With The Child In His Eyes
Egypt
L'amour Looks Something Like You
Violin
The Kick Inside

Interlude - John Carder Bush poetry reading

In The Warm Room
Fullhouse *(not performed at the Hammersmith Odeon dates in London)*
Strange Phenomena
Hammer Horror *(not sung live)*
Kashka From Baghdad

Interlude - Chanting

Dont Push Your Foot On The Heartbrake
Wow
Coffee Homeground *(with extended instrumental introduction)*
In Search Of Peter Pan

Interlude - John Carder Bush poetry reading

Symphony In Blue *(contains elements of Gymnopédie No.1 by Erik Satie)*
Feel It *(with instrumental introduction)*
Kite
James And The Cold Gun

First Encore
Oh England My Lionheart

Second Encore
Wuthering Heights

Kate performing 'Kite'.

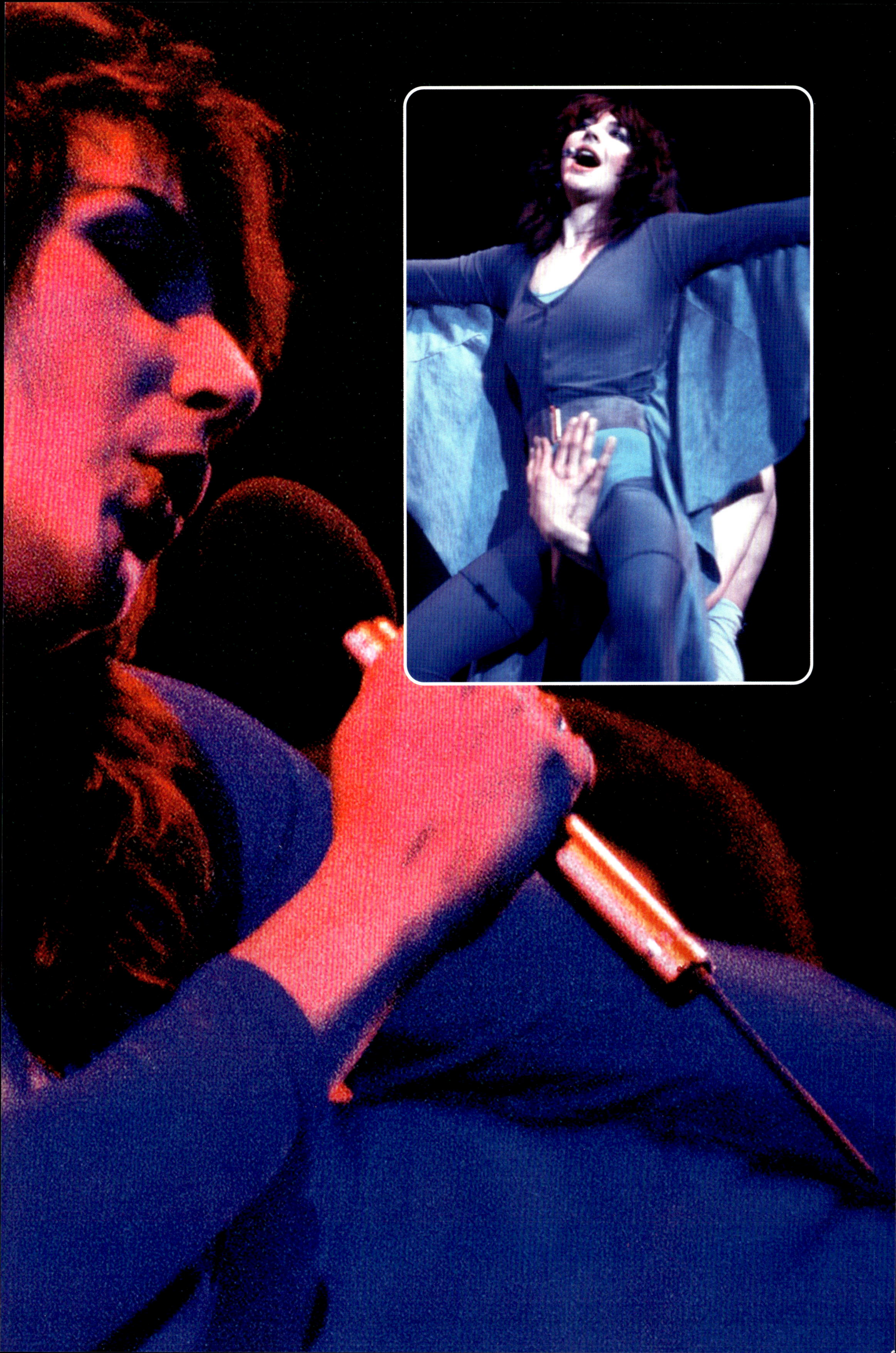

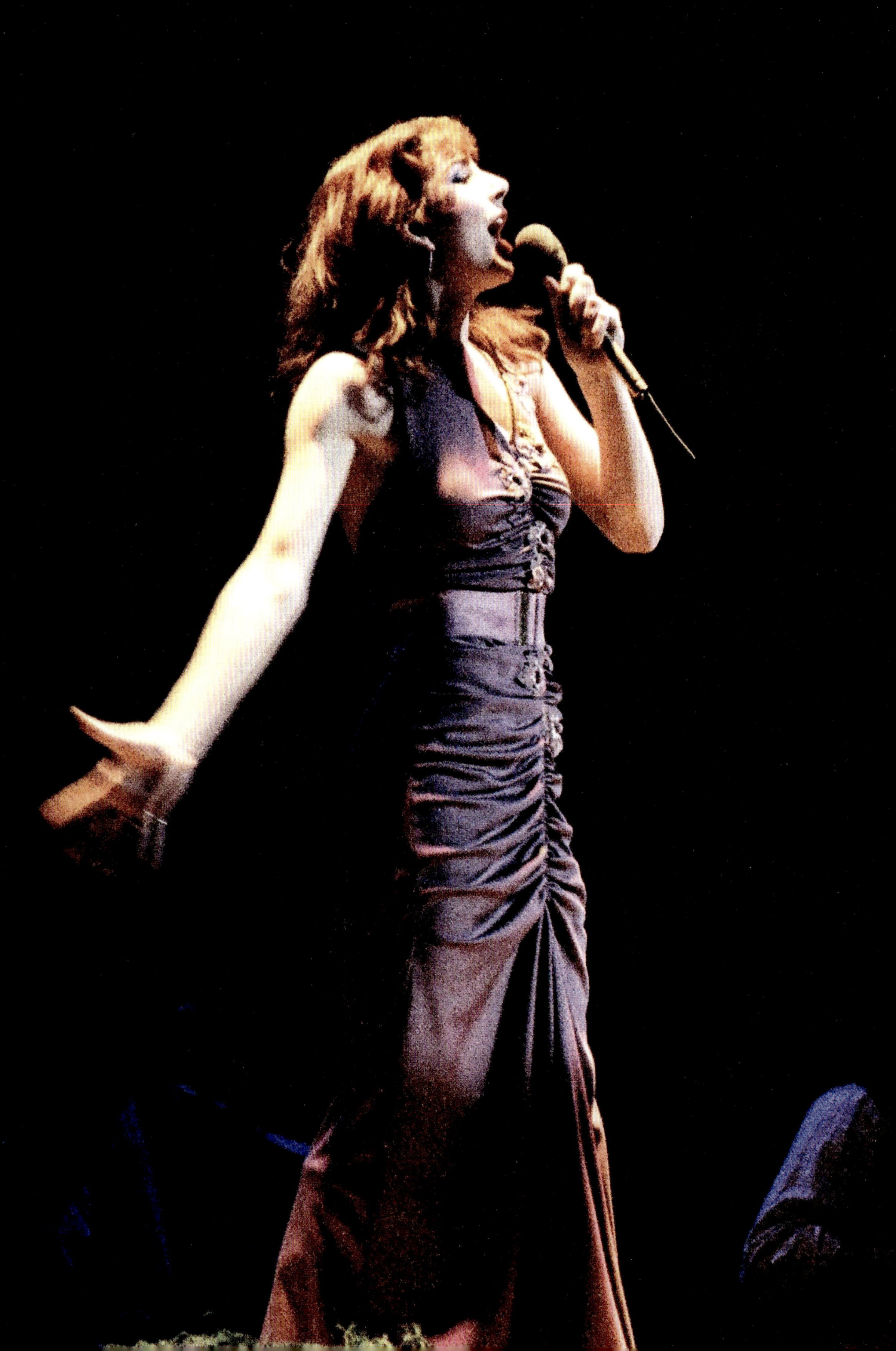

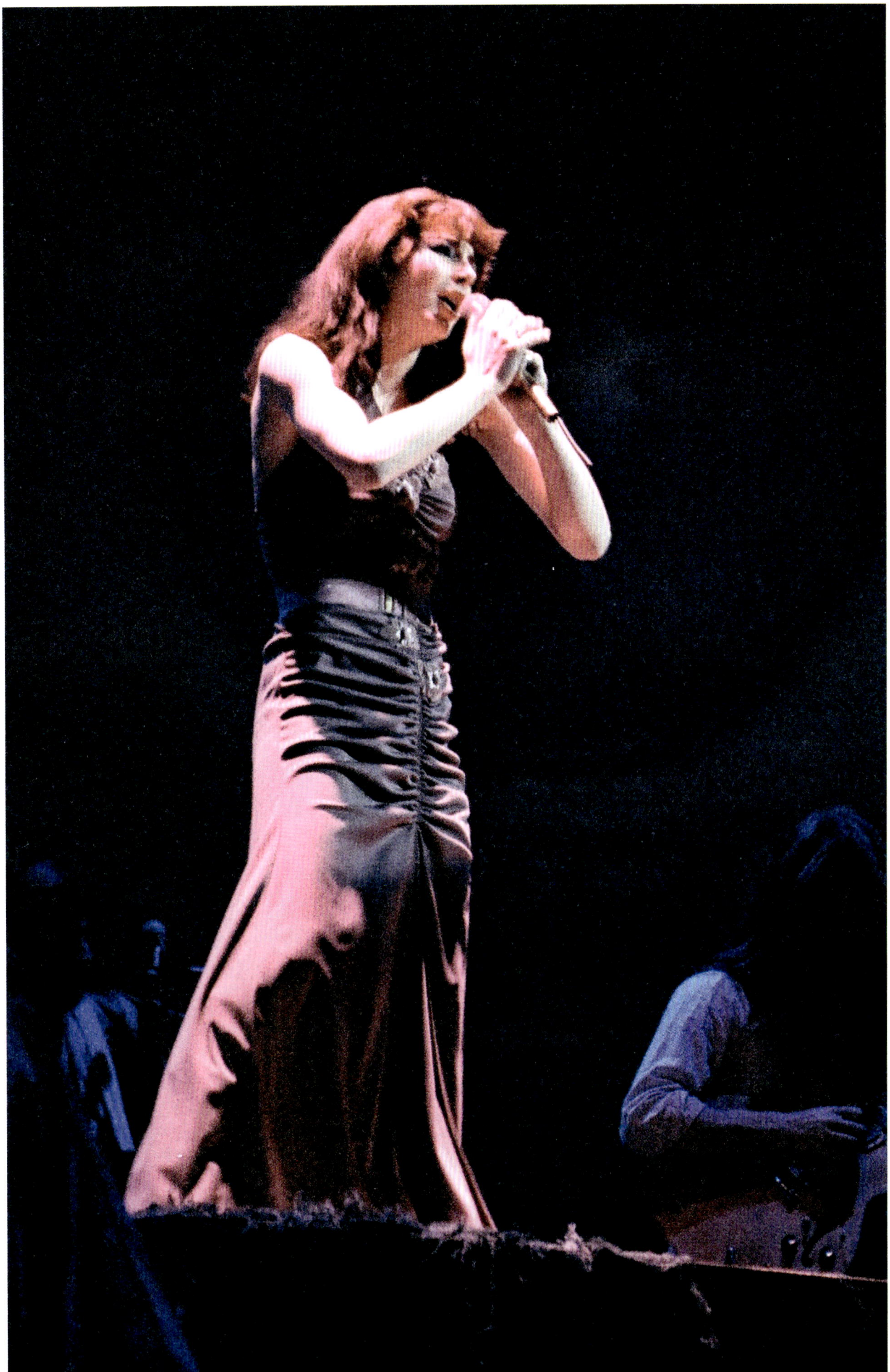

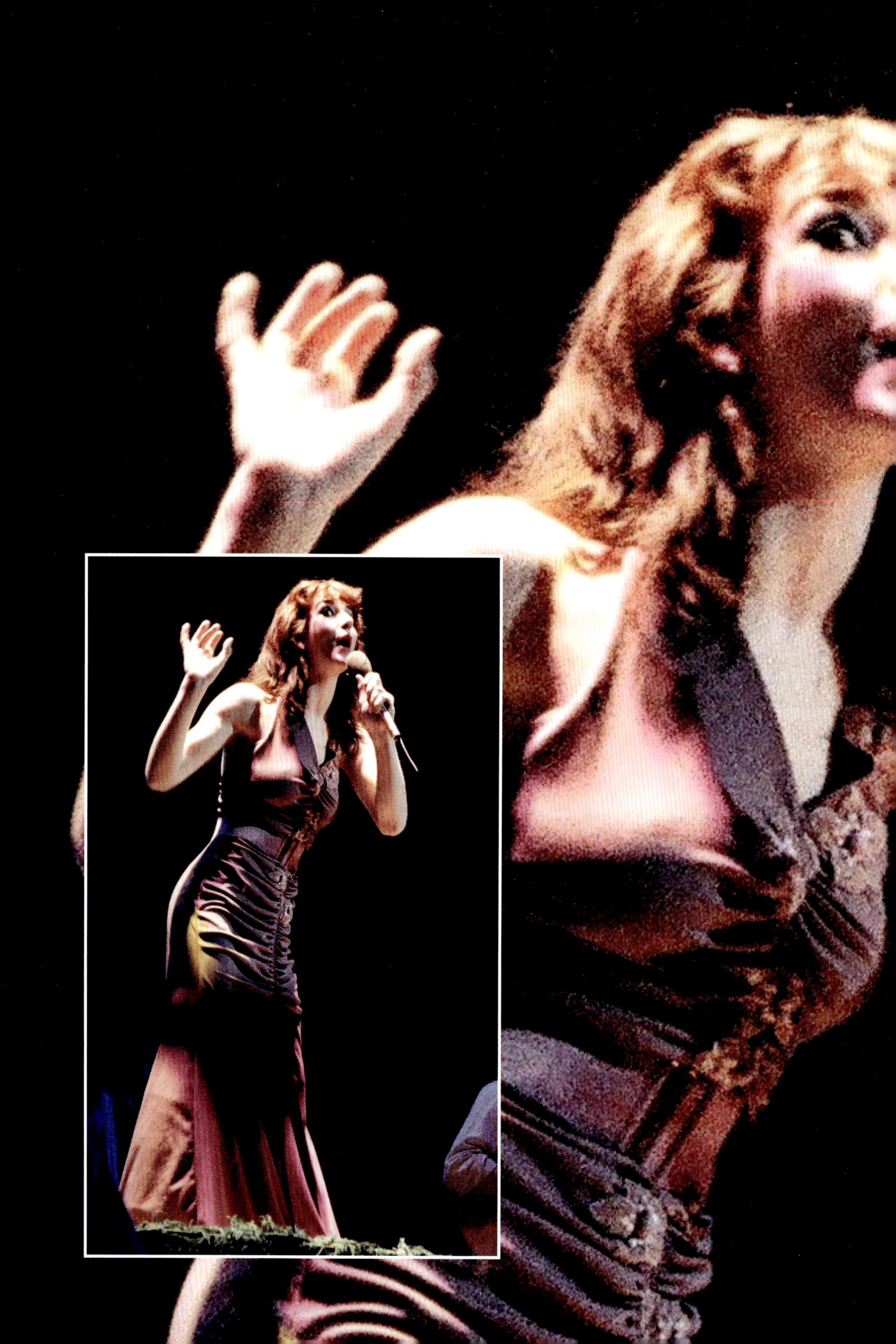

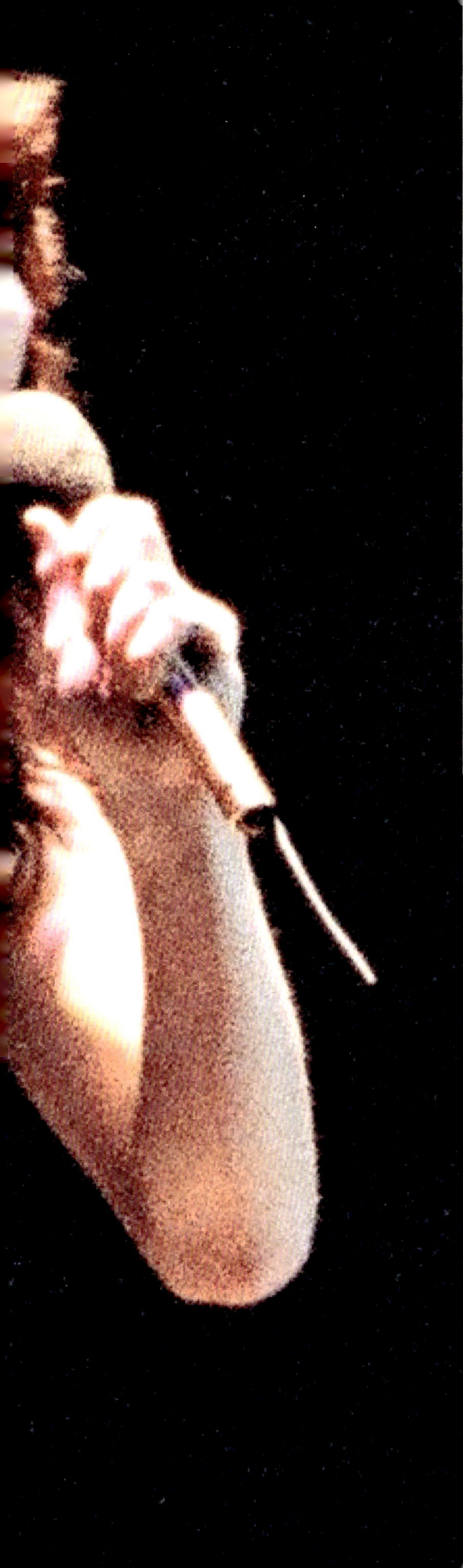

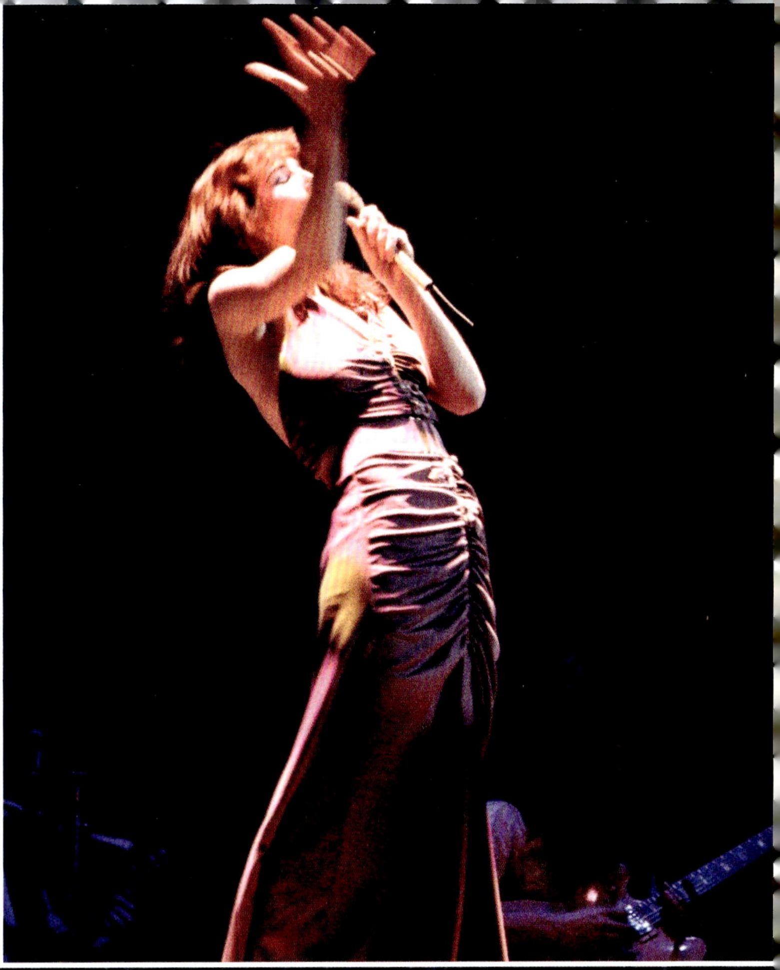

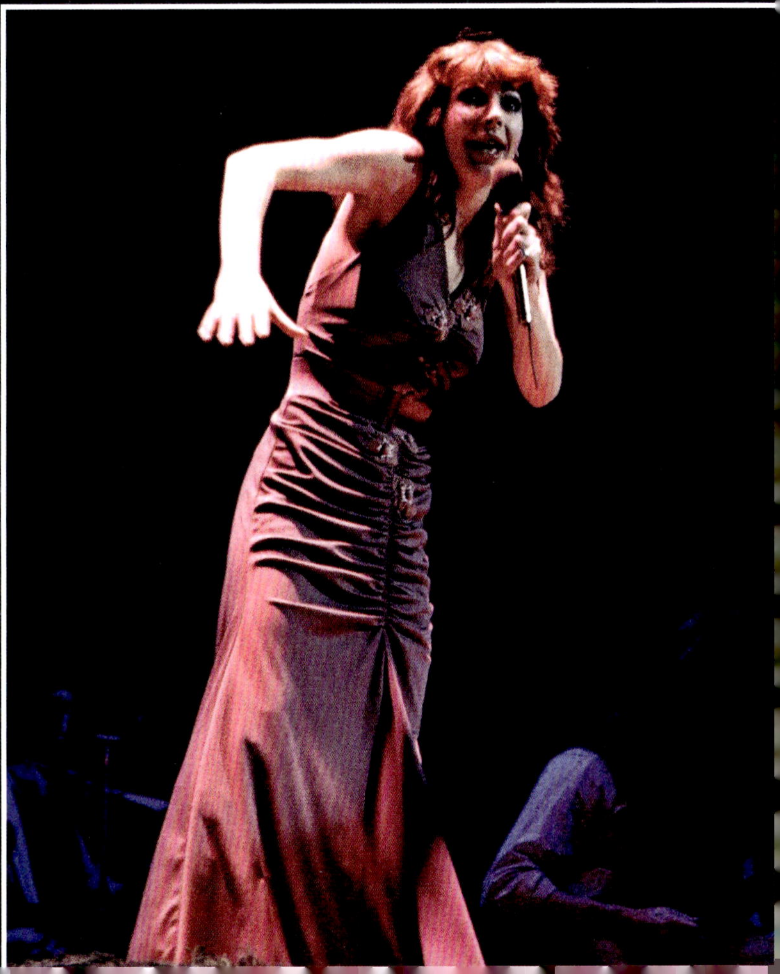

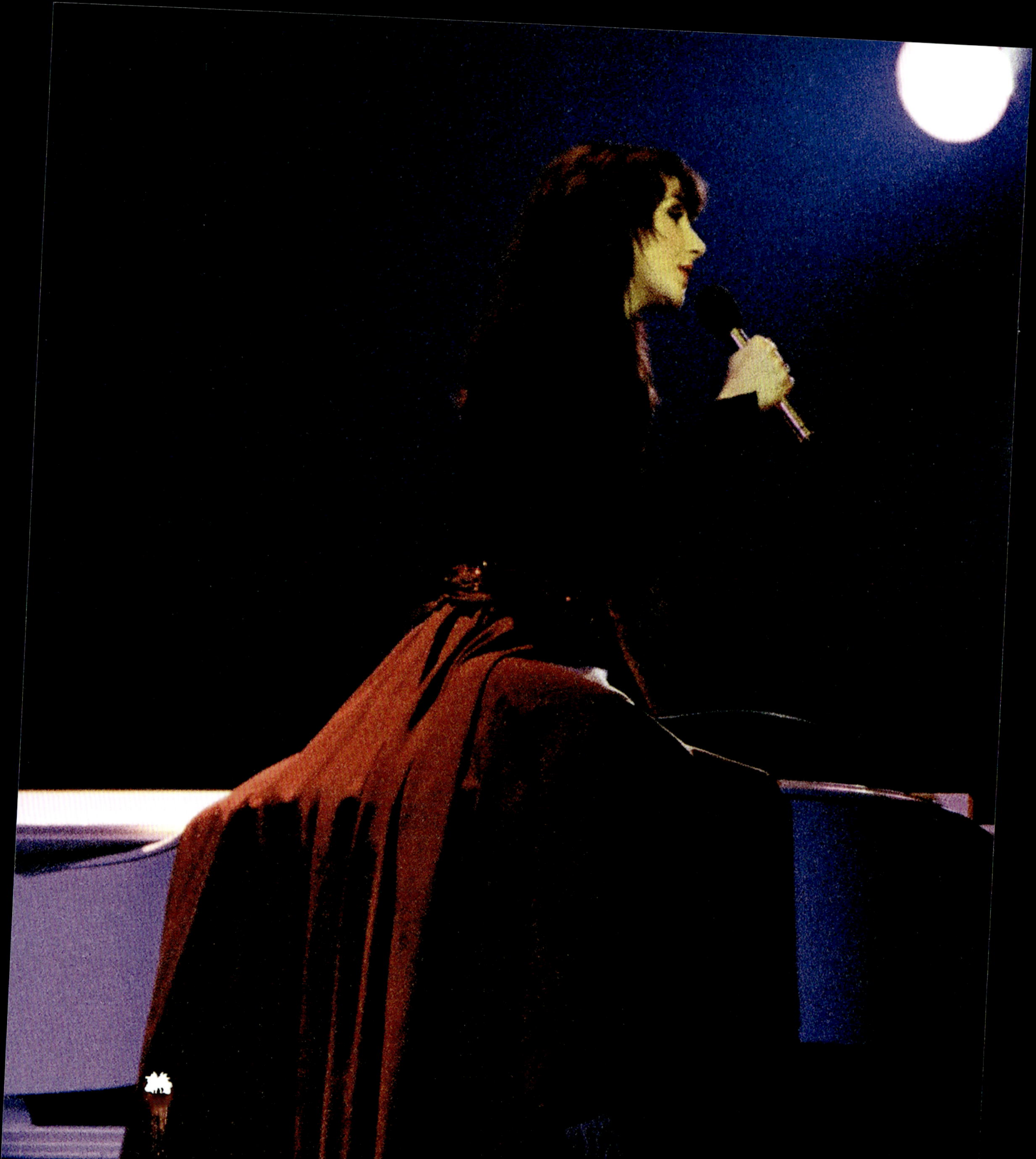

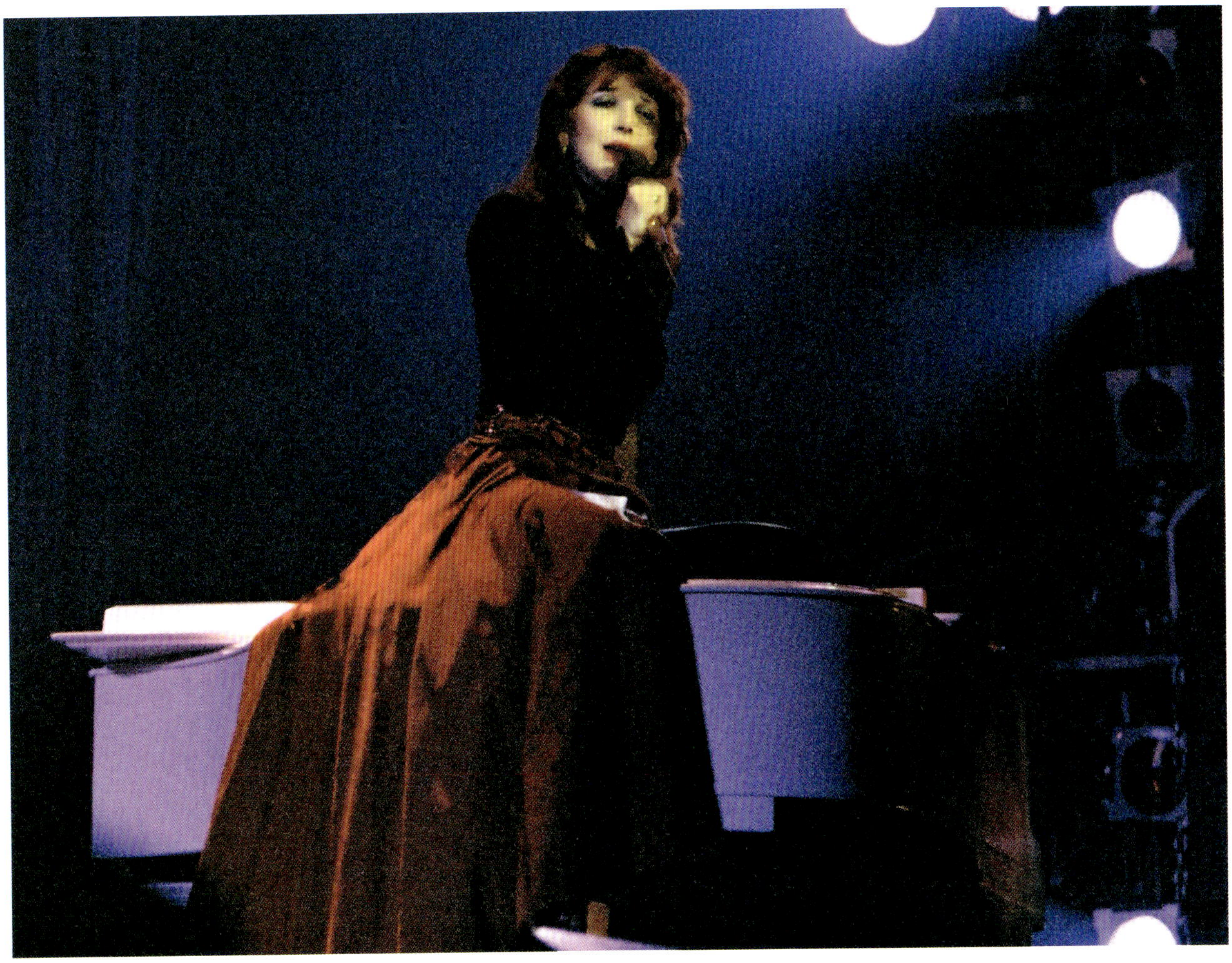

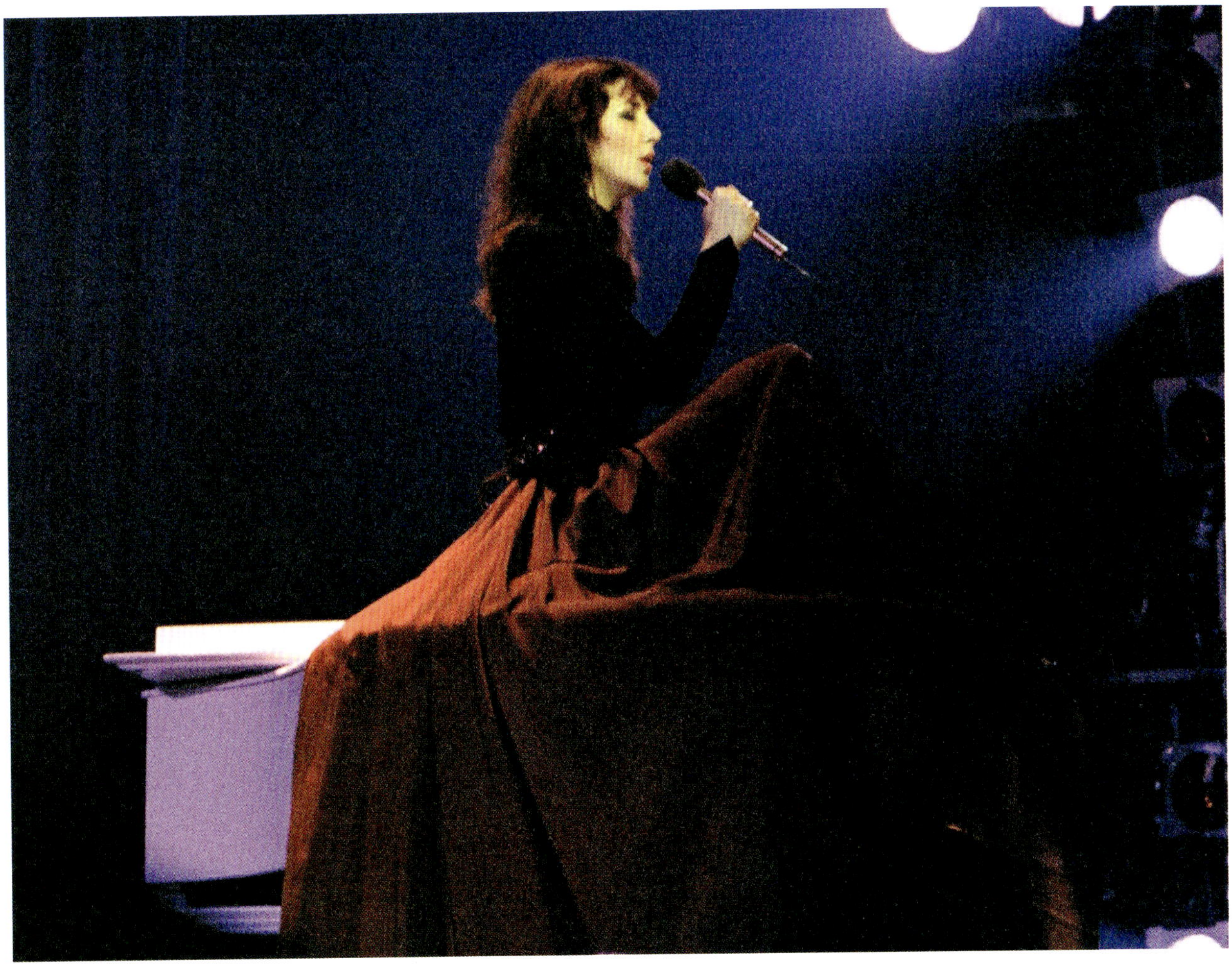

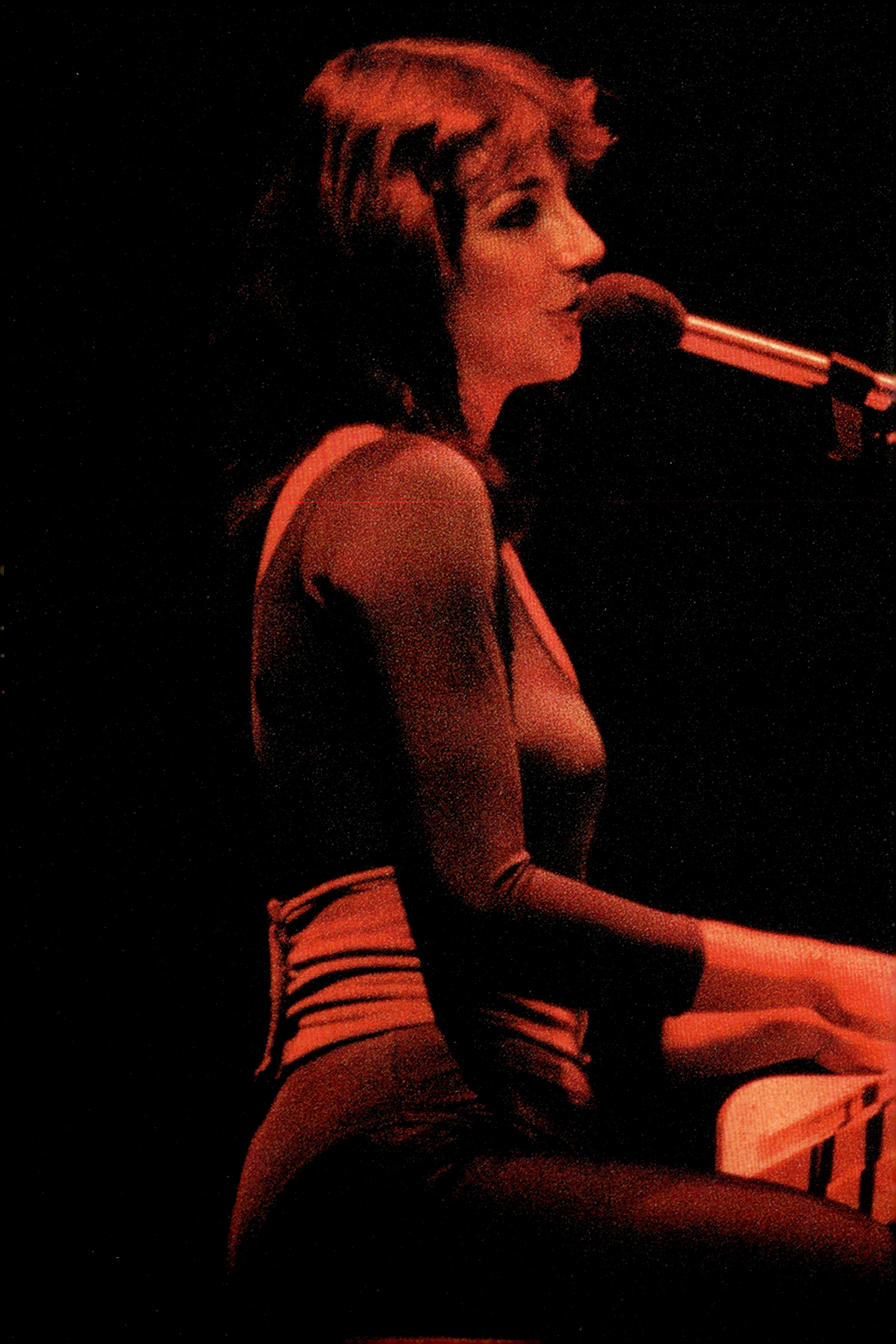

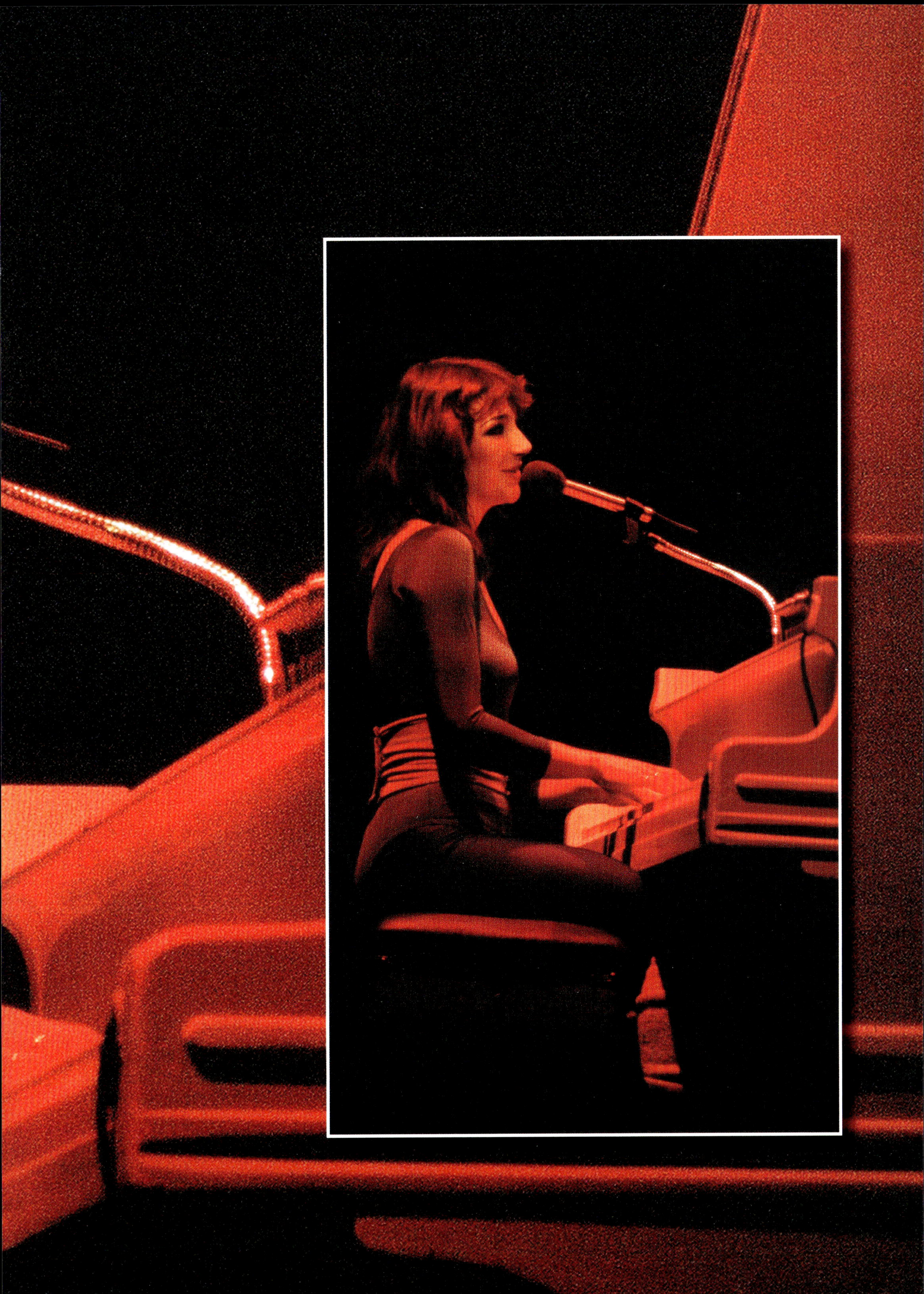

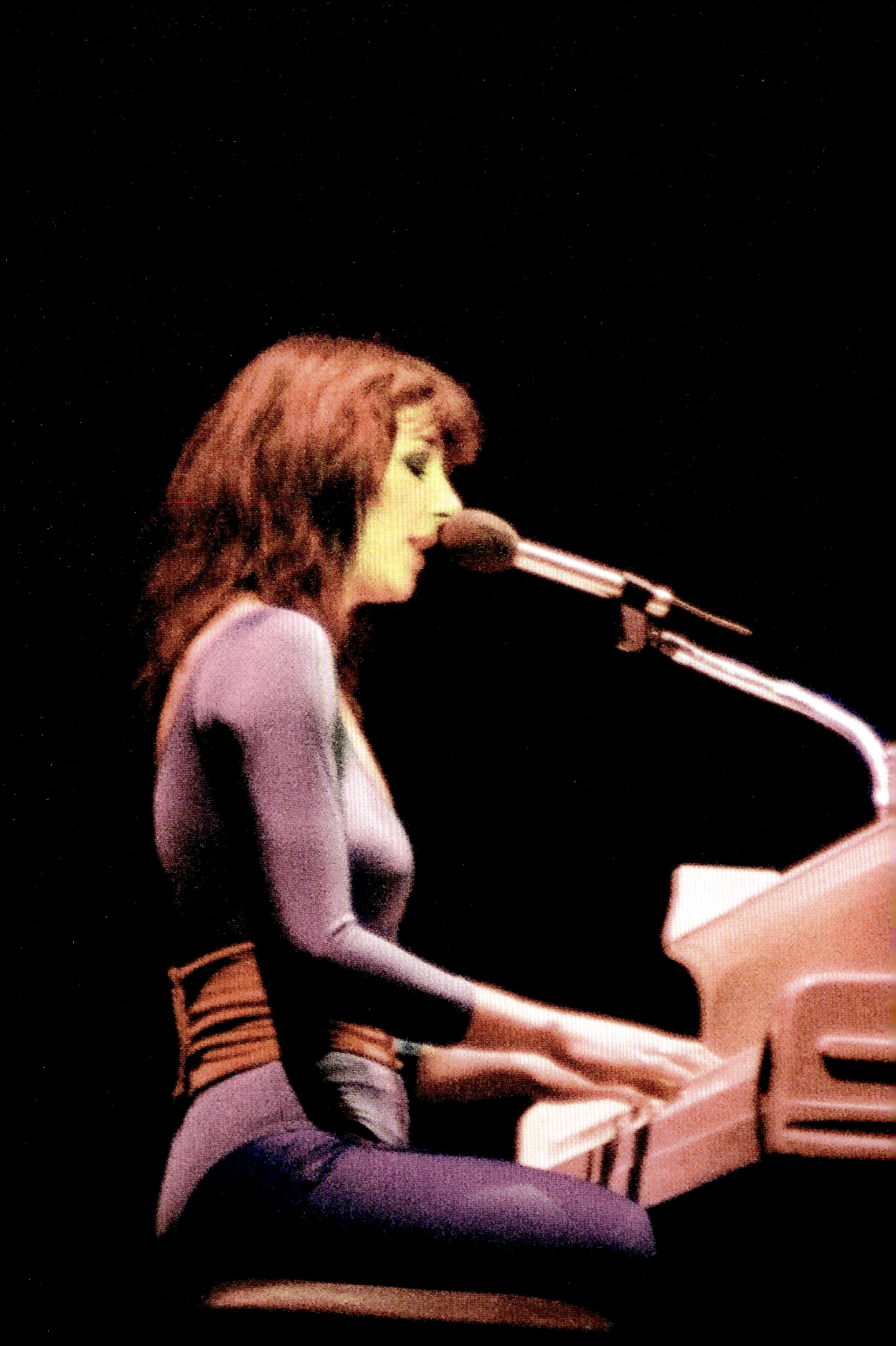

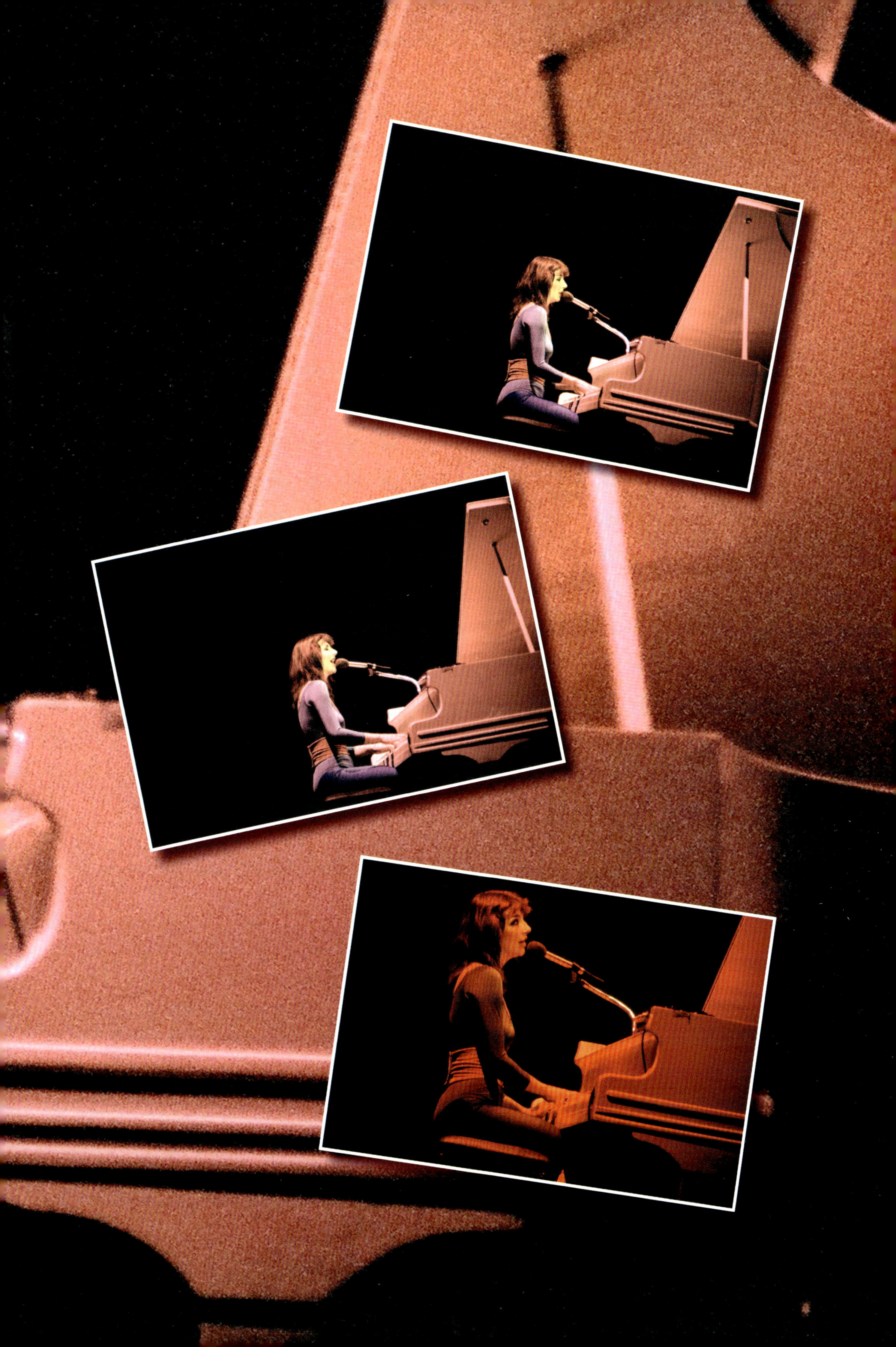

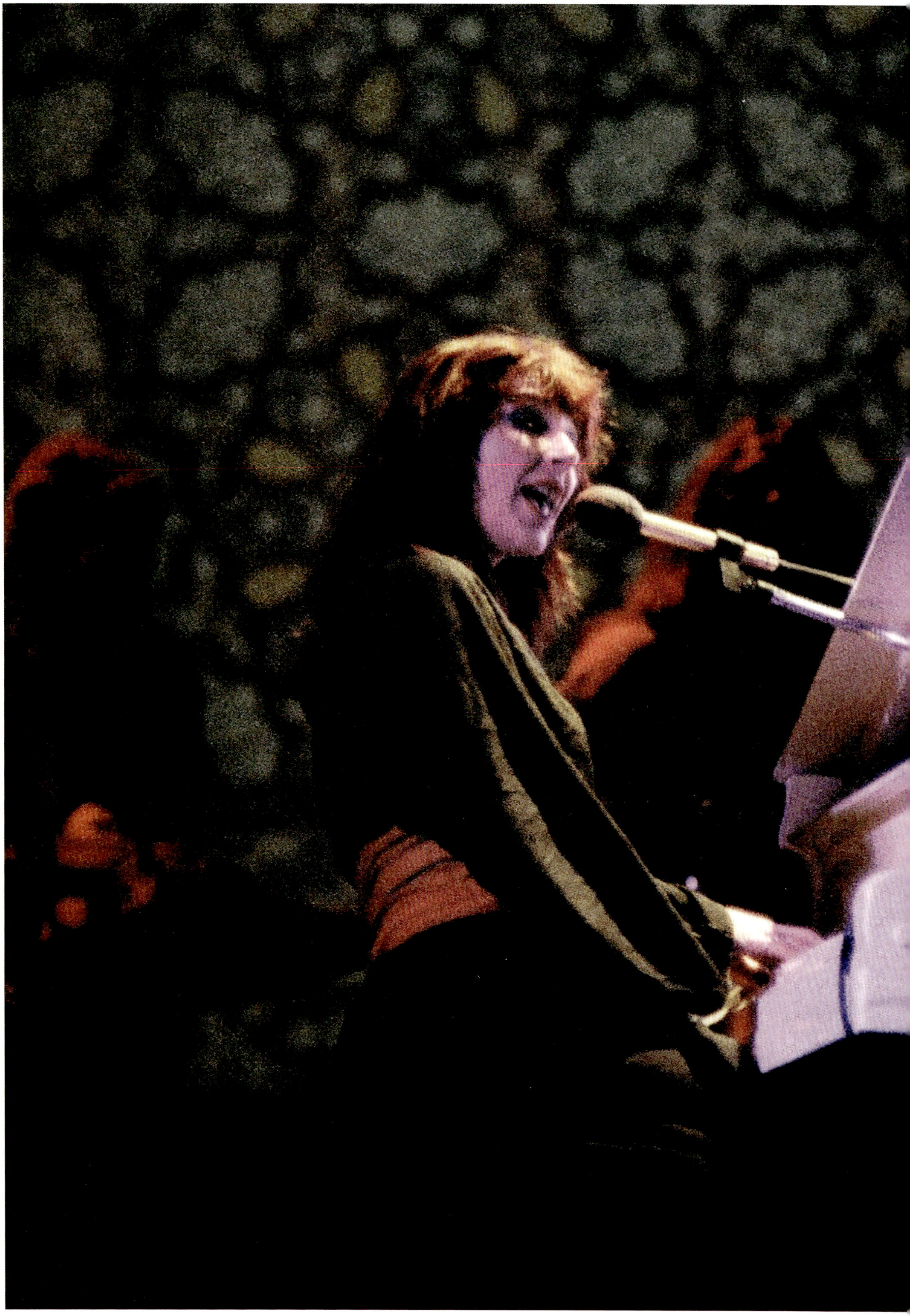

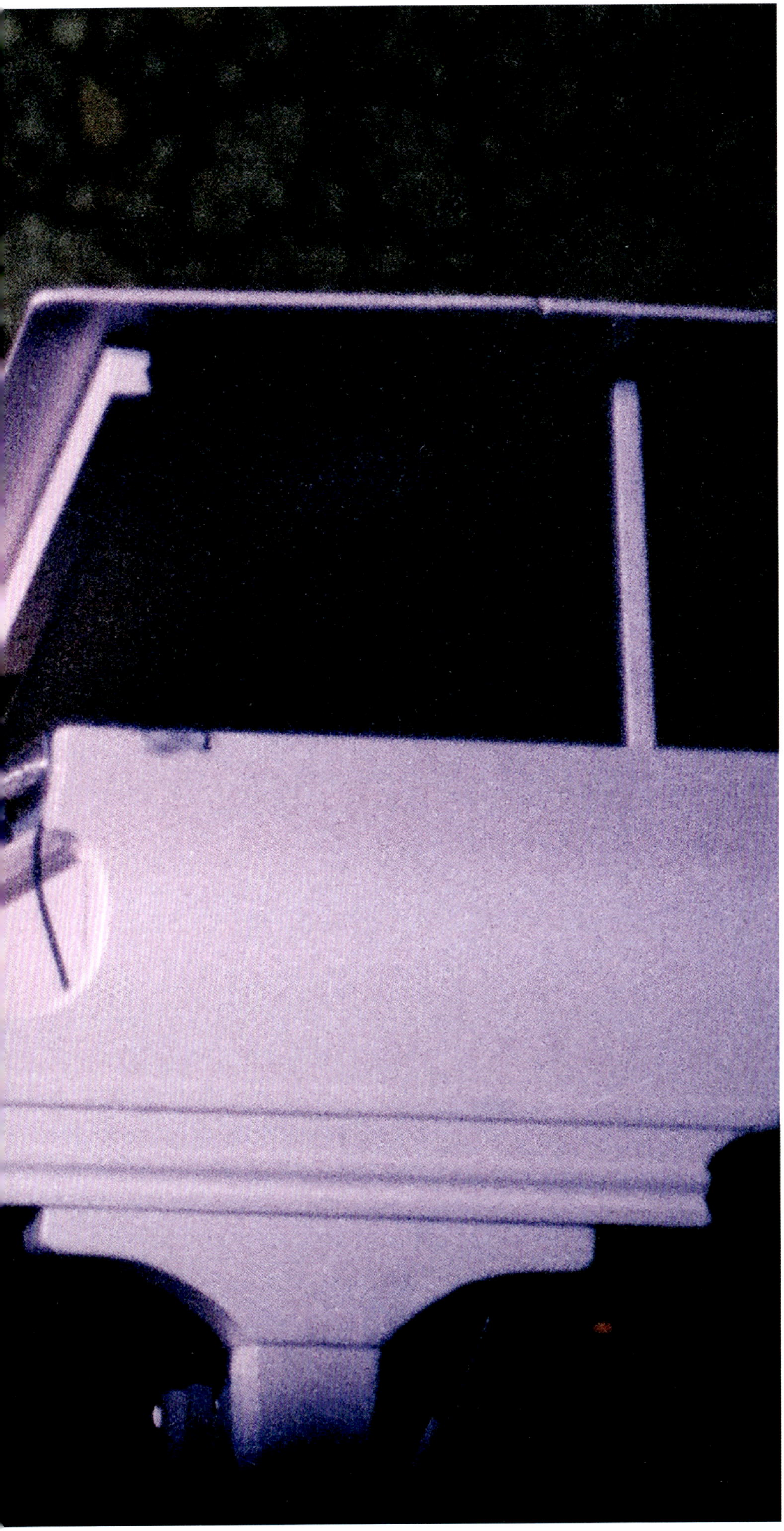

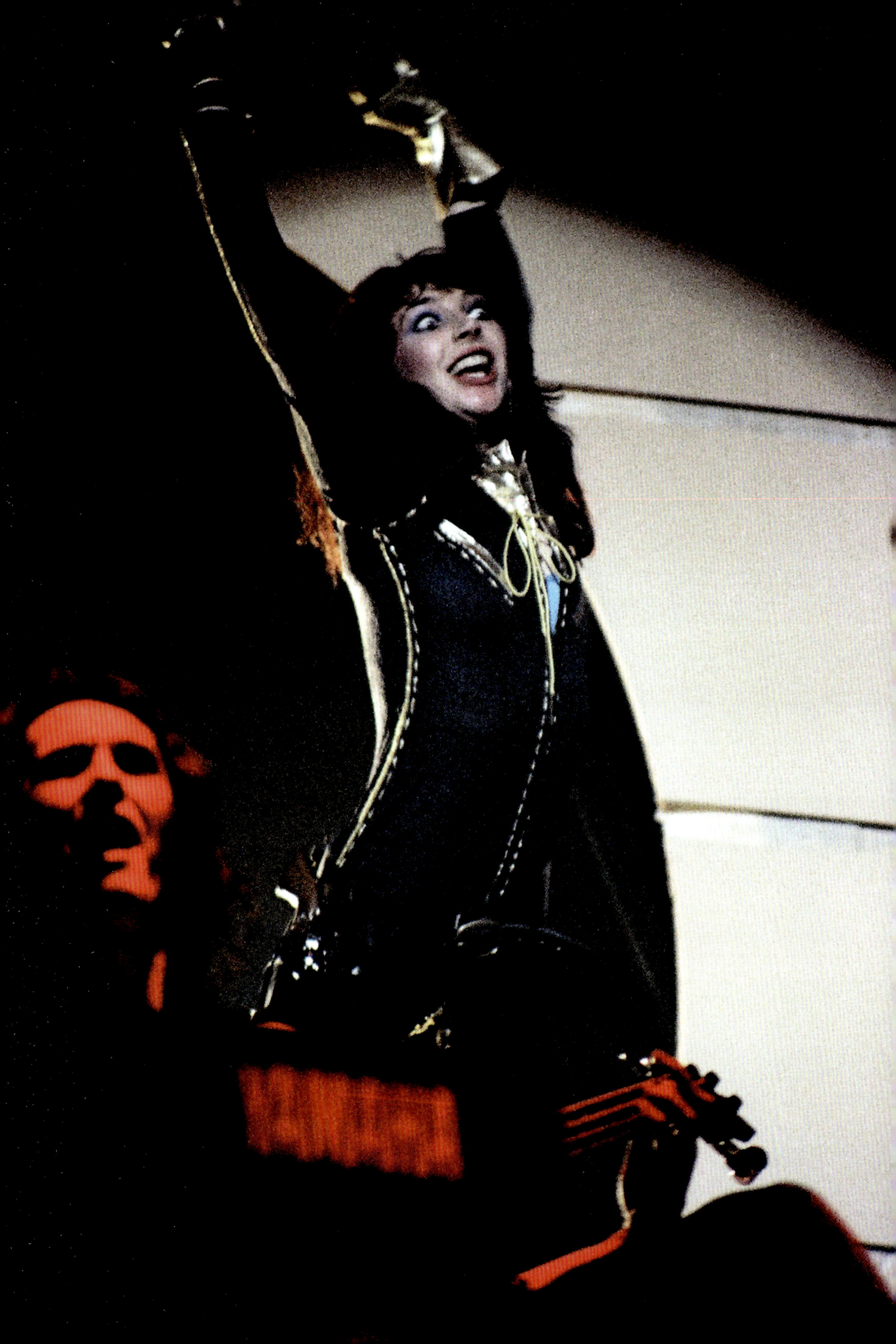

These shots and the next seven pages capture Kate performing 'James And The Cold Gun', which closed the main set. Photographer Alan Perry who was fortunate to shoot this first gig said, "It was the highlight for me — an amazing track when played live!"

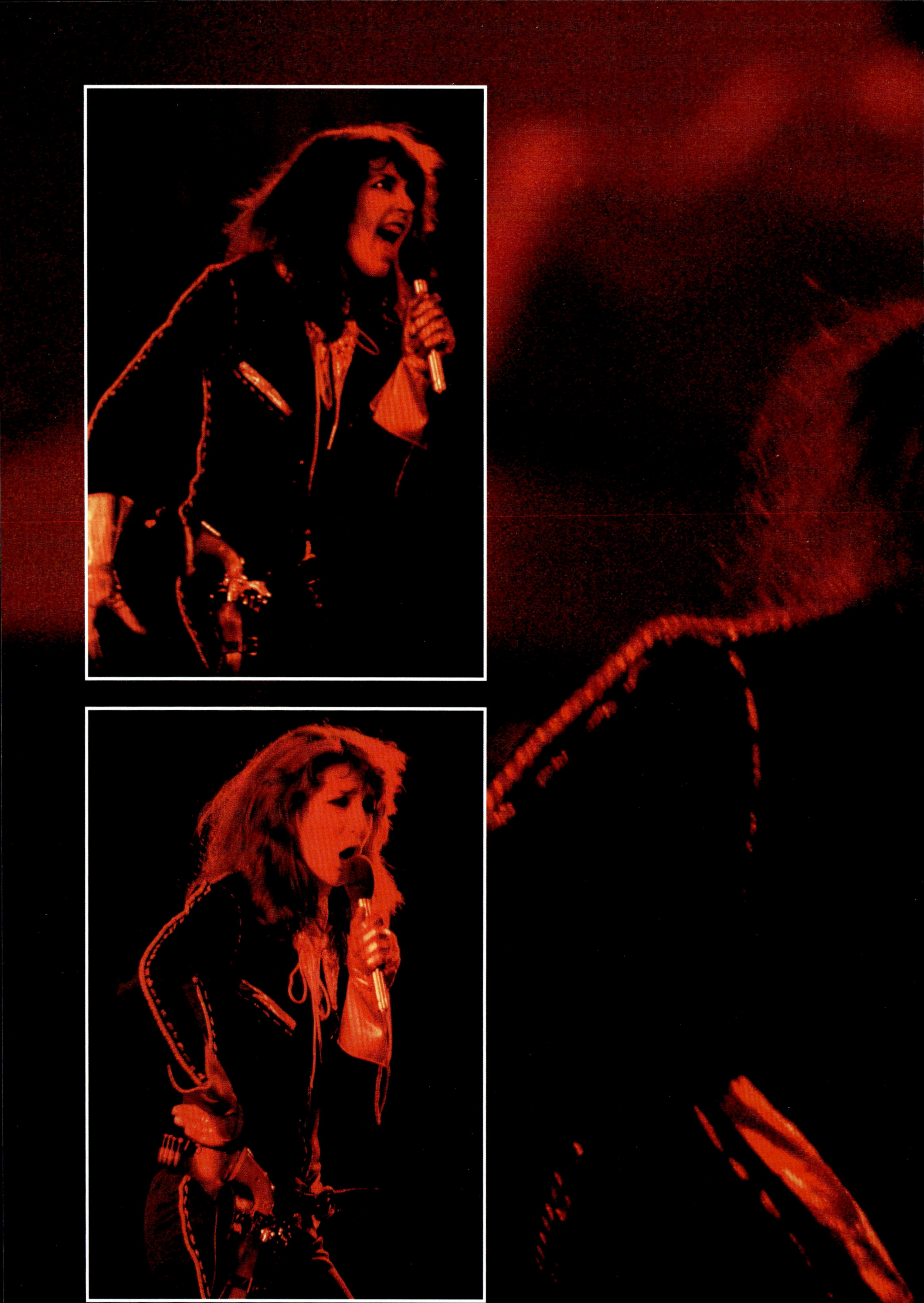

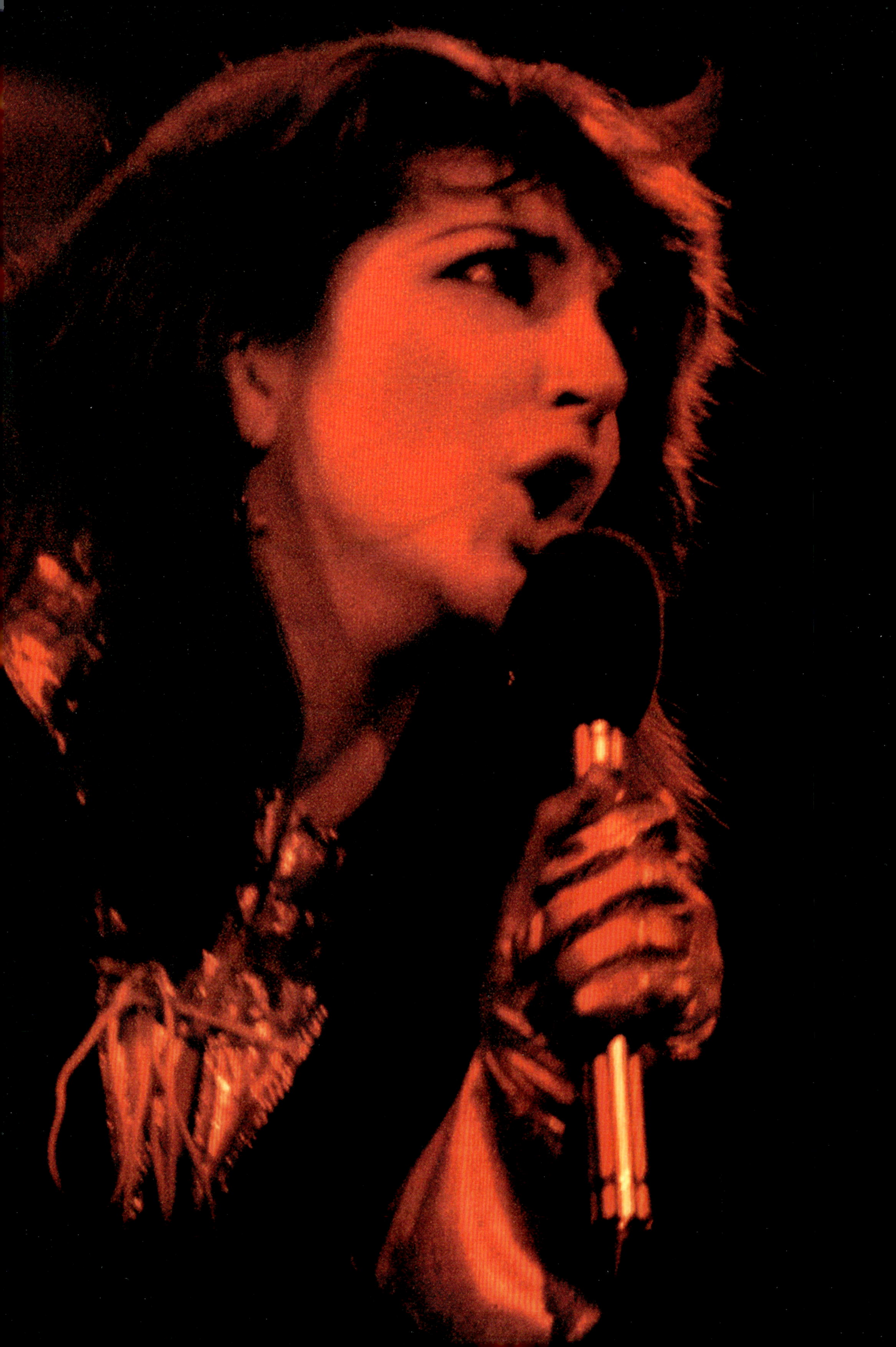

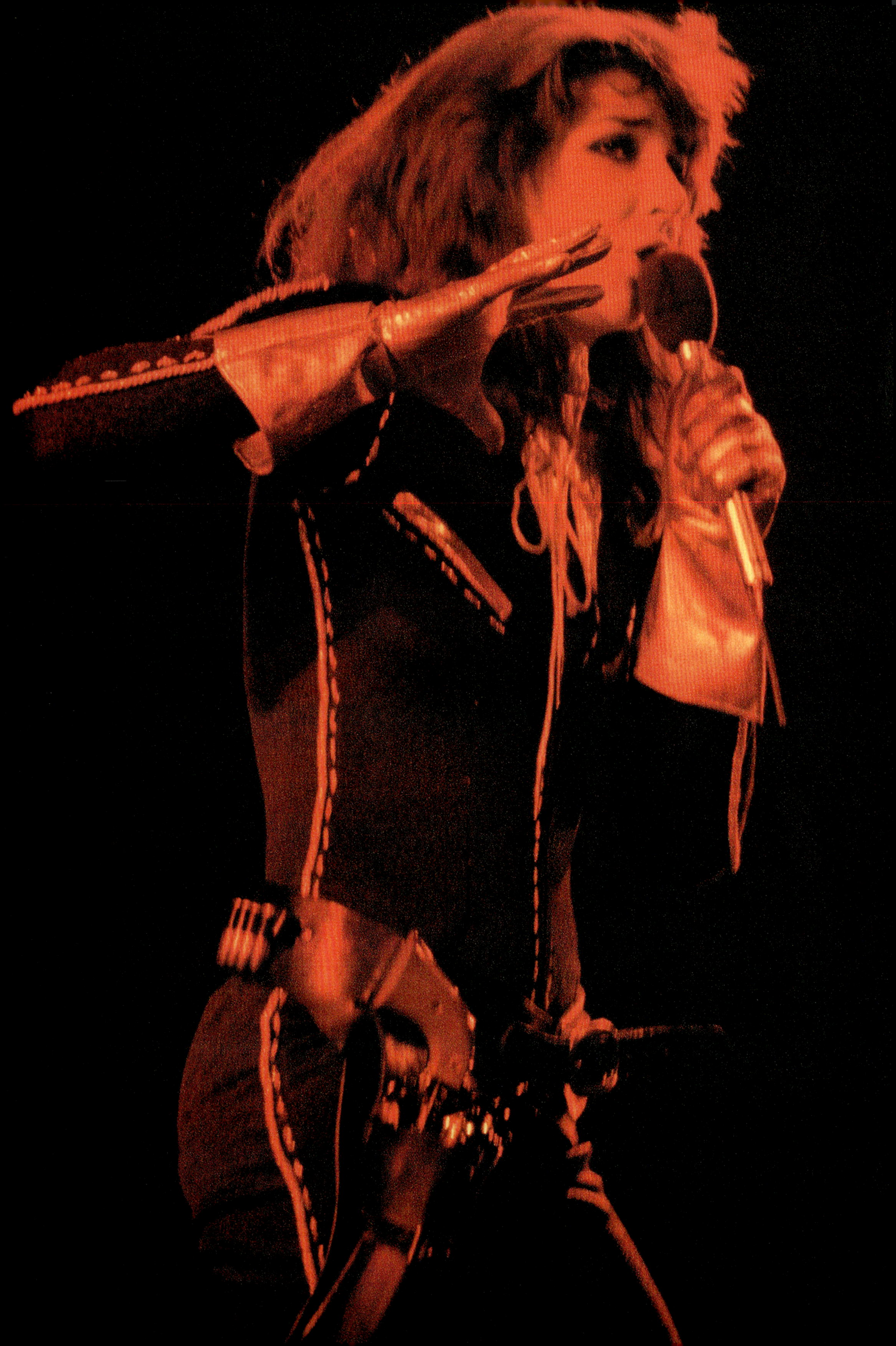

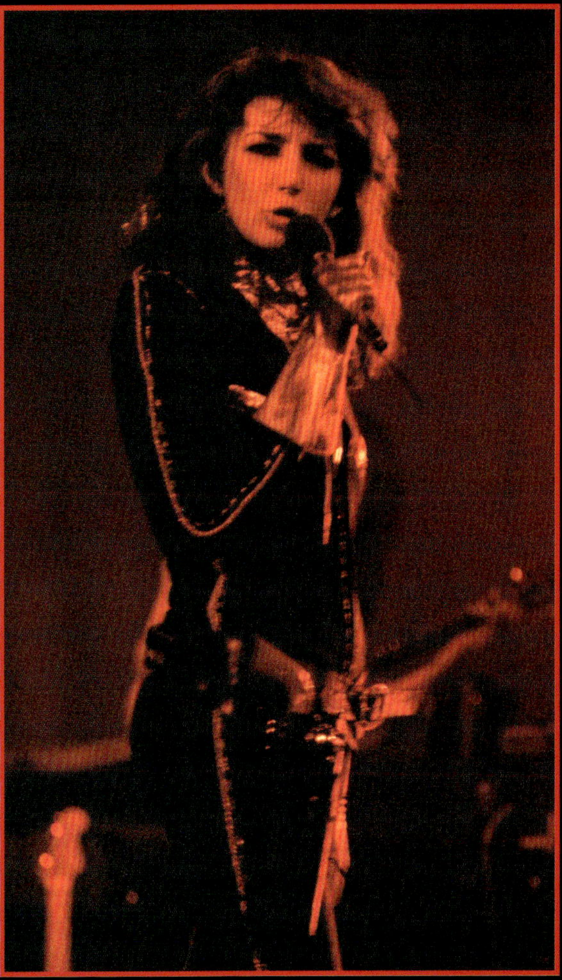

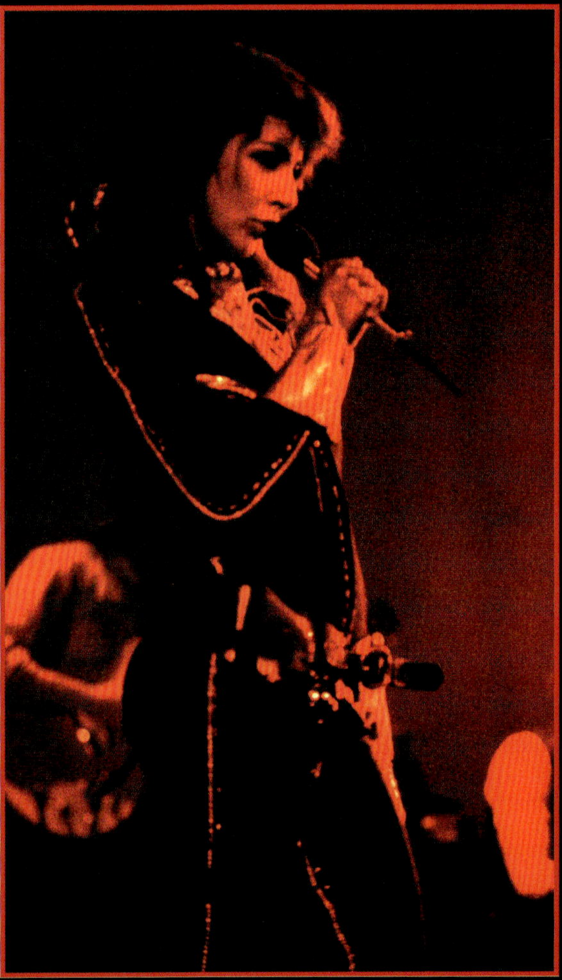

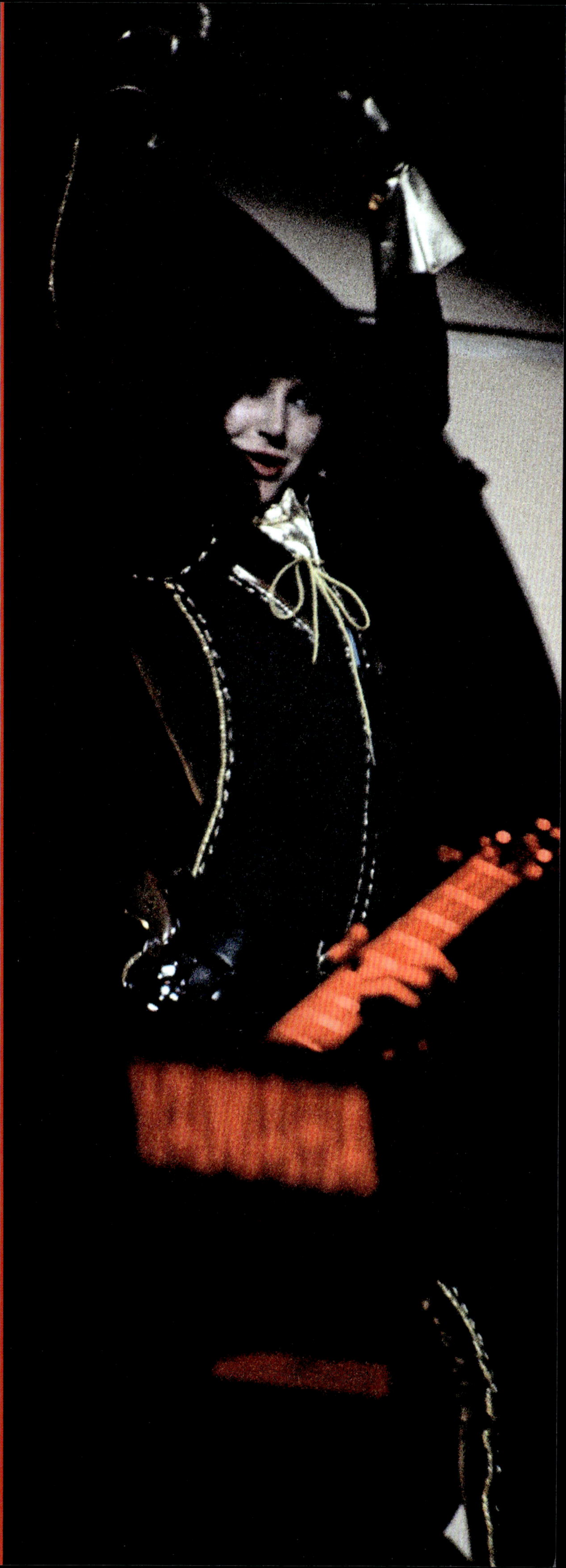

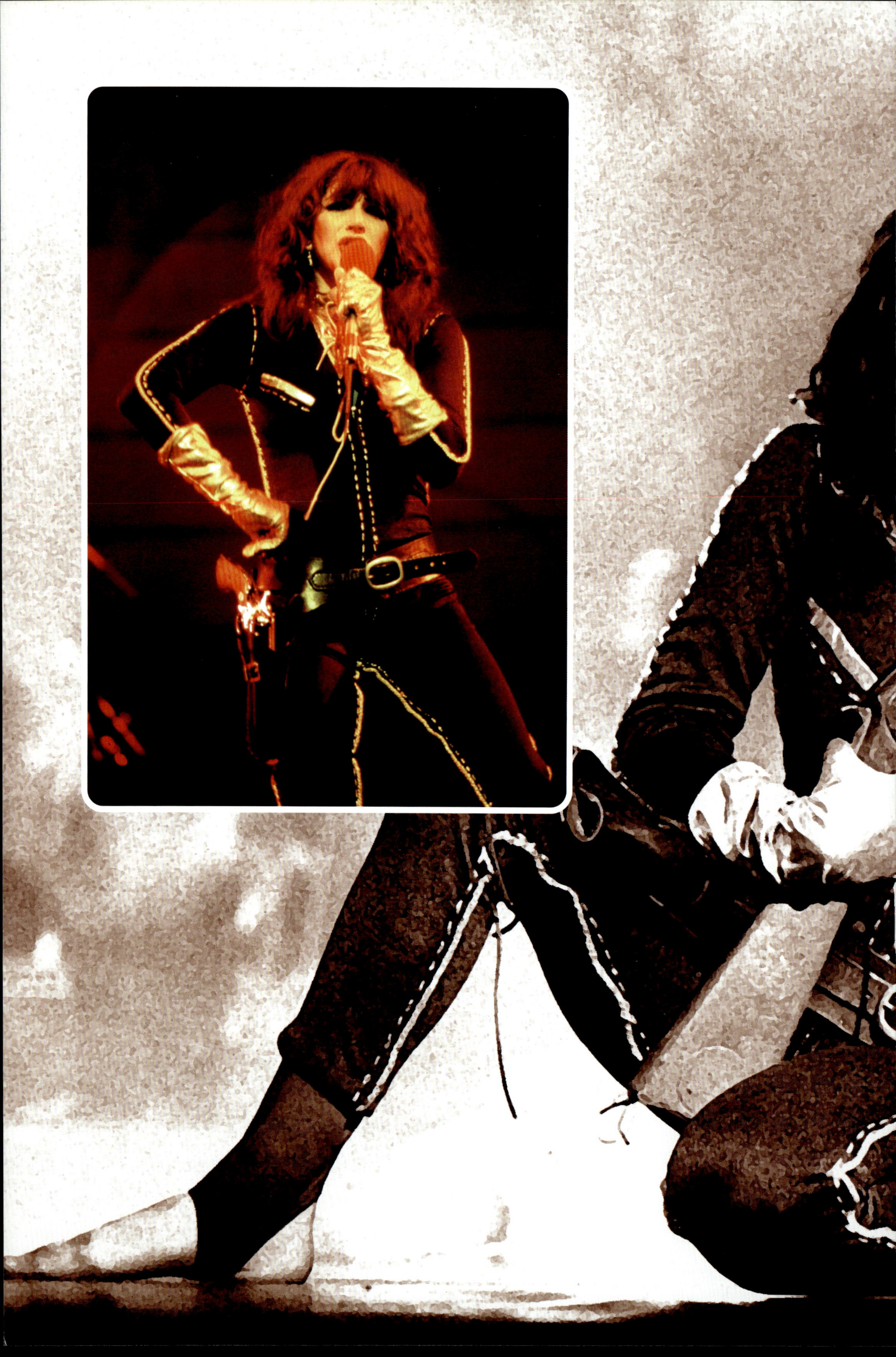

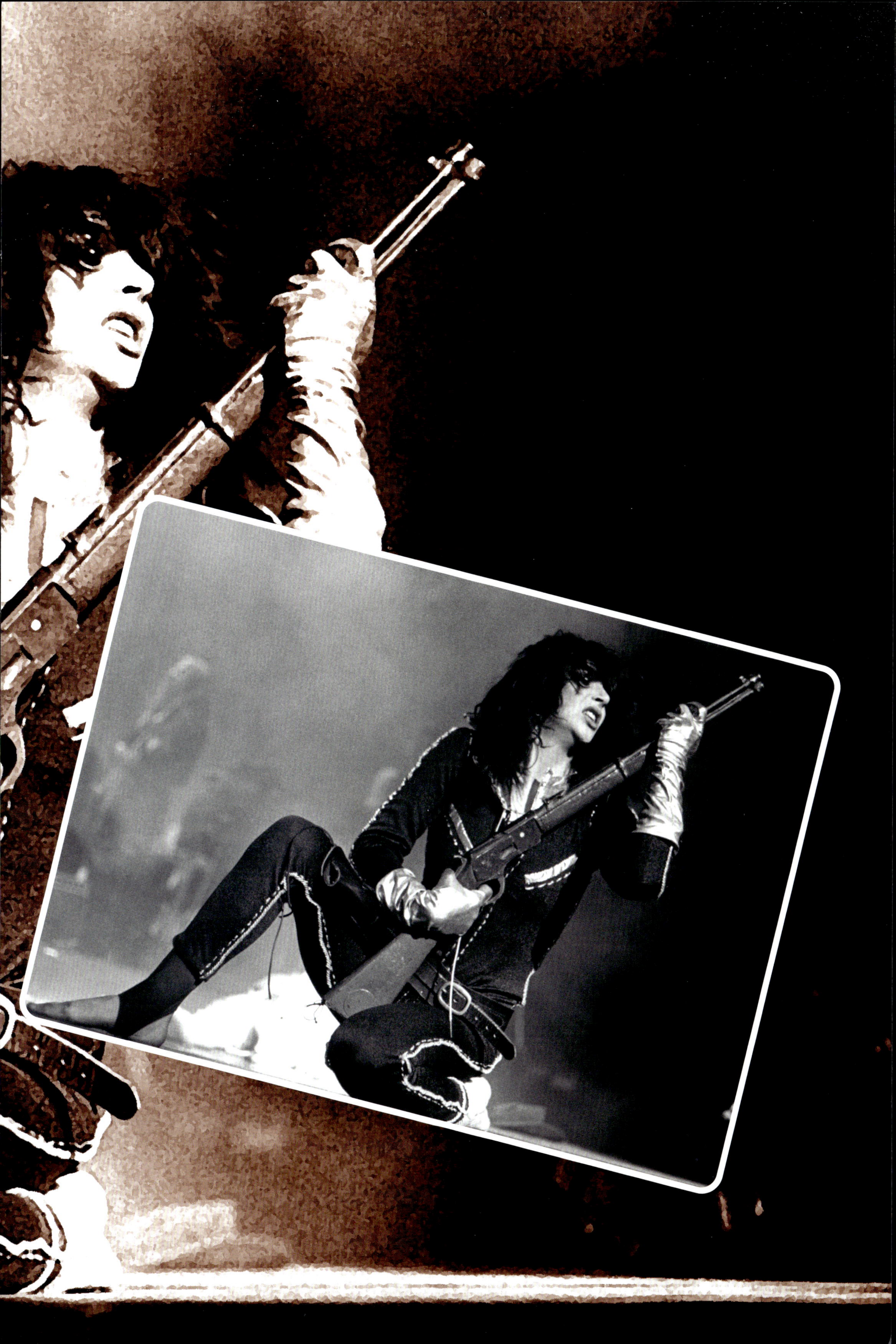

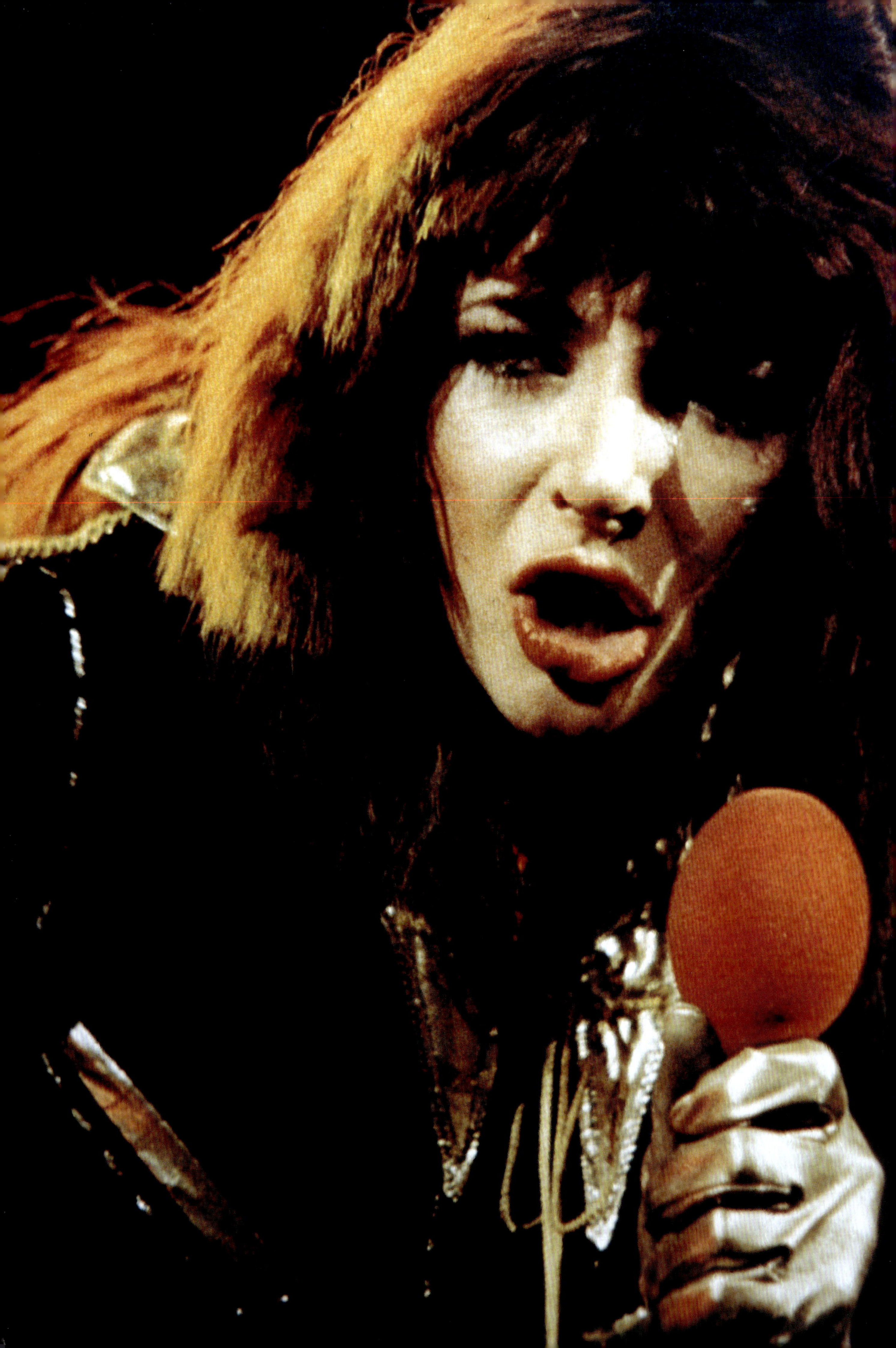

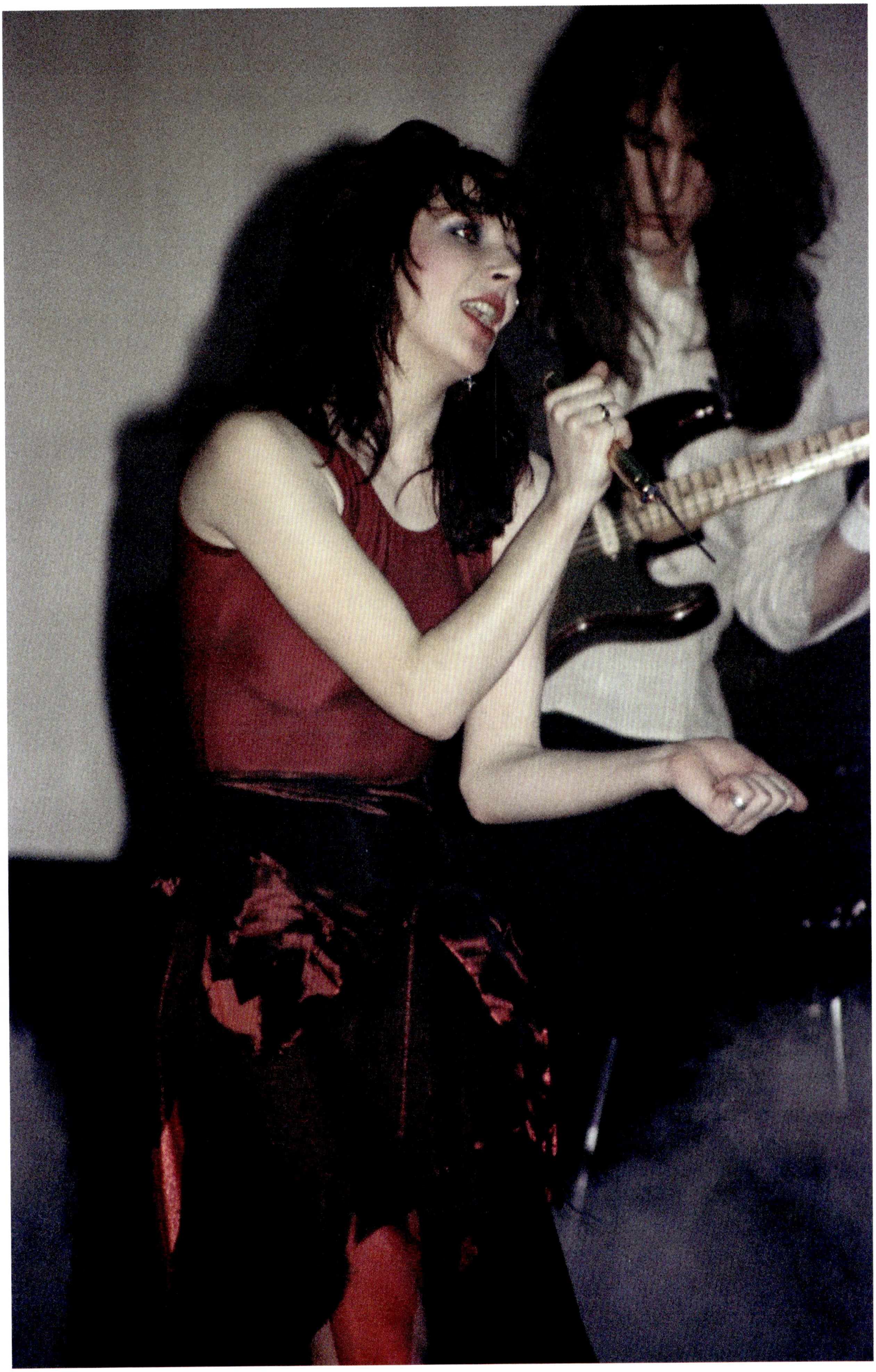

The '79 shows saw Kate perform the concert in several sets, broken up with interludes where her brother read poetry. This gave Kate the time to change costumes, making the shows as much about theatre as music.

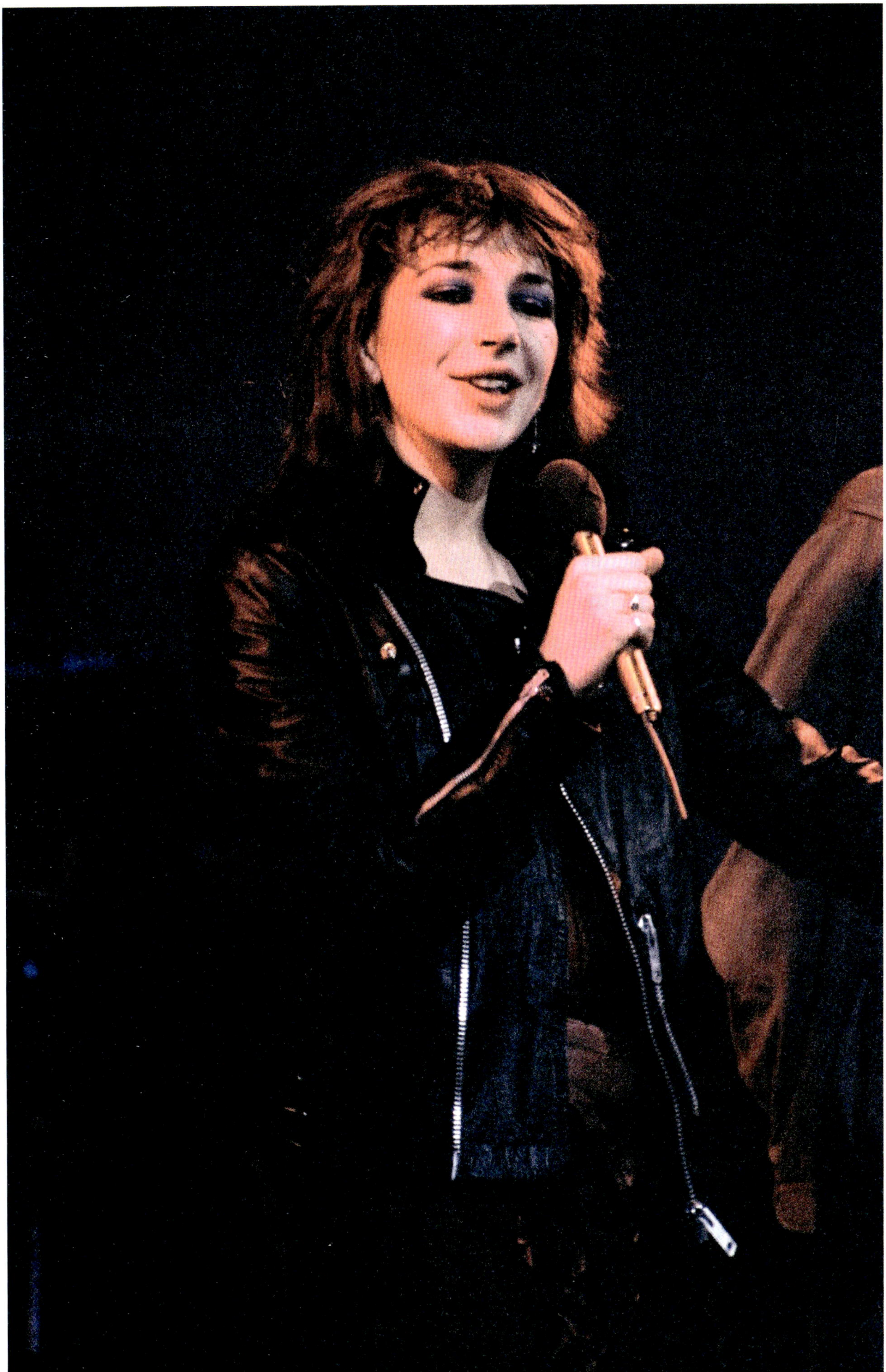

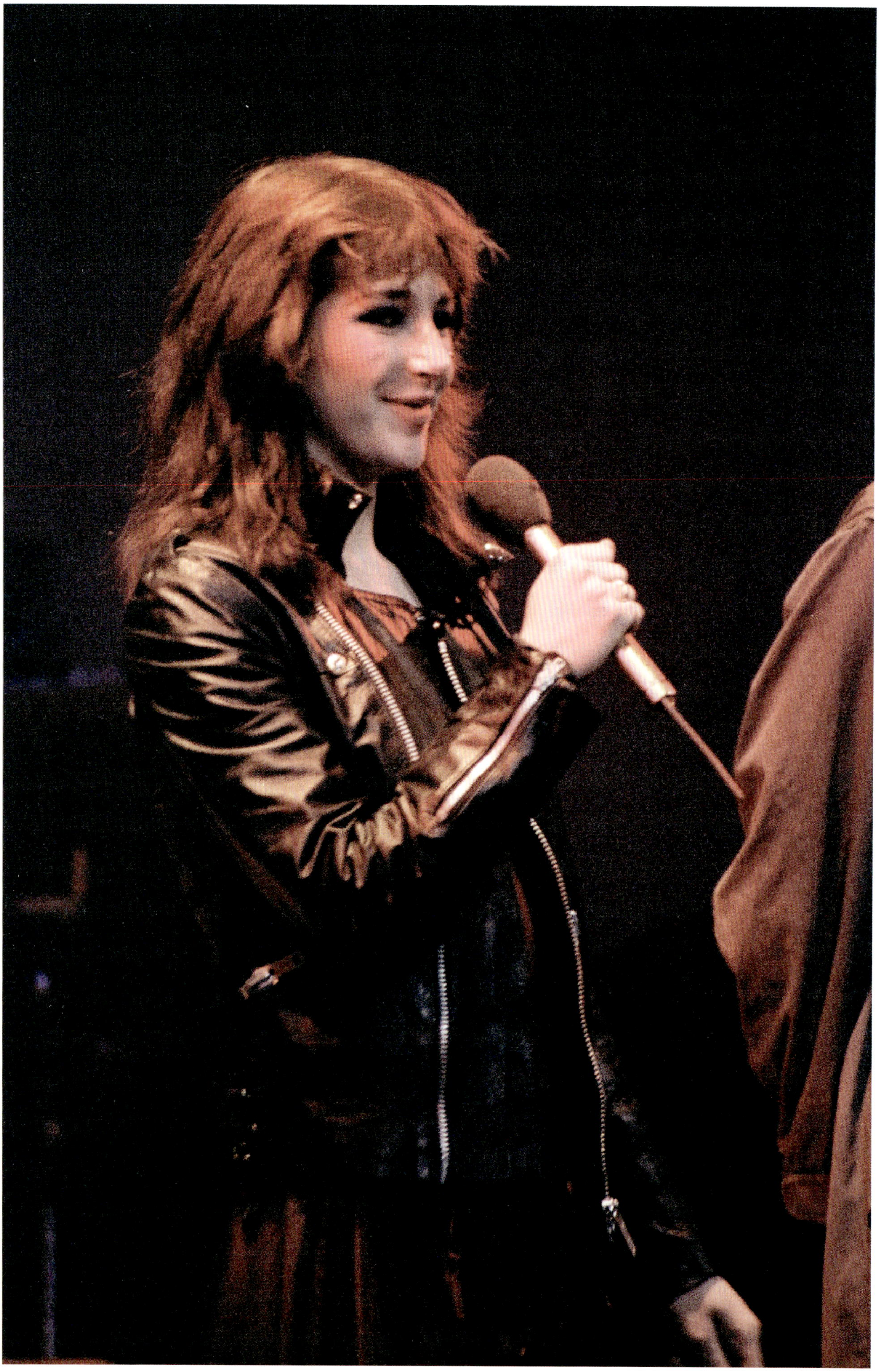

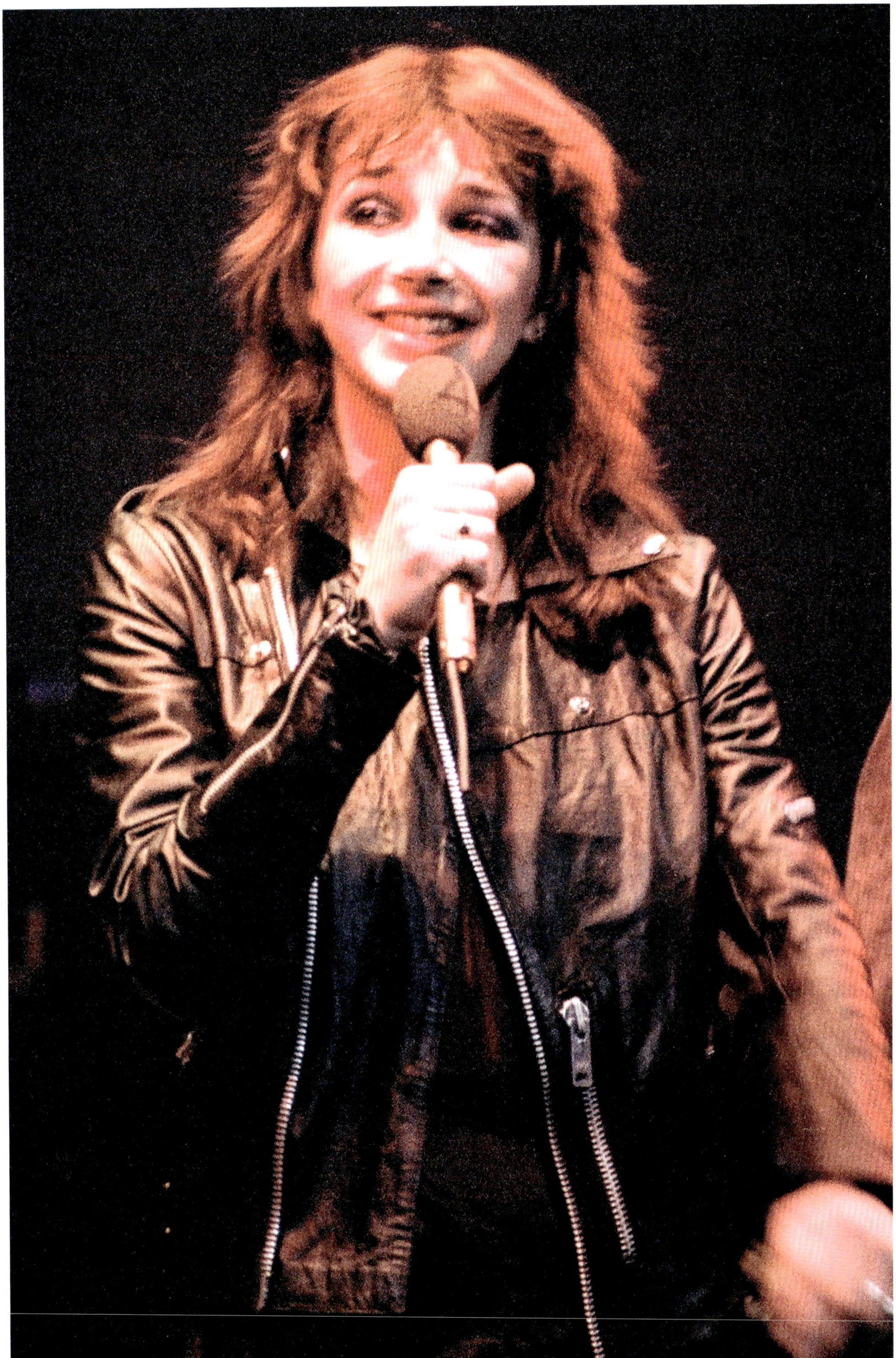

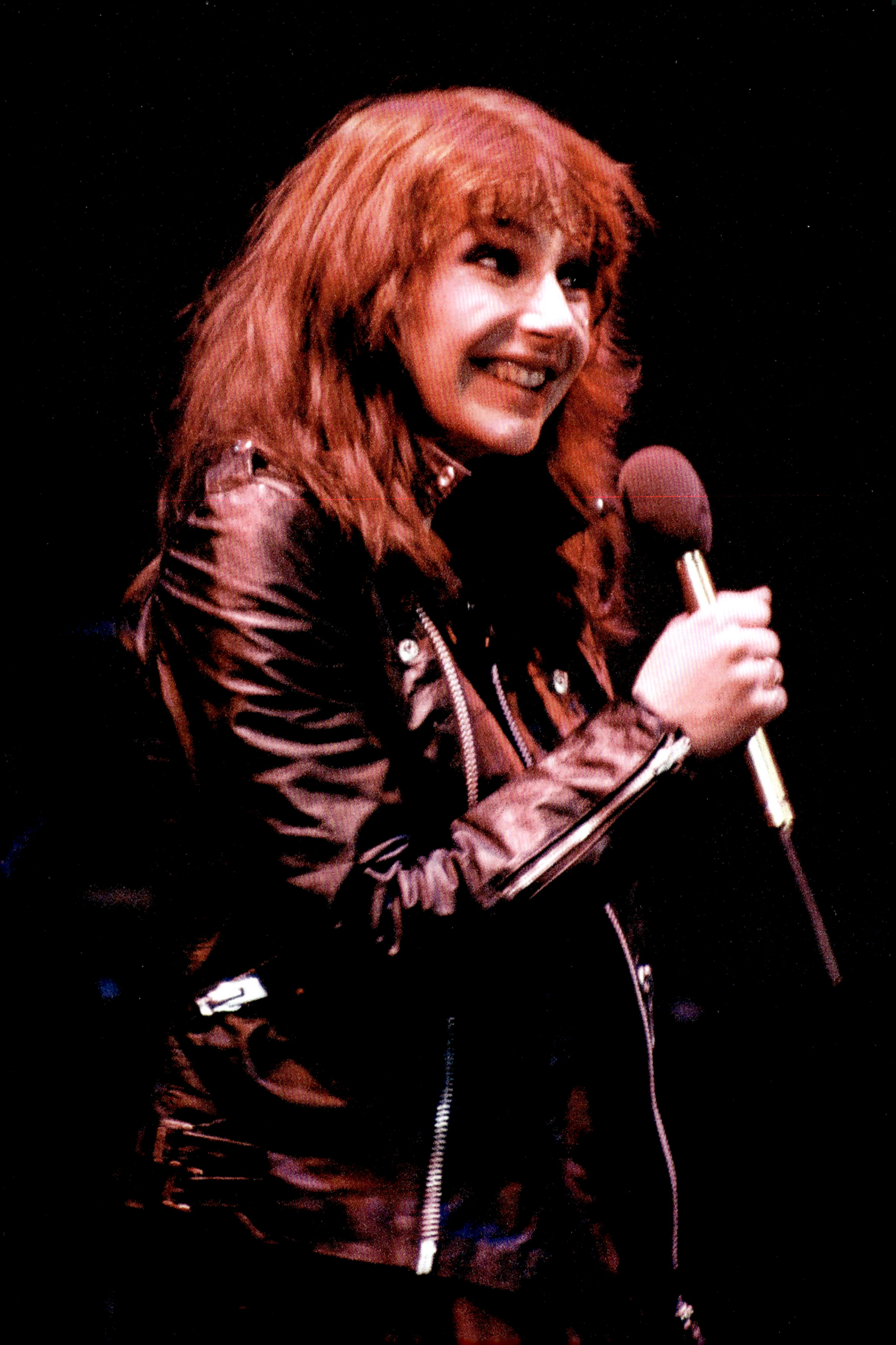

77

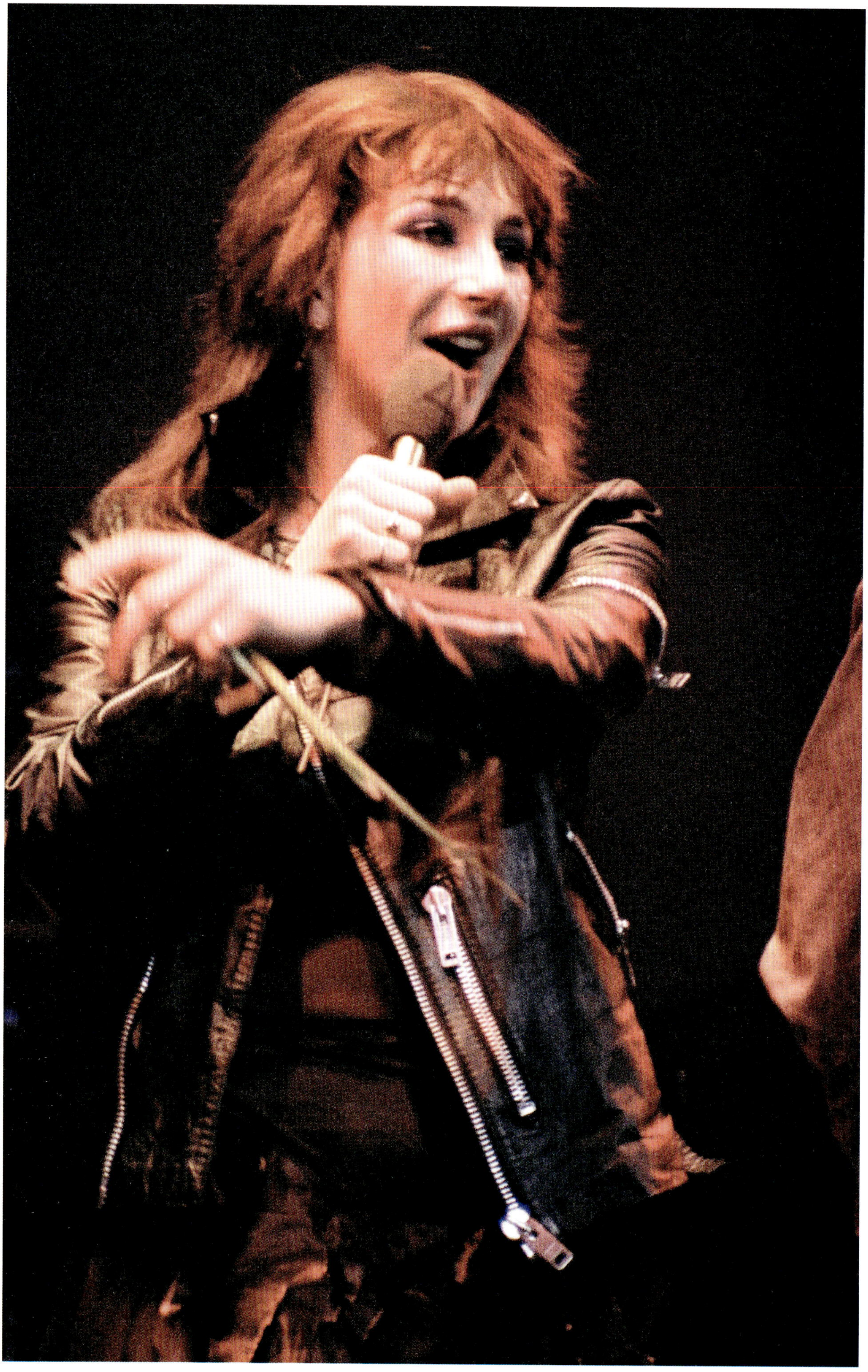

Kate played two nights at the Manchester Apollo, and photographer Alan Perry caught the second of these. Tickets were a mere £3.50.

Following the UK tour, ten shows were played throughout mainland Europe, including Amsterdam, as captured here.

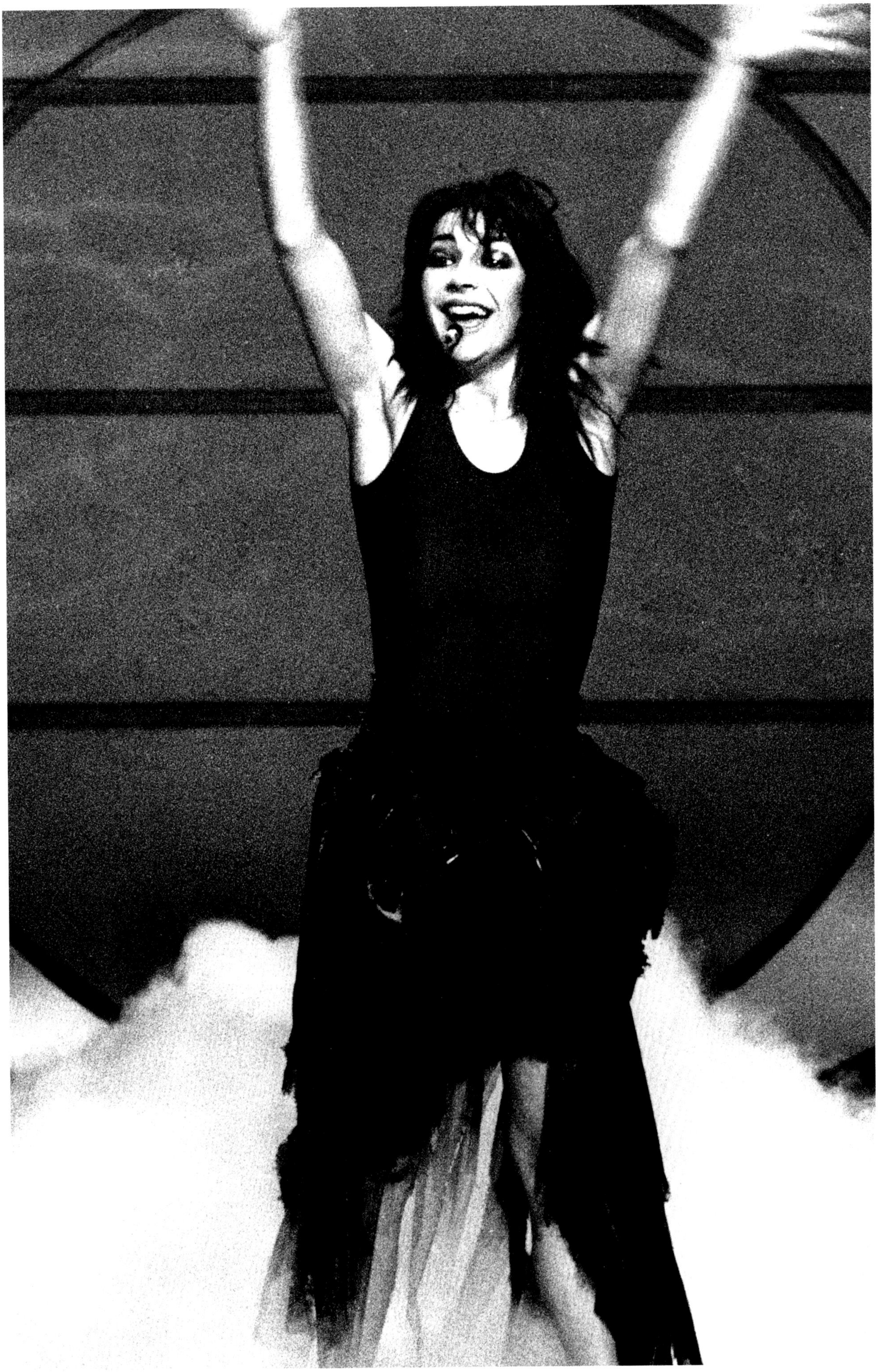

not only was the tour a success at the time, but it would go on to be held in high regard years later. As *The Guardian* noted in 2010, British reviews of the tour were almost universally "euphoric". (The bad reviews were notably from Chas Shaar Murray in the NME and from John Blake writing for the *London Evening Standard*).

The Telegraph described Kate as a "stunningly original stage performer", commenting on the setlist of the show as being "dazzling testimony to a remarkable talent, evidently intense rehearsal and technological know-how". A review in *Melody Maker* praised Kate's vocals for her lower and higher-pitched registers, whilst noting that she had created "a series of tableaux vivants of peerless visual and aural dazzle that added immeasurably to the complexity and variable excellence of her songs". Another reviewer for *Melody Maker* described the tour's performance in Birmingham as "the most magnificent spectacle ever encountered in the world of rock".

The day after the Liverpool show that took place on 3rd April, *The Daily Mail* reported; "She exploded onto the stage, a waif-like elfin figure in tight jeans, and her voice pierced the auditorium with the bewitching quality of the wind shrieking over 'Wuthering Heights'... Kate relies not so much on the quality of her voice, but on the drama with which she sings her songs."

It was reported in the *Liverpool Echo*; "What she gave the 2,500 fans — many of whom had queued all night when tickets went on sale a month ago — was much more than a concert: it was a show which combined ballet, theatre and rock into what the Americans are apt to call "a total experience". The simple fact is that Kate — virtually unknown twelve months ago, when she produced her first hit, 'Wuthering Heights' — does have real talent. Her music is real music, and not a collection of readily assembled chords. Her lyrics are intelligent, provocative, even poetic... She may only be 5ft 3in tall but she's a giant of a show woman. Then there's the personal charisma." To which Kate was quoted, 'I'm probably the person who knows least about myself. To make music I need to be alone with my piano. I lock myself away.'"

A performance was reviewed in the *Birmingham Daily Post*; "The Hippodrome was a highly appropriate venue for Kate Bush's Birmingham debut. It lent itself perfectly to the dramatic content of her show, which unfolded delightful effects. A specially-designed set was complemented by the rapid costume changes, back projection slides, quick-fire lighting,

Kate pops up from the daffodils at the Inn-on-the-Park, London, 17th April 1979.

darkness, ingenious props and some attractive illusionism in a generous show that stretched across three acts. Her highly-personalised songs are well suited to such treatment. Like Genesis, her music follows a meandering path, washed through with a mix of subtle and exotic textures. The grandiose treatment that it embodied in the current show served to strengthen emotions that on vinyl are sometimes a trifle thin. It also served to reveal aspects of Kate Bush unbeknown to the record-buying public. She is an accomplished dancer and freed from the handheld microphone, she illustrated her emotions expressively, accompanied by two male dancers who complemented her movements. If the attractive setting was a bonus then we were not let down musically either. Kate Bush's voice is stunning, running the gamut from childlike high pitch through womanly maturity to a sexy rasp at the bottom, often twisting and turning its way rapidly over scattering phrases. And she gave every song in the Bush catalogue its due. Some such as the gorgeous 'The Man With The Child In His Eyes' were simple affairs backed only by her attractive piano playing. Others, such as the storming 'Don't Push Your Foot On The Heartbrake' were full-blooded. And all to rapturous applause from the capacity house. In the meantime, her eight-piece band, which had the unenviable task of being both faultless and inconspicuous, achieved both admirably."

It was reported in the *Bristol Evening Post*; "On last night's show, she is a major artist by any standards. She wrote the songs, she sang them, and she danced beautifully with a sinuous grace... Each aspect was perfect in itself, together with imaginative staging, brilliant production, and a tight and disciplined backing group of musicians and dancers... It made for spectacular entertainment... A remarkable stage debut by a rare talent."

Later on, the BBC would imply that Kate may have declined to tour again due to a fear of flying, or because of lighting engineer Bill Duffield's fatal accident. Bob Mercer considered that touring was "just too hard... I think [Bush] liked it but the equation didn't work... I could see at the end of the show that she was completely wiped out."

In 2011, speaking to *Mojo* magazine, Kate described the tour as "enormously enjoyable" but "absolutely exhausting". She also added however, that "I still don't give up hope completely that I'll be able to do some live work, but it's certainly not in the picture at the moment because I just don't quite know how that would work with how my life is now". Essentially, even just three years before the announcement of her 2014

Story continues on page 101...

Michael Palin presenting an award to Kate Bush at a *Melody Maker* Poll Awards ceremony in London, England, in 1979.

Photo shoot, 27th September 1979,
London, England.

Photo shoot, 27th September 1979,
London, England.

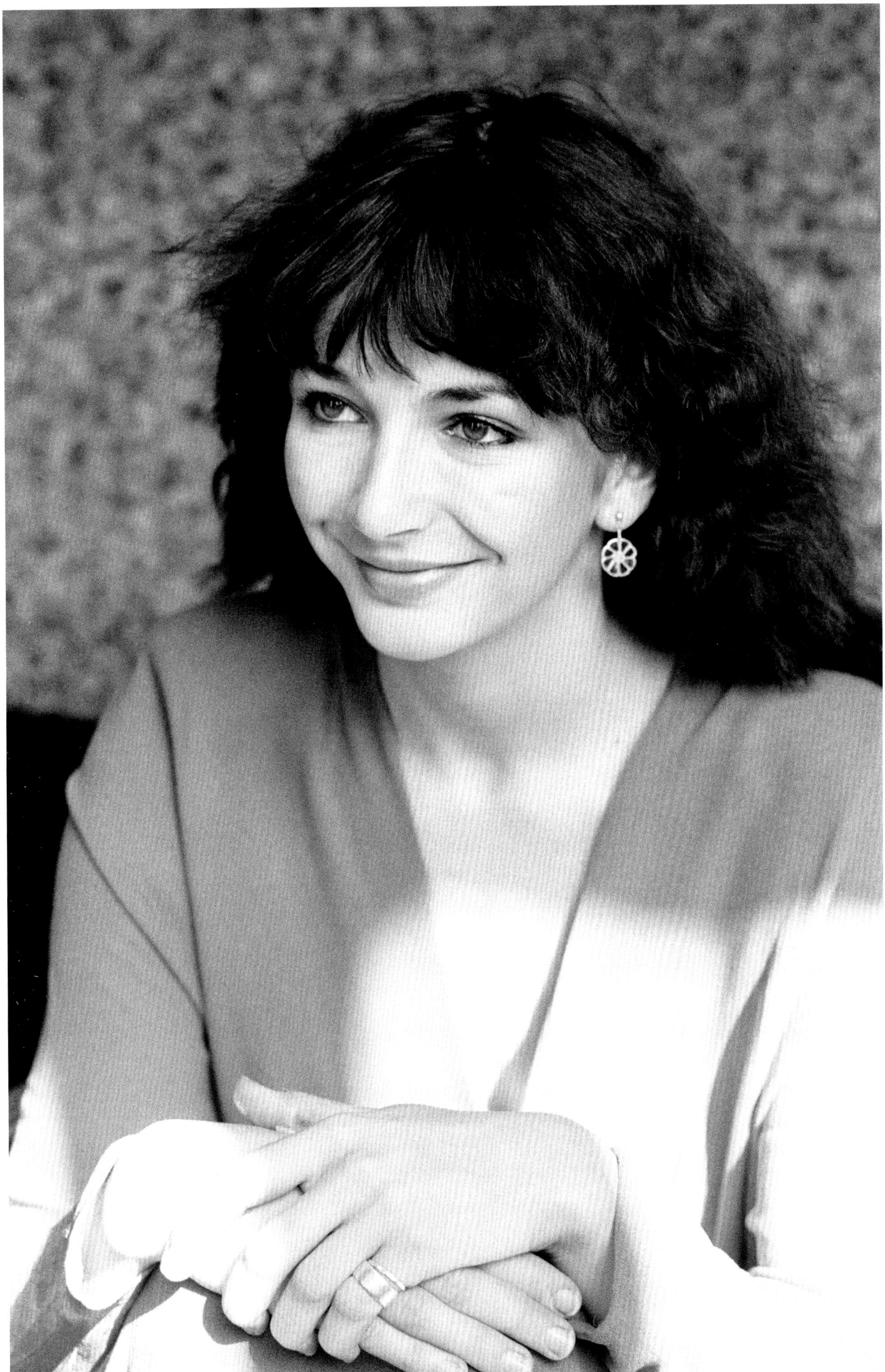

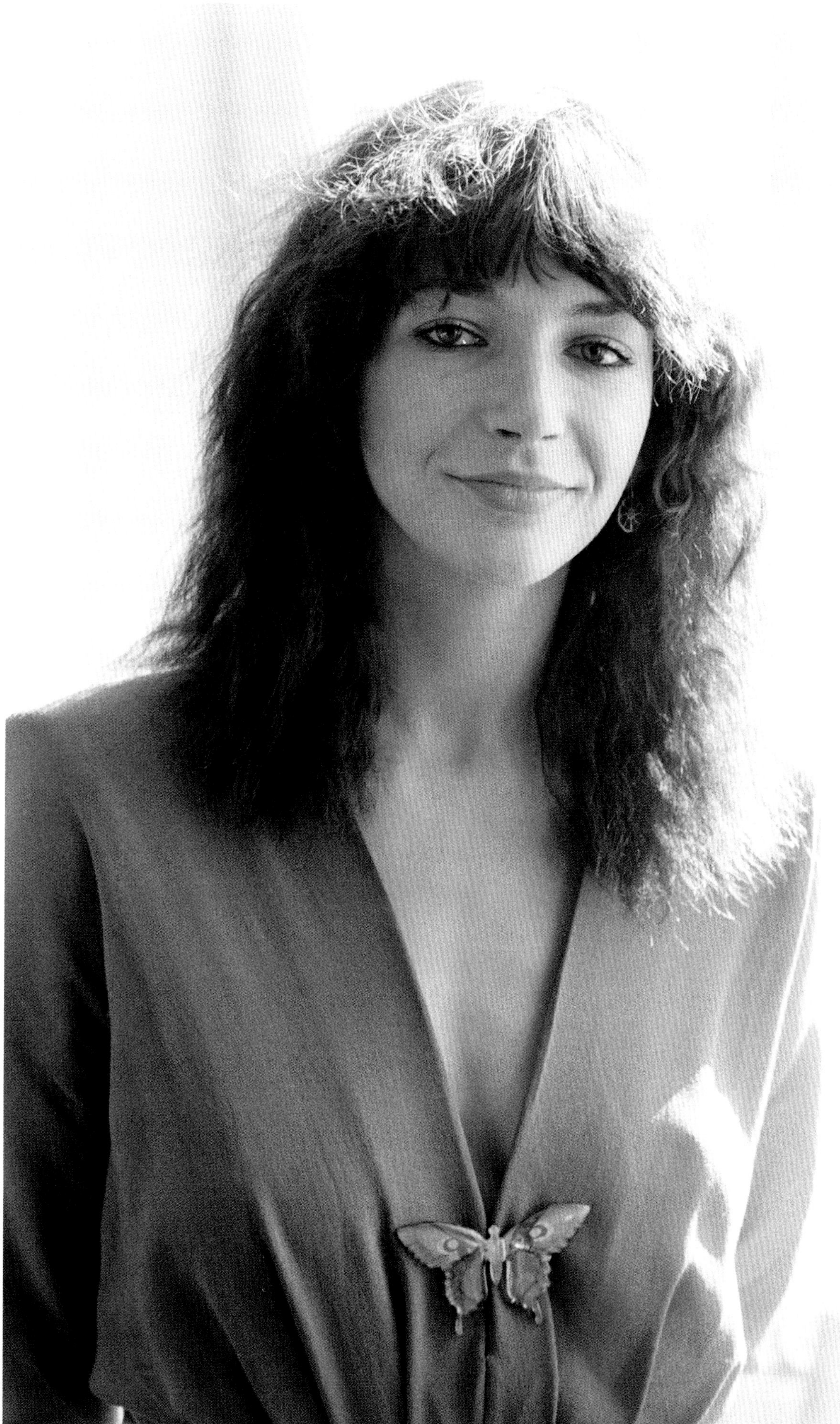

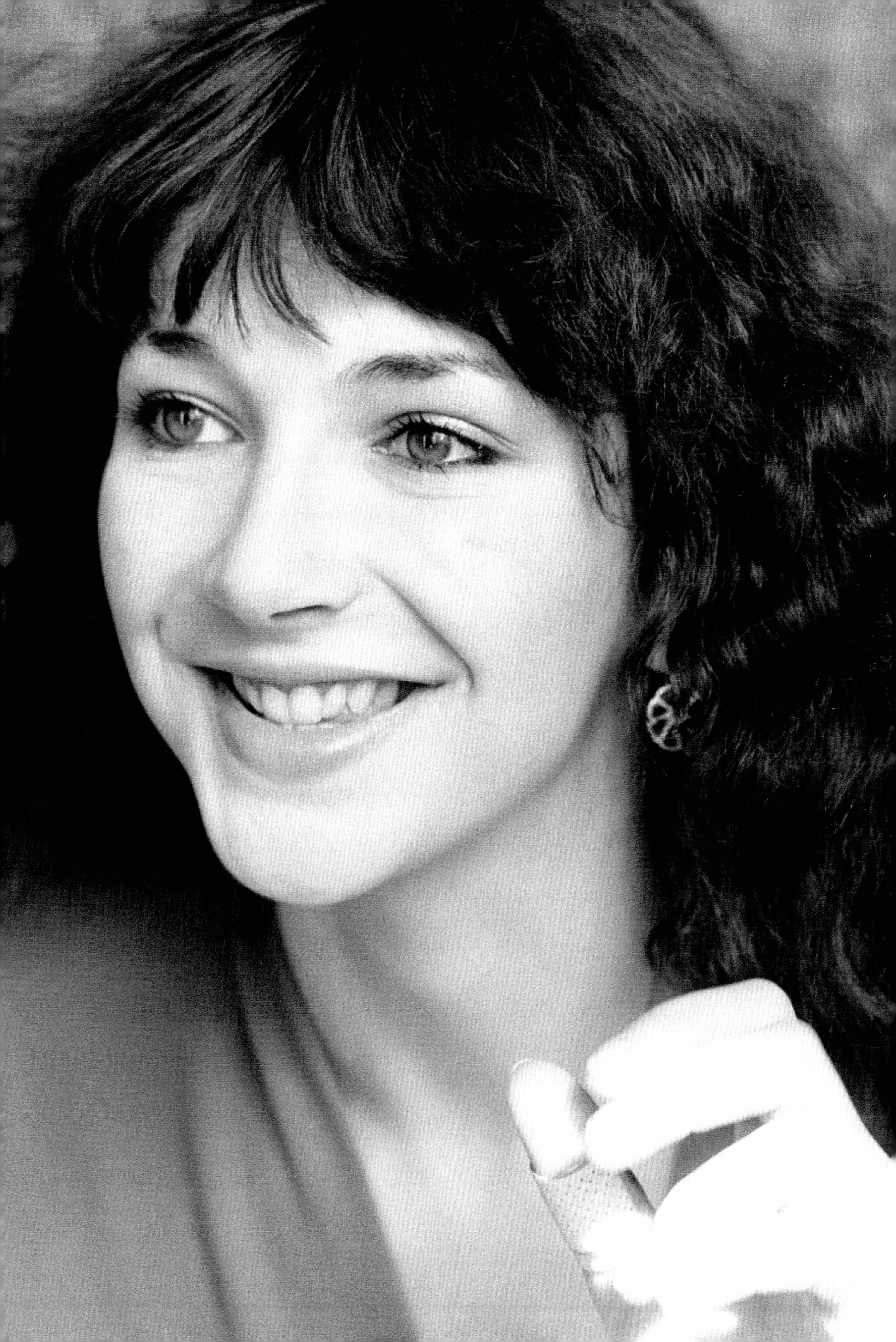

Kate with Lesley Duncan, Pete Townshend, Phil Lynott, Joe Brown and Paddy Bush release 'Sing Children Sing', a charity single for International Year Of The Child, November 1979.

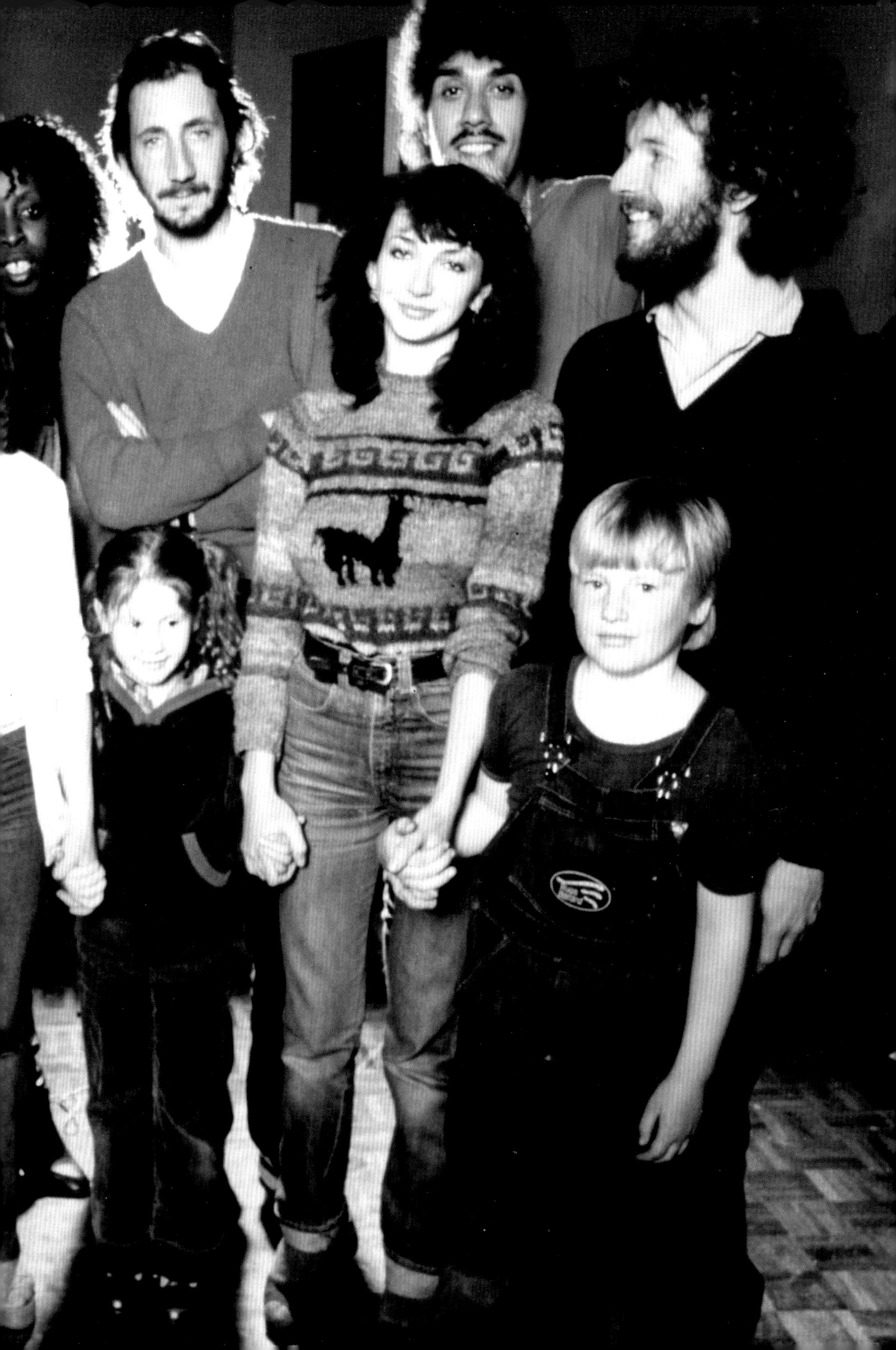

28th November 1979, both Kate and Bob Geldof collecting their best single awards.

Amsterdam, Netherlands, 1979.

Kate receiving an award from David "Kid" Jensen at the British Rock and Pop awards, 11th April 1979 (with Hank Marvin of the Shadows behind).

At the Capital Radio Music Awards at Grosvenor House, 3rd March 1980. The award for the best British Female artist went to Kate, with Ian Dury (seated) taking the best Male artist award.

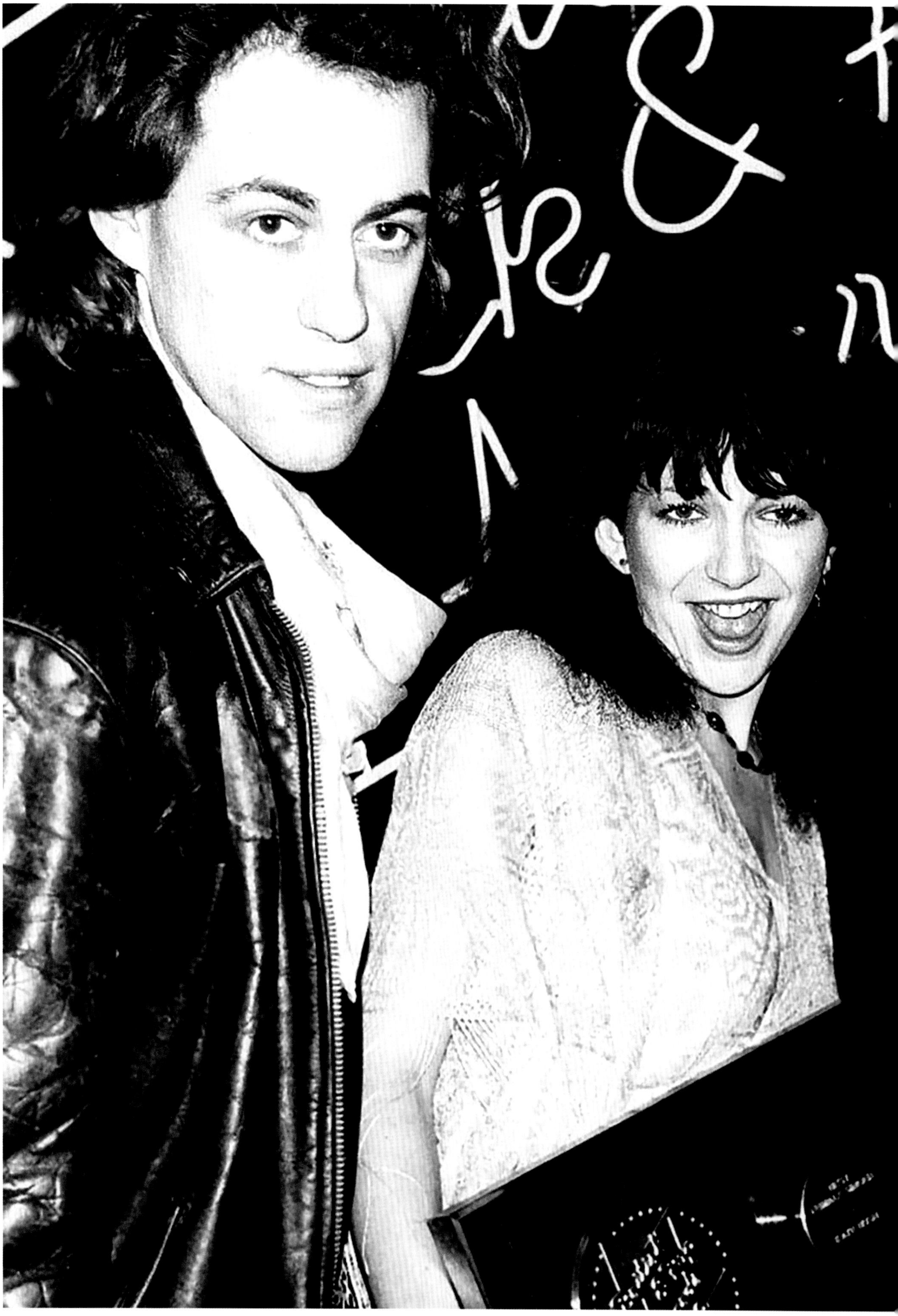

With Bob Geldof and
Paul McCartney at
The British Rock and Pop Awards
26th February 1980.

December 1979.

live shows, the prospect of such endeavour could have gone either way.

By the end of 1979, Kate had a number of key television performances under her belt. As well as appearances on multiple programmes, and several on *Top Of The Pops* by that point, to end what had been an incredibly prolific year for her, on 28th December, BBC TV aired the *Kate Bush Christmas Special*. Along with musical performances, she presented the forty-five-minute programme herself, on which Peter Gabriel was present as a special guest.

Throughout her career, Kate has always spoken more favourably of being in it for the music than for any kind of fame in and of itself. She said in a 1980 interview: "Artists shouldn't be made famous. They have this huge aura of almost god-like quality about them, just because their craft makes a lot of money. And at the same time it is a forced importance… It is man-made so the press can feed off it."

Kate's third studio album was released in September 1980. Titled *Never For Ever*, it marked her second foray into production whereby she co-produced it with Jon Kelly.

Notably though, even throughout her earlier days in the studio, Kate had always been certain about what she wanted to achieve from a sonic perspective. Of the sessions for *The Kick Inside*, Kelly told *Sound On Sound* in 2004; "Kate would certainly get involved, poking her head all around to see where it sounded nice. There was a good feeling of camaraderie, so I never felt nervous, just insecure! I recorded the celeste with a Coles ribbon mic positioned on the soundboard at the back, and that worked out fine. You couldn't keep Kate away from her sessions even if you had wild dogs and bazookas. She was just drinking it all up, learning everything that went on. The first moment she walked into the control room, I could tell that's where she wanted to be, in control of her own records. She was so astute and intelligent, and she was also phenomenally easy to work with. An absolute joy. I can't remember any bad moments at all… She was the shining light of the entire sessions. You couldn't deny her anything."

"Kate herself was just fantastic. Looking back, she was incredible and such an inspiration, even though when she first walked in, I probably thought she was just another new artist. Her openness, her enthusiasm, her obvious talent — I remember finishing that first day, having recorded two or three backing tracks, and thinking 'My God, that's it. I've peaked!'… Kate always recorded live vocals, and they were fantastic, but then she'd want to redo them later. In the case of 'Wuthering Heights', she was imitating this witch, the mad lady from the

December 1979.

At Virgin Records in Eldon Square, Newcastle, signing autographs on the 10th September 1980.

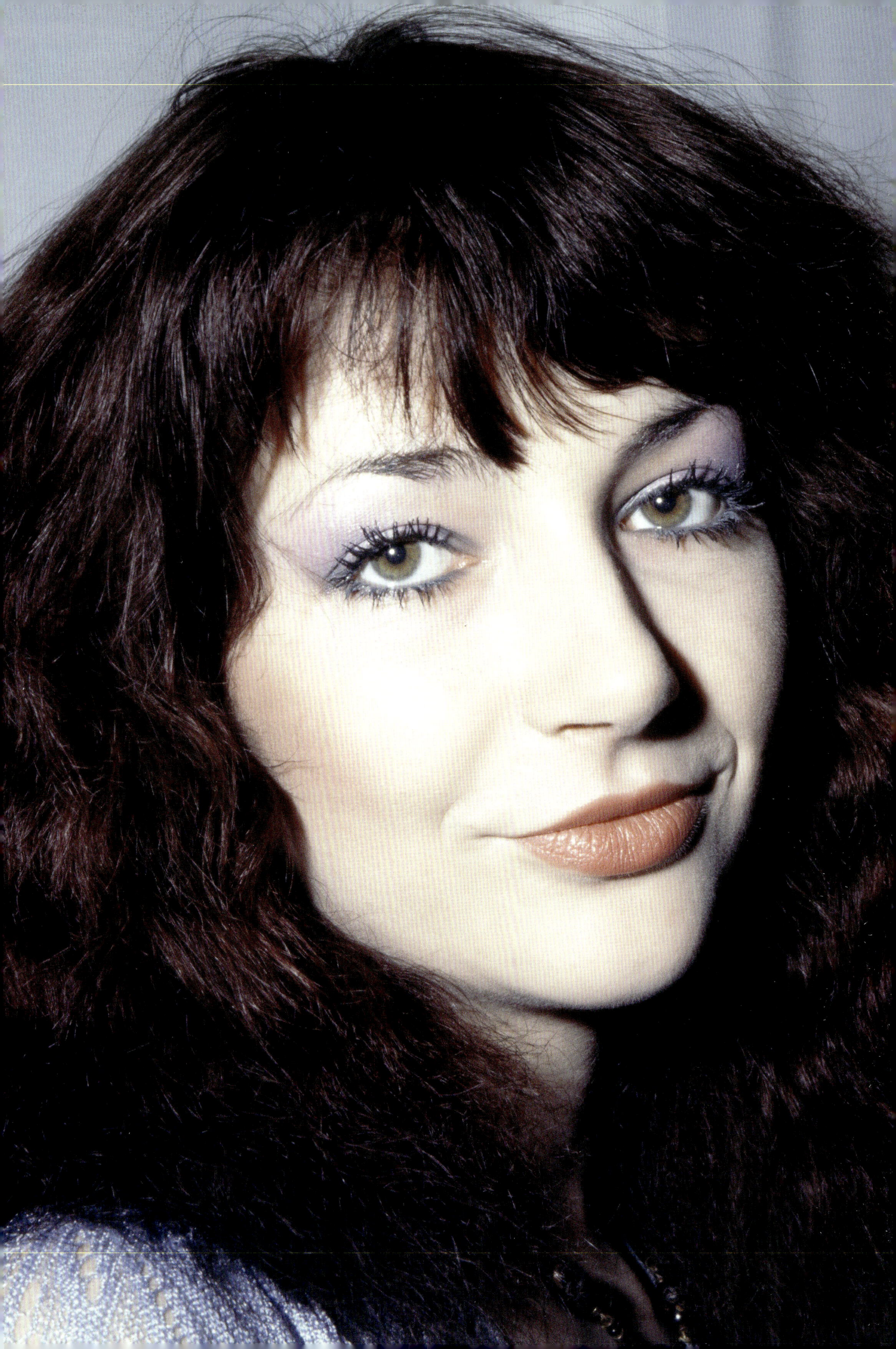

British Rock and Pop Awards,
26th February 1980.

KATE BUSH
HER NEW ALBUM
NEVER FOR EVER

Featuring 'BREATHING' & 'BABOOSHKA'
and the new single 'ARMY DREAMERS'

To hear a preview
of Kate's new album
telephone
01-409 2961
or 01-499 9471

EMI

Kate at an album signing in Glasgow,
October 1980 *(and overleaf)*.

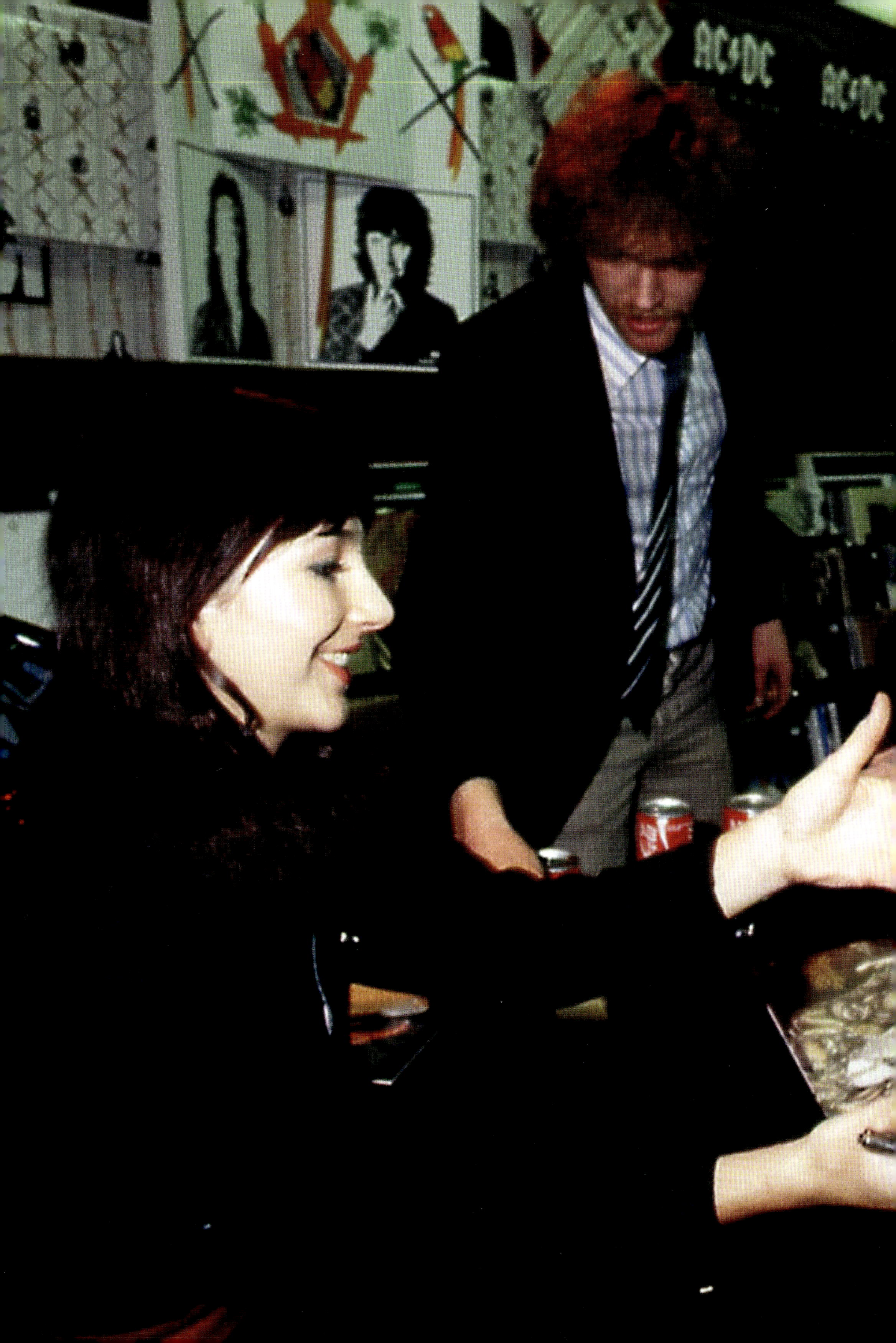

AC/DC
AC/DC

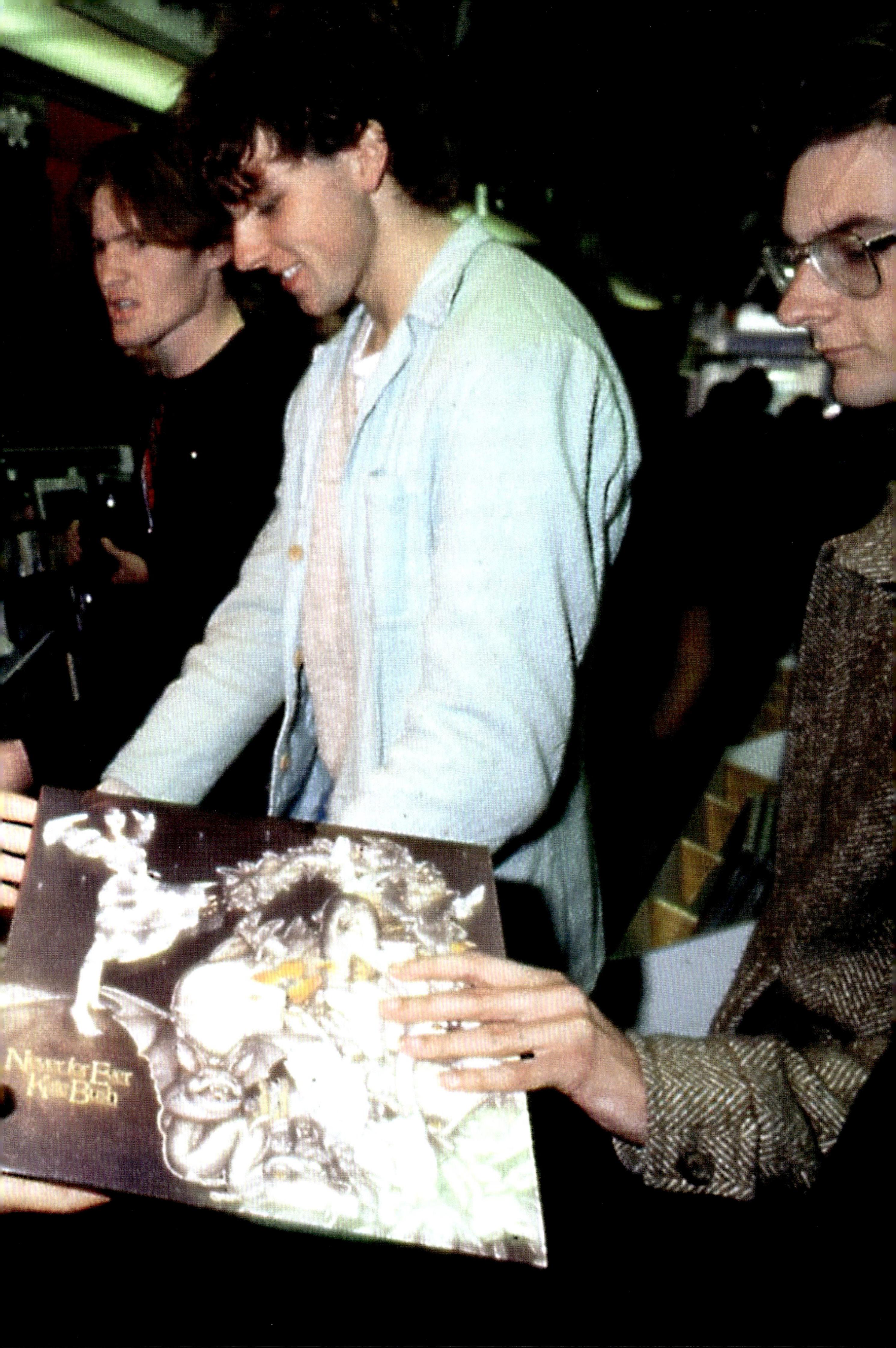
Never for Ever
Kate Bush

Kate poses in the studio wearing lycra leggings and pop sox.
18th August 1980.

Yorkshire Moors, and she was very theatrical about it. She was such a mesmerising performer — she threw her heart and soul into everything she did — that it was difficult to ever fault her or say 'You could do better.'"

On balance, Kate spoke keenly of how the musicians she had worked with had been empathetic to her artistic vision; "The first album was all down to the producer, Andrew Powell, and the engineer, Jon Kelly. As far as I know, it was mainly Andrew Powell who chose the musicians, he'd worked with them before and they were all sort of tied in with Alan Parsons. There was Stuart Elliot on drums, Ian Bairnson on guitar, David Paton on bass, and Duncan Mackay on electric keyboards. And, on that first album, I had no say, so I was very lucky really to be given such good musicians to start with. And they were lovely, because they were all very concerned about what I thought of the treatment of each of the songs. And if I was unhappy with anything, they were more than willing to redo their parts. So they were very concerned about what I thought, which was very nice. And they were really nice guys, eager to know what the songs were about and all that sort of thing. I don't honestly see how anyone can play with feeling unless you know what the song is about. You know, you might be feeling this really positive vibe, yet the song might be something weird and heavy and sad. So I think that's always been very important for me, to sit down and tell the musicians what the song is about."

Whilst Kate's first two albums had resulted in a definitive sound evident in every track, with orchestral arrangements supporting the live band sound, the range of styles on *Never For Ever* is much more diverse. They cover a straightforward rock style, such as that which features on 'Violin', right across to the melancholic waltz of 'Army Dreamers'.

Never For Ever was Kate's first album to feature synthesisers and drum machines, and of course, the Fairlight CMI. She was introduced to the latter when she contributed backing vocals on Peter Gabriel's eponymous third album in early 1980. *Never For Ever* was the first of Kate's albums to reach peak position in the UK. It made her not only the first *British* female to achieve the position, but the first female to do it entirely.

The best-selling single from the album was 'Babooshka'. It got to number five in the UK. Following the release of 'Army Dreamers', which got to number sixteen, Kate released the standalone Christmas single, 'December Will Be Magic Again', which got to number twenty-nine.

September 1982 saw the release of *The Dreaming*, the first album that Kate produced entirely on her own. With the enhanced scope for creativity in such regard, she experimented

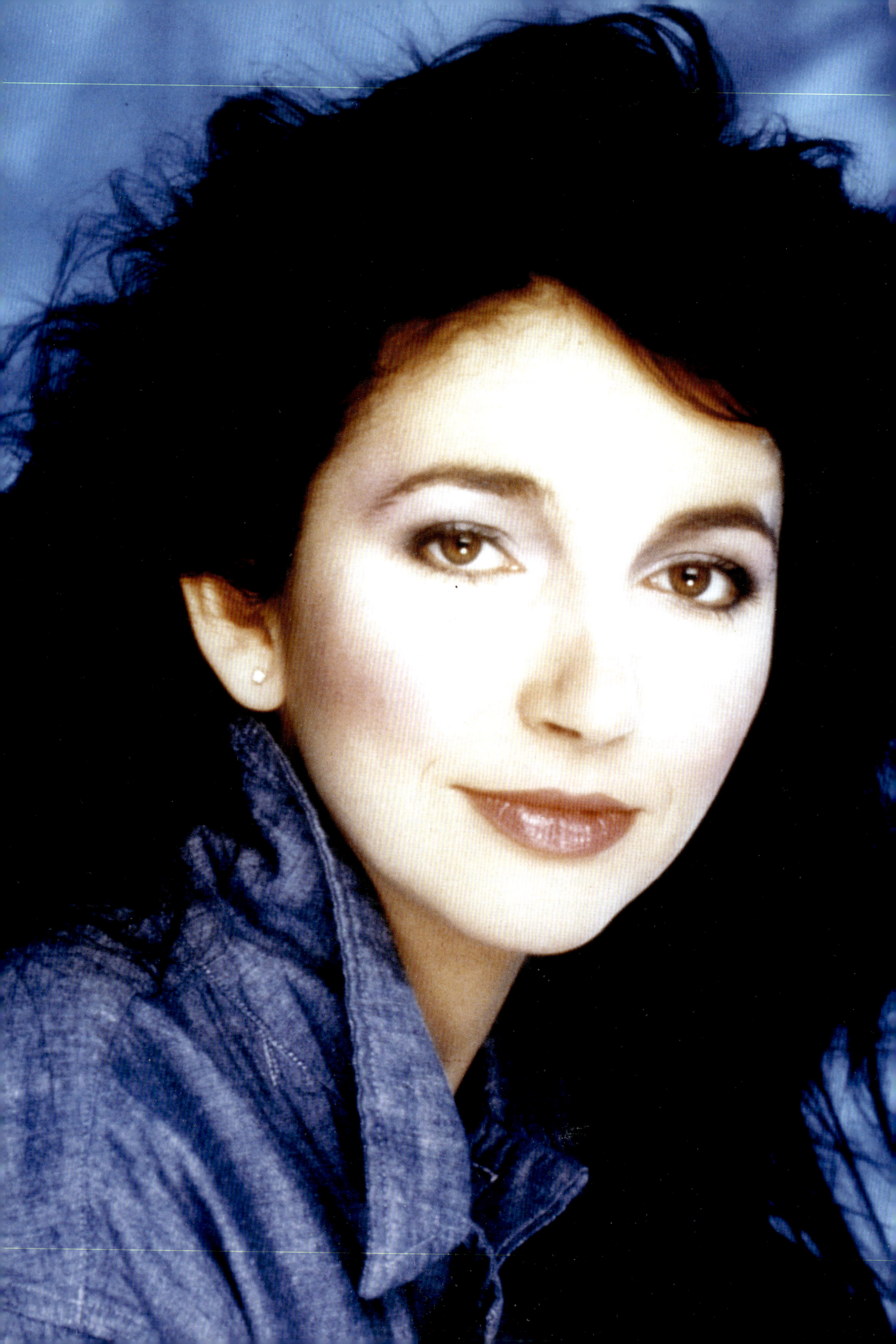

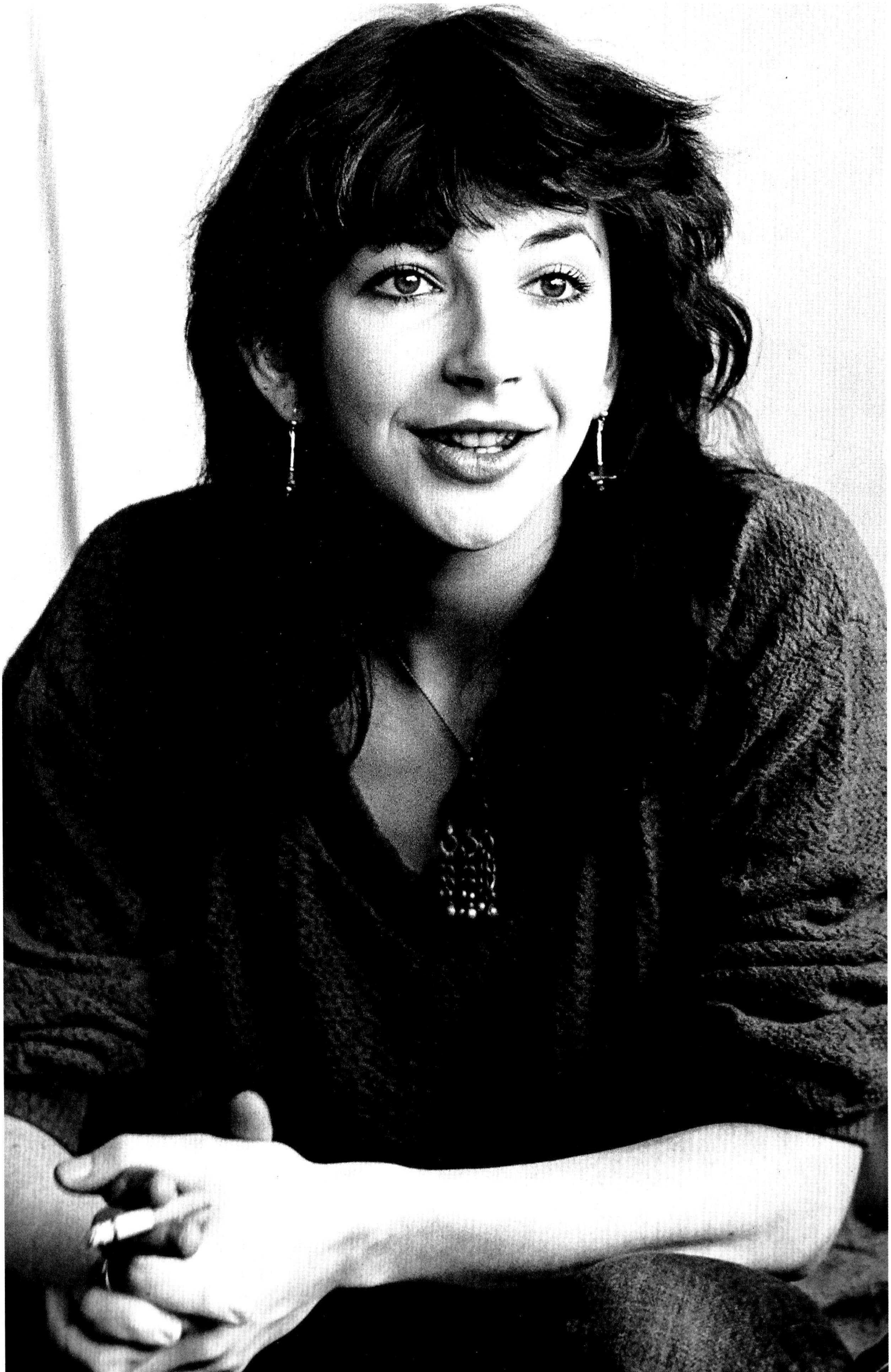

Kate with
Rowan Atkinson
at NME awards
1st October 1980.

KATE BUSH
THE DREAMING

HER NEW ALBUM AND CASSETTE

ALBUM EMC 3419 — EMI — CASSETTE TC/EMC 3419

Page 28 SOUNDS October 30, 1982

THE LONG-HAIRED, denim-clad figure who emerged from the recesses of *Kerrang!* stopped in his tracks, listening intently to the record on the turntable.

"This Kate Bush?" he queried. "Good, isn't she, I really like her stuff."

When I told my mum I'd be interviewing the lady she was so impressed I thought for one awful moment that she was going to ask me to get her autograph. Now, I can't think of many artists with that kind of across the board appeal, and the funny thing is that Kate Bush makes some very strange records.

Her first album for two years is 'The Dreaming', and it's as far removed from the current chart sounds as you could possibly imagine (or hope for), but in it went at number three, proof that you don't have to conform to commercial formulae to be (or stay) successful.

A surprisingly slight but strangely attractive figure with a direct gaze, clad in baggy jumper and jeans, Kate Bush is nothing like her dreadful public image — that of a breathless squeaky voiced girl whose vocabulary is limited to words like 'wow' and 'incredible'. I wondered if she finds it disconcerting that people have such a weird image of her.

"Oh yeah, and it worries me a bit too," she says. "That image was something that was created in the first two years of my popularity though, when people latched onto the fact that I was young and female, rather than a young female singer/songwriter.

"Now it's much easier for females to be recognised as that because there are more around, but when I started there was really only me and Debbie Harry and we got tied into this whole body thing — it was very flattering but not the ideal image I would have chosen."

Because people *see* that rather than hear the songs....

"Right, and I've spent so much time trying to prove to those people that there's more to me than that. Just the fact that I'm still around and my art keeps happening should convince them.

"I can't go around all the time telling people where I'm at now, I just have to hope that there are people who see the changes and change with me. I think it was just that the media didn't know how to handle it because it was so unusual at the time."

Did you ever feel like you were being treated as a child prodigy?

"I felt that because I was so young people weren't taking me seriously, they couldn't accept that I could be so involved in what I was doing.

"I was very lucky because when I left school I knew what I wanted to do and it worked out, and I suppose I did grow up fairly fast because in a way I was working in an area two or three years ahead of myself."

Kate is now 24, and 'The Dreaming' is undoubtedly her most mature work to date. It took over a year to make and the result is an intricate, complex web of ideas and images, with sounds used to create pictures which are sometimes too abstract for easy comprehension. I wondered if she was occasionally being deliberately obscure.

"No, not at all, because although there's a lot going on in some of the tracks, to me they're kept on a simple basic within themselves — all the ideas are aiming towards the same picture.

"Like, some people have said it's over-produced, but I don't think it is because I know what I was trying to get at. I think of over-produced albums as the ones that have strings, brass, choirs, that sort of thing."

What about the lyrics, though; as I sat struggling with them I felt that you had made them consciously oblique in places.

"I don't intend them to be that way, it's just the way they come out. The thing is, when I have a subject matter the best way I could explain it would be across ten pages of foolscap, but as I've got to get it in a song I have to precis everything.

"Maybe the album *is* more difficult for people than I meant it to be, it isn't intended to be complicated but it obviously is for some. A lot of it is to do with the fact that the songs are very involved, there's lots of different layers.

"Hopefully the next one will be simpler, but each time it gets harder because *I'm* getting more involved, I'm trying to do something better all the time."

Do you worry about losing fans?

"Yeah, I do, because obviously from a purely financial point of view I depend on money to make albums and if they're not successful it's quite likely I won't have the scope to do what I want on the next one.

"But, I'd rather go artistically the way I want to than hang onto an audience, because you have to keep doing what you feel — it's just luck if you can hang onto the people as well."

THE TIME and cost of 'The Dreaming' has already been fairly well documented — did you intend to spend that long recording it?

"No, not at all but I find that a lot of things I do now take so much longer than I thought they would."

What is it that takes the time, translating your ideas onto record?

"Yeah, that's what's really hard, in so many cases you need to be in the studio to get the sounds and it can maybe take a couple of days just to get one idea across — sometimes you wonder if you should just leave them."

How do you feel about your early records now?

"I don't really like them — a lot of the stuff on the first two albums I wasn't at all happy with, I think I'm still fond of a lot of the songs but I was unhappy about the way they came across on record.

"Also, until this album I'd never really enjoyed the sound of my own voice — it's always been very difficult for me because I've wanted to hear the songs in a different way."

Why didn't you like it?

"I think a lot of people don't like the sound of their own voices, it's like you have to keep working towards something you eventually *do* like. It was very satisfying for me on this album because for the first time I can sit and listen to the vocals and think, yeah, that's actually quite good."

Were you pushing it more to create different sounds?

"In a way, but I probably used to push it more in other ways. I went through a phase of trying to leap up and down a lot when I was writing songs, I used to try to push it almost acrobatically, now I'm trying more to get the song across and I have more control. When I'm trying to think up the character is when it needs a bit of push."

Do you always try to put yourself in the role of a character then?

"Yeah, normally, because the song is always about something and always from a particular viewpoint — there's normally a personality that runs along with it.

"Sometimes I really have to work at it to get in the right frame of mind because it's maybe the opposite to how I'm feeling, but other times it feels almost like an extension of me, which it is in some ways."

You have been accused in the past of living in some kind of fantasy world — would you say you refuse to face up to reality?

"No, I think I do actually, although there are certain parts of me that definitely don't want to look at reality. Generally speaking though I'm quite realistic, but perhaps the songs on the first two albums created some kind of fantasy image so people presumed I lived in that kind of world."

Where do you get the ideas for songs from?

"Anywhere really, there's two or three tracks that I had the ideas for on the last album but never got together, others come from films, books or stories from people I know, that kind of thing."

What about 'Pull Out The Pin', a song about Vietnam — was that something you'd always wanted to write about?

"No, I didn't think I'd ever want to write about it until I saw this documentary on television which moved me so much I thought I just had to."

The title track concerns the abuse of Aborigines by so-called civilised man. Where did that interest come from?

"That's something that's been growing for years, it started when I was tiny and my brother bought 'Sunarise'. We though it was brilliant, to me that's a classic record, I started to become aware of the whole thing, that it's almost an instinctive thing in white man to wipe out a race that actually owns the land — it's happening all over the world."

Do you hope to change people's opinions by what you write?

"No, because I don't think a song can ever do that, if people have strong opinions then they're so deep rooted that you'll never be able to change the situation anyway. Even if you can change the way a few people think you'll never be able to change the situation anyway.

"I don't ever write politically because I know nothing about politics, to me they seem more destructive than helpful. I think I write from an emotional point of view, because even though a situation may be political there's always some emotional element, and that's what gets to me."

THE THOUGHTS and ideas are expressed through a variety of sounds, an adventurous use of instruments and people, from Rolf Harris on digeridu to Percy Edwardes on animal impressions! Kate has also discovered the Fairlight, a computerised synthesiser.

"It's given me a completely different perspective on sounds," she enthuses. "You can put any sound you want onto the keyboard, so if you go ugh, you can play ugh all the way up the keyboard — theoretically any sound that exists you can play.

"I think it's surprising that with all the gear around at the moment people aren't experimenting more."

Whatever you may think of Kate Bush, you could never say that she's not been prepared to take risks. In the four years that have passed since her startling first single 'Wuthering Heights' she has grown increasingly adventurous and ambitious, creating music that she hopes will last longer than much of todays transient pop.

Of 'The Dreaming' she says: "I wanted it to be a long lasting album, because my favourite records are the ones that grow on you, that you play lots of times because each time you hear something different."

Never particularly a public fave, her last live shows were three years ago, and although she plans to do some in the future they'll take at least six months to prepare.

She admits she found her initial success hard to cope with at times.

"I still find some things frightening, I've adjusted a hell of a lot but it still scares me. There are so many aspects that if you start thinking about them are terrifying. The best thing to do is not even to think about it — just try to sail through."

Steve Rapport

BUSHY TALES
KATE BUSH TELLS KAREN SWAYNE ABOUT HER LATEST DREAM

A brand of make-believe

KATE BUSH
'The Dreaming'
(EMI TC-EMC 3419)**

KATE BUSH does provoke reaction.

You can't wash her down with a glass of vermouth while posing on the patio.

The world suddenly becomes black and white. She's not a walk-over or something to toss over your shoulder.

I'm a blank sheet. Three hearings later, I feel sick. My stomach has turned.

My first reaction was revulsion at the over-production. This is Ms Bush's utopia. She has realised her fantasy in the studio. It reminds me of how I felt after seeing *All That Jazz* where Bob Fosse indulges in a director's orgy. Here, Kate Bush unleashes every special effect available in sound engineering. It's a barrage with no real roughage.

My second reaction was confusion. I felt swamped by Ms Bush's constant flight to the symbolic and esoteric. She takes pathos and rams it against a thick wall of sickly strings. I can't escape. Every song becomes an epic endeavour; a *Ben Hur* with shades of *Don Giovanni*.

My third reaction was shock. I read the lyric sheet. I'm sitting there under the impression that Ms Bush is floating on a terminal cloud nine when I stumble across some real thoughts.

'Dreaming' deals with the abuse and wiping out of the aborigines by the white man. Beneath the grandiose veneer lies a hard core. You would never dream it but there's more.

'Pull Out The Pin' is about the nobility of the Vietnamese in war. They put their silver Buddhas in their mouths before they went into action. It's a worthy theme but a horribly romantic treatment and you can hear Bush sighing at the aesthetic beauty of it all.

My fourth reaction is depression. After the positive ideas of the first side in 'Leave It Open', 'Sat In Your Lap' and 'There Goes A Tenner' comes a sentimental fog. The melodrama is hammed up to the hilt. Ms Bush falls easily into the maudlin mood with those prize tearjerkers 'All The Love' and 'Houdini'.

On reflection after initial reactions, I can't help admiring her eccentric spirit and her *voice*.

She has to be praised for bringing in Rolf Harris on his didgeridoo, Percy Edwards with his animal noises, an Irish jig band and a choirboy. Her sense of adventure is evidently intact but she crammed in too much.

I'm drowning in a sea of vocal over-dubs. My taste buds have been over-stimulated.

It took a year, five studios and five engineers to make this record. It shows.

ROSE ROUSE

KATE BUSH: 'sickening and stomach-turning' says our reviewer

with production techniques (including further exploration into embracing the technology of the Fairlight). The result was an album abundant in diverse blends of musical styles. Due to its eclectic nature, The Dreaming received a mixed reception in the UK. Some critics were baffled by the dense soundscapes on it and thus considered it to be "less accessible" than her earlier work.

Nevertheless, it was something that Kate stood proudly by, and creatively, she was in her element and enjoying the ride. She said at the time; "After the last album, Never For Ever, I started writing some new songs. They were very different from anything I'd ever written before — they were much more rhythmic, and in a way, a completely new side to my music. I was using different instruments, and everything was changing; and I felt that really the best thing to do would be to make this album a real departure – make it completely different. And the only way to achieve this was to sever all the links I had had with the older stuff."

In later years, with the advantage of hindsight, Kate told

Laugh? I could have Di-ed

Prince's Trust Royal Gala
Dominion

FOUR WEEKS of are they/aren't they speculation about who was actually going to **play** this exclusive charity do didn't apparently help to sell tickets to the glitterati.

The remainder, Lord preserve us, had to be sold to the **public at large** and a good thing too. Instead of portly executives and self-absorbed 'celebrities', it was peopled mainly by music lovers and **that** rather than the presence of HRH, is what flavoured the atmosphere.

That, and the fact of having a selection of the very best of British musicians under one roof made it quite a unique occasion.

Madness kicked off with a party version of the national anthem, and weren't all that inspiring. HRH didn't think so either and spent the time peering at the TV monitor, scratching his left ear, and smiling wanly.

Maybe he was trying to remember the carefully rehearsed speech he was going to deliver about the winners of the Trust Fund music competition, Brummie reggae outfit Unity who, despite the fawning adjectives laid at their door, were quite acceptable. Who's to bet that **they** won't be allowed to slip back into obscurity!

Formalities over, we were refreshed by the all too brief appearance of Joan Armatrading and, you know, it gives me a kick still to see an audience held captive by the basic power of one guitar and the impact of a voice. The hell with techno-rock and electro-bop, gimme emotion in simplicity anytime. 'Love & Emotion' was imbued with more pathos than can **ever** be reproduced on vinyl.

And from the sublime to...? Britain's most famous fish-farmer bedecked in tam o'shanter and tights with a bulge that'd put Nureyev to shame?

Jethro Tull of course, and for ten minutes we were transported to the excesses of the Wembley Arena with flash lighting, the whole works and Ian Anderson weaving about the stage like a drunken morris dancer. Maybe he imagined he was dodging snipers. I heard he'd arrived early afternoon to personally check out the stage for suspect devices although the grotesqueries of the previous day had us all covertly looking under our seats.

Phil Collins was guesting in the percussion hotseat which he then vacated to render a disappointingly dull version of 'In The Air Tonight'. We were then 'entertained' by the Masai Dance Company, muscular black guys in shorts with an embarassingly unco-ordinated routine — an obvious filler.

But the climax was worth the wait. To see Townshend, Ure, Karn, Collins, Brooker, Plant and Bush onstage at once was third degree culture shock! Everyone did their party piece, the highlights being a superbly textured version of 'No Regrets' with Townshend adding backing vocals, a nostalgic blast from Brooker et al with 'Whiter Shade of Pale' and an intriguingly poignant song from Townshend seeing him forsake guitar for piano. Shamefully, I've no idea of its origins but I intend to find them out.

Kate Bush made a brief but well received appearance, especially well received when her straps broke and she had to make a sidestage exit clutching modestly to her bosom! And then Robert Plant joined the party, and disorientation gave way to sheer disbelief!

I mean, see Mick Karn shuffling little pirouettes around Robert Plant and Pete Townshend does little to imbue you with a great sense of reality!

The grand finale was a grossly top-heavy version of 'Gonna Take You Higher' with Masai Dancers and pelvic thrusts in wild abundance. Even HRH seemed to be in the groove! And the evening wasn't even marred by Kid Jensen's cloying attempt at being MC.

HELEN FITZGERALD

KATE BUSH seen moments before the strain proved too much: Robert Plant thumps away regardless

Q magazine in 1993; "That was my "she's gone mad" album." Still though, *The Dreaming* was her first album to enter the US Billboard 200 chart, albeit only getting to number 157. In the UK, although the album initially sold less than its predecessors, it still got to number three, and has since been certified silver by the BPI.

The first single to be released from the album was 'Sat In Your Lap'. Preceding the album's release date by over a year, it got to number eleven in the UK. The title track, featuring Rolf Harris and Percy Edwards, stalled at number forty-eight, and the third single, 'There Goes A Tenner', only got as far as number ninety-three. 'Suspended In Gaffa' was released as a single in Europe, but not in the UK.

Continuing in her storytelling tradition on her forth album, Kate looked beyond her own frame of reference as a source of inspiration. She drew on old crime films for 'There Goes A Tenner', a documentary about the Vietnam War for 'Pull Out The Pin', and the plight of Indigenous Australians for the title track. 'Houdini' is about the magician's death, and 'Get Out Of My House' was inspired by Stephen King's novel, *The Shining*.

For the first benefit concert in aid of The Prince's Trust, in July 1982, Kate sang 'The Wedding List', backed by a band consisting of Pete Townshend, Phil Collins, Midge Ure, Mick Karn, Gary Brooker, Dave Formula and Peter Hope Evans. The performance was later released on VHS video, Laserdisc and CED disc.

The Dreaming had been expensive to make owing to the costs of hiring studio space – Kate had worked at four different London studios at various points during the recording timeline: Advision, Odyssey, Abbey Road and Townhouse. In response to this, by the summer of 1983, it made economic sense for Kate to build a private studio near her home, allowing her to work at her own pace.

Kate started to record demos for *Hounds Of Love* in January 1984. Instead of re-recording the material, she enhanced the demos during further sessions. Five months thereafter, she set to work on overdubbing and mixing the album, which took a year to do. Once again she made use of the Fairlight CMI synthesiser, as well as the piano, traditional Irish instruments, and layered vocals.

Hounds Of Love took advantage of the vinyl and cassette formats whereby it was produced as two suites. Side one is subtitled Hounds Of Love, and contains five, predominantly accessible, pop songs: 'Running Up That Hill', 'Cloudbusting', 'Hounds Of Love', and 'The Big Sky' (all of which were released as singles) and 'Mother Stands For Comfort'. Side two – a seven-track concept piece – is subtitled The Ninth Wave. The album

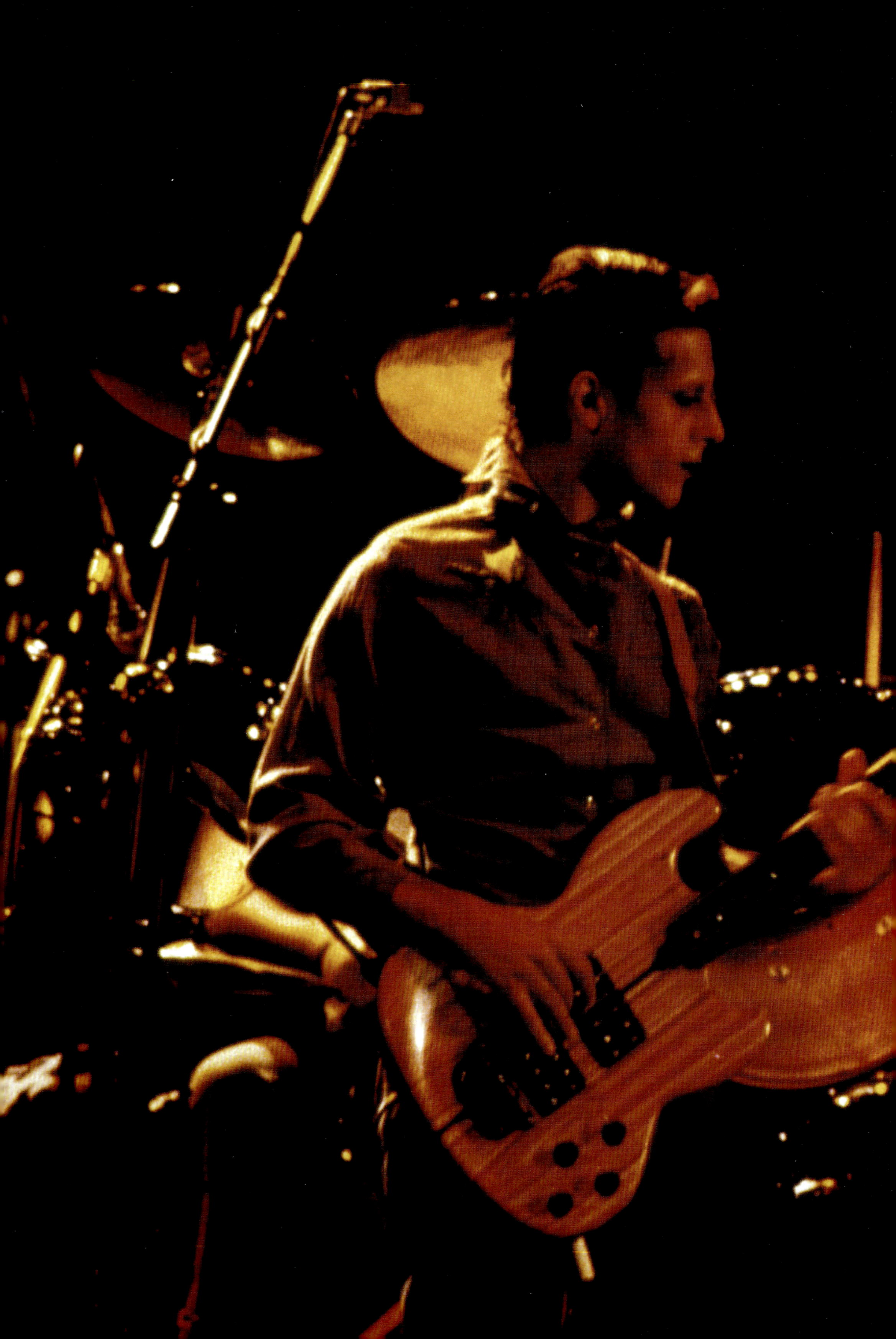

The Prince's Trust Concert, 21st July 1982, Dominion Theatre, London. Kate performed 'The Wedding List' with a band that featured Midge Ure, Mick Karn, Phil Collins, Pete Townshend and Gary Brooker.

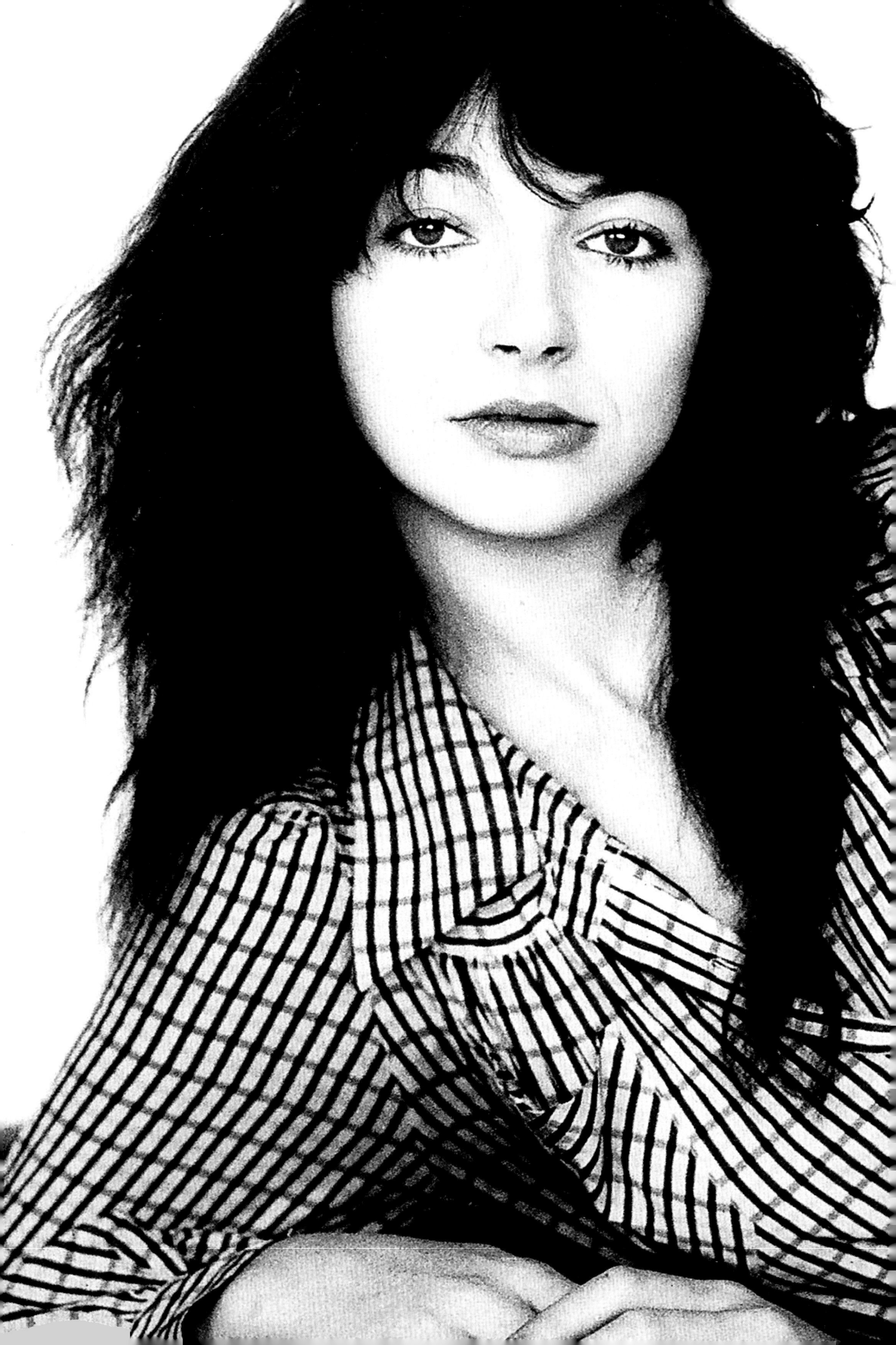

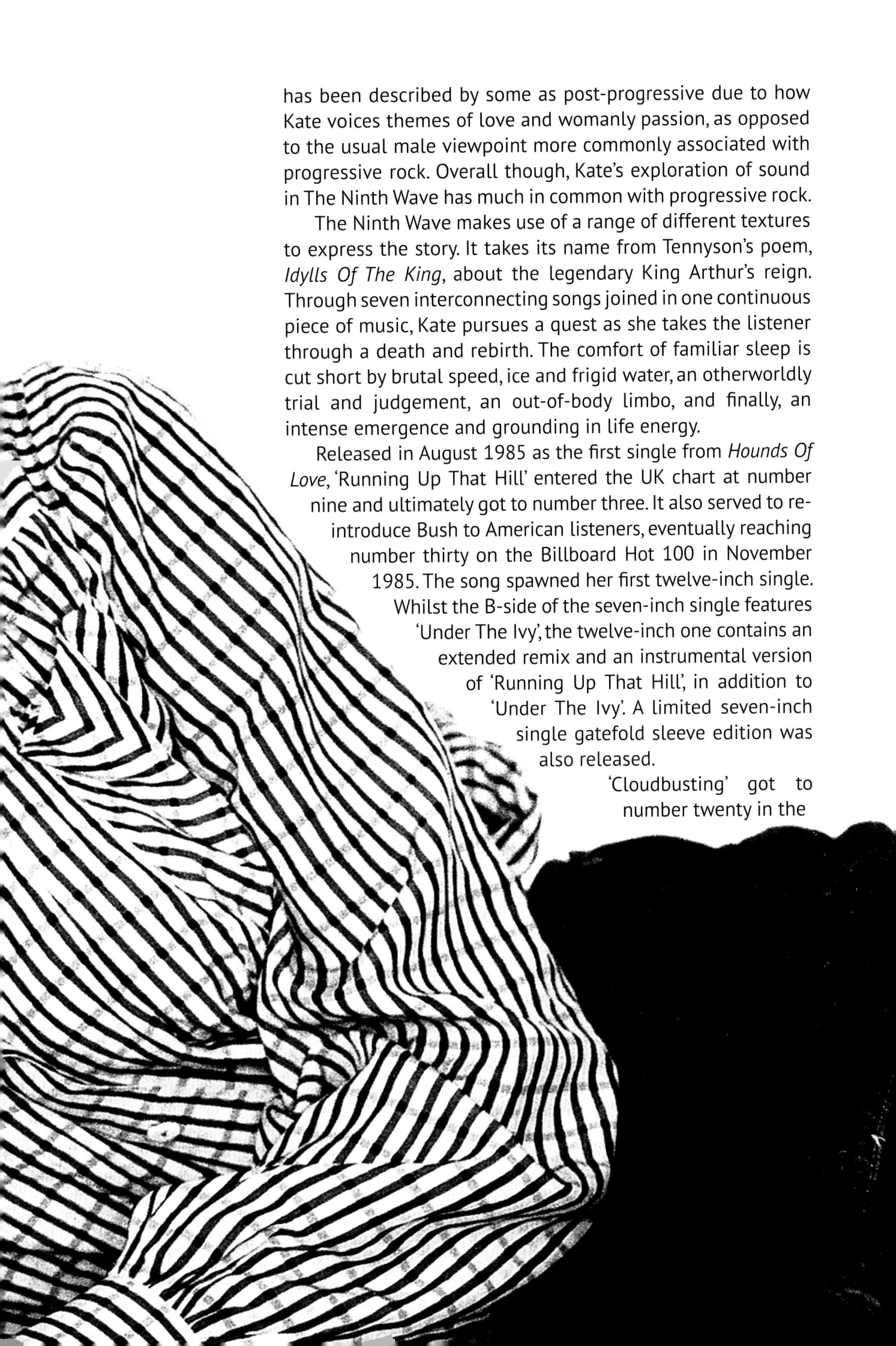

has been described by some as post-progressive due to how Kate voices themes of love and womanly passion, as opposed to the usual male viewpoint more commonly associated with progressive rock. Overall though, Kate's exploration of sound in The Ninth Wave has much in common with progressive rock.

The Ninth Wave makes use of a range of different textures to express the story. It takes its name from Tennyson's poem, *Idylls Of The King*, about the legendary King Arthur's reign. Through seven interconnecting songs joined in one continuous piece of music, Kate pursues a quest as she takes the listener through a death and rebirth. The comfort of familiar sleep is cut short by brutal speed, ice and frigid water, an otherworldly trial and judgement, an out-of-body limbo, and finally, an intense emergence and grounding in life energy.

Released in August 1985 as the first single from *Hounds Of Love*, 'Running Up That Hill' entered the UK chart at number nine and ultimately got to number three. It also served to re-introduce Bush to American listeners, eventually reaching number thirty on the Billboard Hot 100 in November 1985. The song spawned her first twelve-inch single. Whilst the B-side of the seven-inch single features 'Under The Ivy', the twelve-inch one contains an extended remix and an instrumental version of 'Running Up That Hill', in addition to 'Under The Ivy'. A limited seven-inch single gatefold sleeve edition was also released.

'Cloudbusting' got to number twenty in the

UK. The music video was conceived as a short film by Kate with Terry Gilliam. Directed by Julian Doyle, it features Canadian actor Donald Sutherland playing the role of Wilhelm Reich, with Kate in the role of his young son, Peter.

As the third single from *Hounds Of Love*, the title track was released in February 1986 and got to number eighteen in the UK. Released in the April, the fourth and final single released from *Hounds Of Love*, 'The Big Sky', got to number thirty-seven in the UK.

When *Hounds Of Love* itself topped the charts in the UK upon its release in September 1985, it knocked Madonna's *Like A Virgin* from the number-one spot. The album did wonders for Kate's career at the mid-peak of the eighties, especially compared to how her previous two albums of the decade had performed. As *Record Mirror* put it; "Now more than eight years into her chart career, Kate Bush has singlehandedly written all fifteen of her hit singles, a figure unrivalled by any other female singer/songwriter in the world. Kate also shares the distinction of being one of only three women to pluck more than three top forty hits off an album (Tina Turner and Madonna are the other two). Kate's *Hounds Of Love* has been raided for 'Running Up That Hill', 'Cloudbusting', 'Hounds Of Love' and 'The Big Sky'. In addition to spawning these hits, the *Hounds Of Love* album has sold over 400,000 copies in its own right, and is the fourth-best selling compact disc ever released in Britain, lining up behind Dire Straits' *Brothers In Arms*, and *Love Over Gold*, and Phil Collins' *No Jacket Required*." The following week, the same publication stated; "Kate Bush's *Hounds Of Love* album, which I conservatively estimated as selling 400,000 copies, has in fact sold over 600,000 copies. Kate's all-time best-seller remains the introductory *The Kick Inside*, which sold over 930,000 copies."

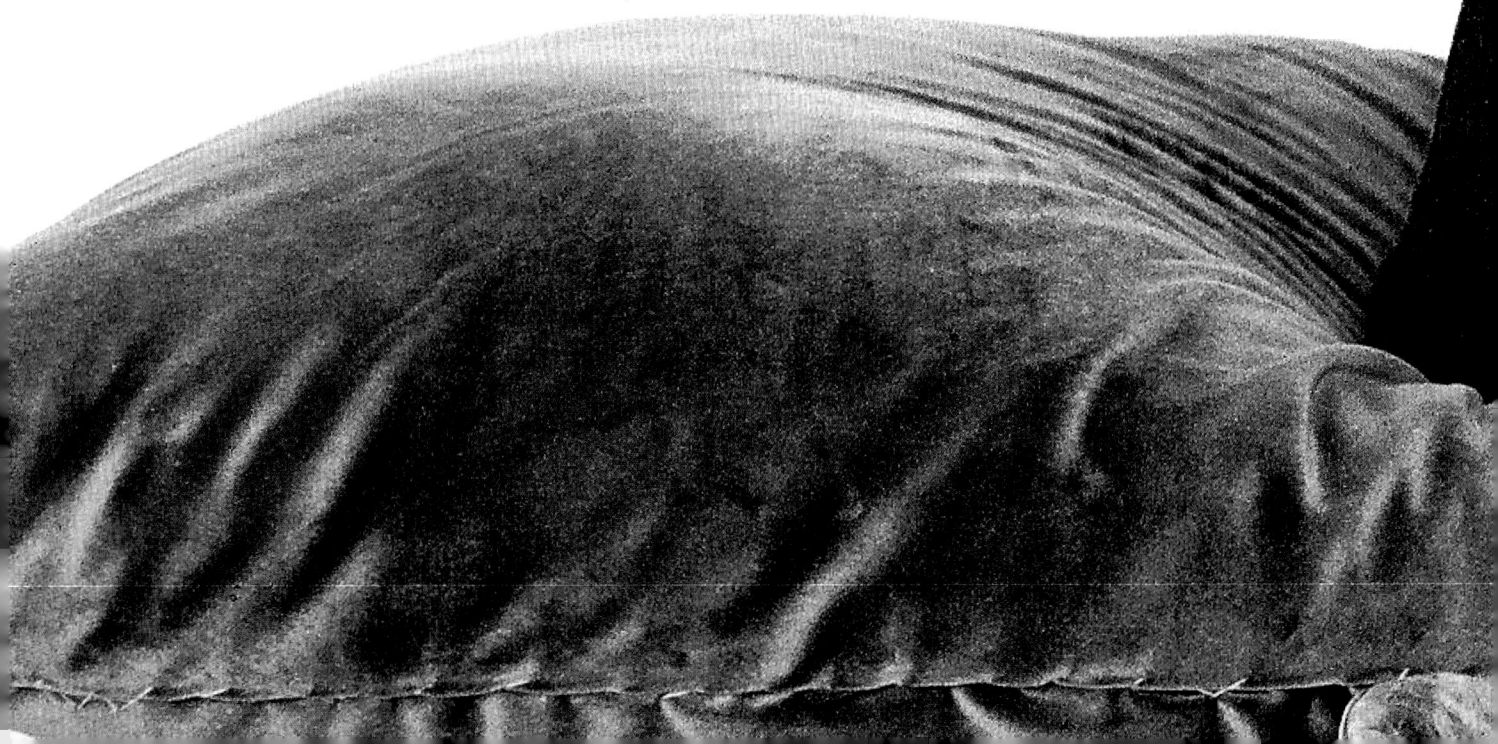

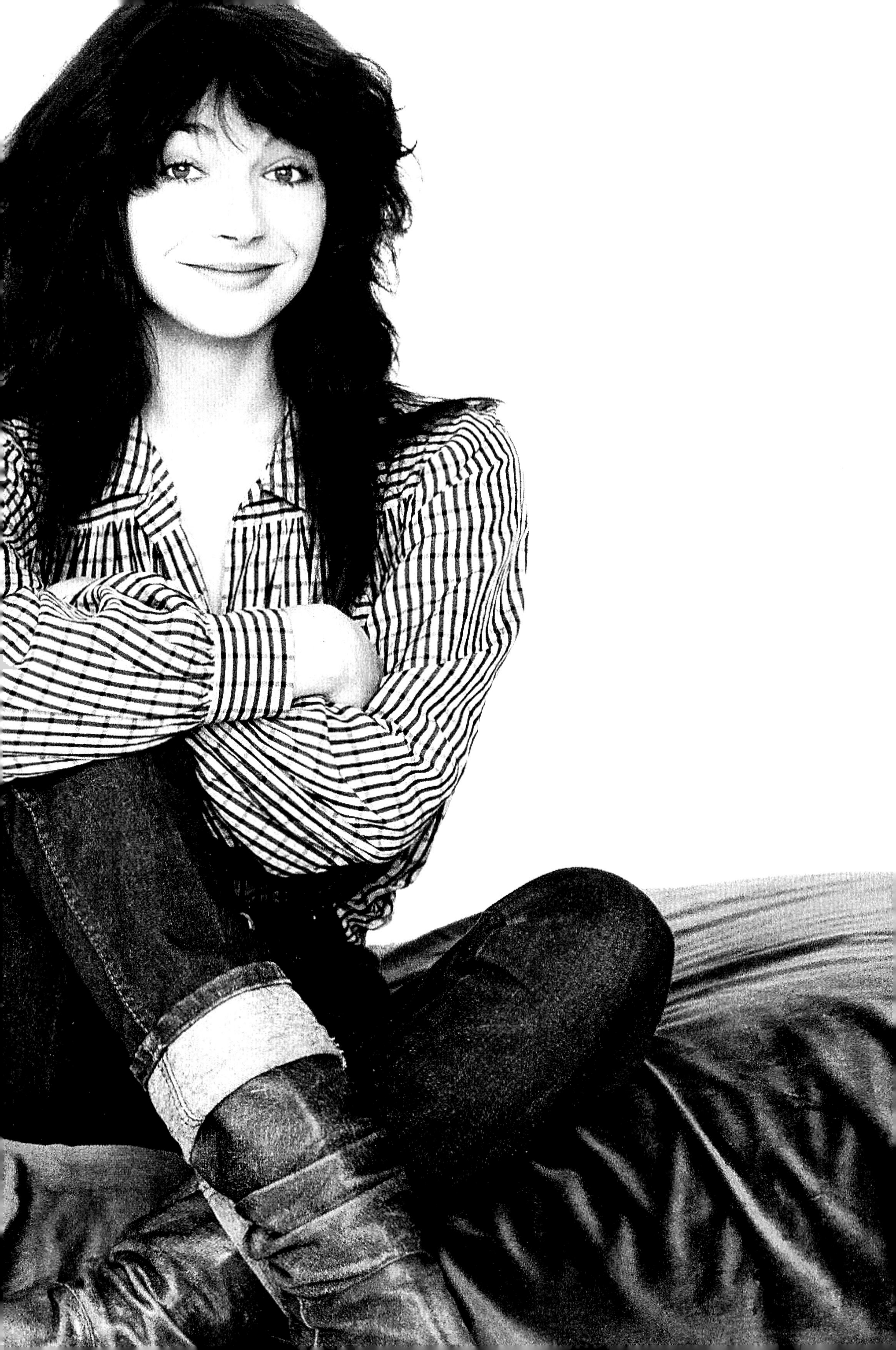

Performing 'Running Up That Hill' on the ZDF Sendung *Peter's Pop Show*, 30th November 1985.

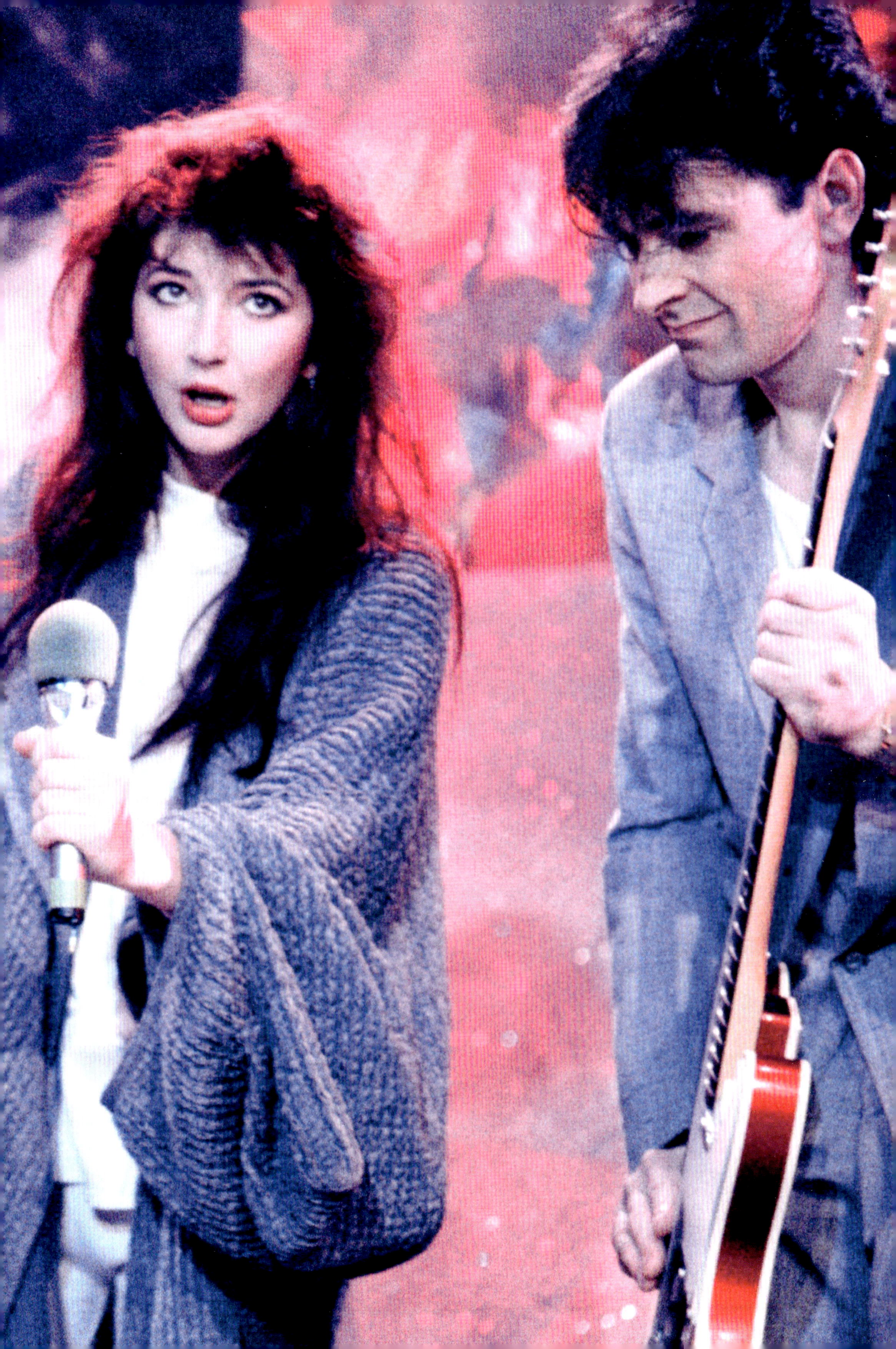

128

Performing 'The Big Sky' on the same TV show.

JAWS

EDITED BY CAROLE LINFIELD

KATE (or is it *Eastenders'* Angie?) closes off the world. Pic: Jane Simon.

PUPPY LOVE

SO THERE we stood in the Baker Street Laserium, eye to eye with Copernicus in a lacquered gold mask. Above our heads, the **Bush** howl yapped about 'Hounds Of Love' while the dogs of Fleet Street barked "Kate! Kate!" Serenely happy in the midst of all this and moving as one with a phalanx of male protectors, the Lionhearted lady seemed to be Dreaming. . .

An offer of a vodka and orange draws all the name drunks, and tonight your *Jaws* correspondent got EMI's money's worth, eyeing up such Romeos as Radio One producer **John Walters, Paul Gambaccini** and a prattle of music hacks.

Presently, the bar was closed, and we trouped forlornly into the Planetarium to be plunged, amid carefree childish shrieking and squealing, into darkness. Kate's undeniably strong voice boomed out and suddenly unbelievably vibrant rays were sketching some hippy's dreams onto several hundred upturned retinas.

Side one of the album, heavily into hearts and flowers, gave us laser Spirographs of writhing red mouths, octagons doing aerobics and *Fantasia*-like blooms exploding exotically into our lashes. Side two was a tale of stream-of-consciousness drowning. . .

Blinking into the light again, heavier drinking and food of the 'bet you can't keep this one down' variety appeared, as did Kate and her bloke, a chap with some of his hair in a plait but most of it in his sideburns.

"Ask her what she sees in that wally," snarled a certain **Brilliant Youth** and, after tripping over a huge promotional Wiemaraner (a dog, it's a *dog*), one intrepid hack decided to be direct about it.

"Are you the boyfriend?" she asked.

"Yeah, I'm Del Palmer," replied the hapless soul.

"Sounds like an Italian cheese. And how long have you been with Kate?"

"Seven years."

"Tell me, why do you think she stays with *you*?" Sniff. "She loves me."

"And why do you think that is?"

"Oh, I know the answer to that one!" interrupted a young Fleet Street journo entering into the spirit. "I've already asked Kate. She says he's sensitive and placid."

"And artistic," said Del. "I play bass on the record."

Bored, *Jaws* scampered over to Kate for a chat. Had she been to this impressive place before?

"No." (Sweet smile.)

Was it your ideal to hold the show here?

"No." (Sweet smile, fluttering lashes.)

The LP has a theme, doesn't it? How did the idea come to you?

"Er. . . I don't know."

Jaws tried to prompt — we mean, be helpful. Was it, perhaps, a dream?

"No."

Ho hum, well, nice to meet you Kate.

Jaws crammed another salmon vol-au-vent into someone's face and stumbled into the night, but one thing remains unsettled. Were there pin-tucks around those pixie ears? We forgot to check. Why, *why* didn't we ask about the last two years, and if she really *did* balloon to 16 stone? Next time. . .

At the 1986 BRIT Awards, *Hounds Of Love* earned Kate nominations for Best Female Solo Artist, Best Album, Best Single, and Best Producer. In the same year, she had a top ten UK hit with Peter Gabriel. For the duet, 'Don't Give Up', Gabriel enlisted the help of Kate after his first choice to sing the female vocal, Dolly Parton, had turned his offer down. Also in 1986, EMI released *The Whole Story*. Considered to be Kate's "greatest hits" album up to that point, she provided a new lead vocal and refreshed backing track on 'Wuthering Heights', and recorded a new single, 'Experiment IV', for inclusion on the compilation album. Dawn French and Hugh Laurie were among those featured in the video for the single. Kate worked with several of Britain's comedy stars that year, performing a live rendition of 'Do Bears...?' with Rowan Atkinson, as well as a solo rendition of 'Breathing', for Comic Relief. In March 1987, accompanied by David Gilmour, she performed 'Running Up That Hill' as part of The Secret Policeman's Third Ball. She would go on to perform with him again at the Royal Festival Hall in London in 2002, singing the Pink Floyd song, 'Comfortably Numb'. At the BRIT Awards of that year, she won the award for Best Female Solo Artist.

Page 34 SOUNDS September 21 1985

LOST AND HOUND

KATE BUSH 'Hounds Of Love' (KAB 1) *****
AS SOMEONE said in 'Falcon Crest' last week, "I've been playing cards for 30 years and I've always found that the person holding all the aces wins. Kate Bush is hogging every last one. If I were allowed to swear, I'd say that 'Hounds Of Love' is f***ing brilliant, but me mum won't let me.

The album version of 'Running Up That Hill' is more elaborate, wordy and subtle than the stormtrooper 12-inch, and to no ill effect. You can trace the roots back four years to barnstorming singles like 'Sat In Your Lap' and back to 'The Dreaming'. Besides the galloping single, the highlight of the five track side one is 'The Big Sky' – another thundering calamity Kate of a noise. The little girl voice is still in evidence, yet its wider, mature range finally lays the ghost of Heathcliffe to rest.

Side two is a seven part concept piece – 'The Ninth Wave', concerning the thoughts of someone alone in water, close to drowning. I see Kate as the primary school teacher announcing, "I'm going to play a record and we will have free dancing. Do anything the music suggests to your imagination." In common with most epic concepts, it takes a bit of earwigging to get into, but then WHAMMO! – hooked, line and sinker. It's a sophisticated series of fleeting and restrained melodies. Macbeth, church bells, whistles, helicopters, fiddles, pipes, narrations, choirs, violins, sythesisers, seagulls, cellos, handclaps, astronauts, Irish jigs, mediaeval riddums, Indian wailing, voice distortions, submarines, poetry, radio static, roaring rowboat men and didjeridoos – all human life contained herein. Dramatic, moving and wildly, unashamedly, beautifully romantic. (Can I say that in *Sounds*?) Give this dog a bone. Bow wow *wow*!

RONNIE RANDALL

KATE BUSH: Love her, love her dog

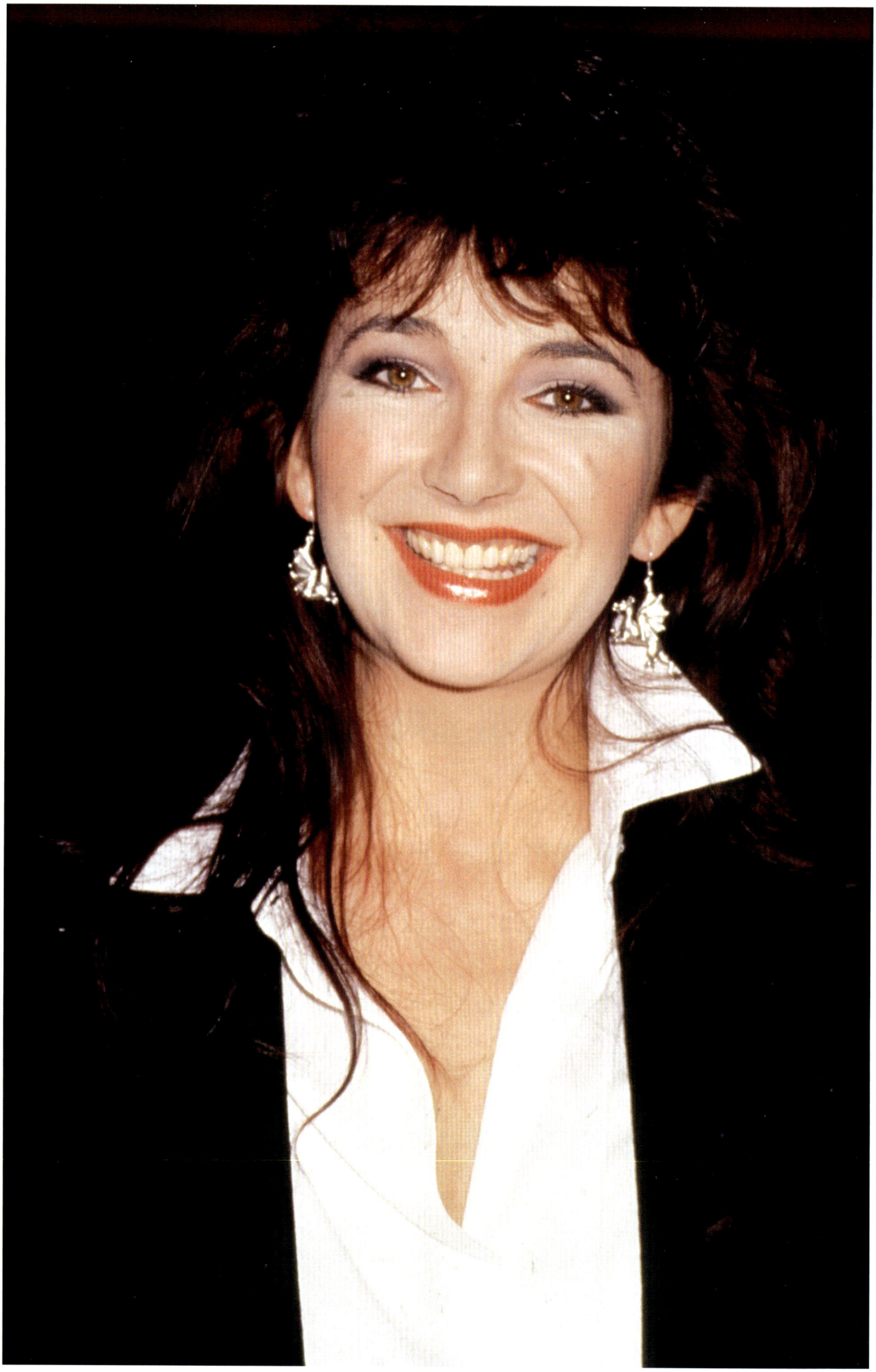

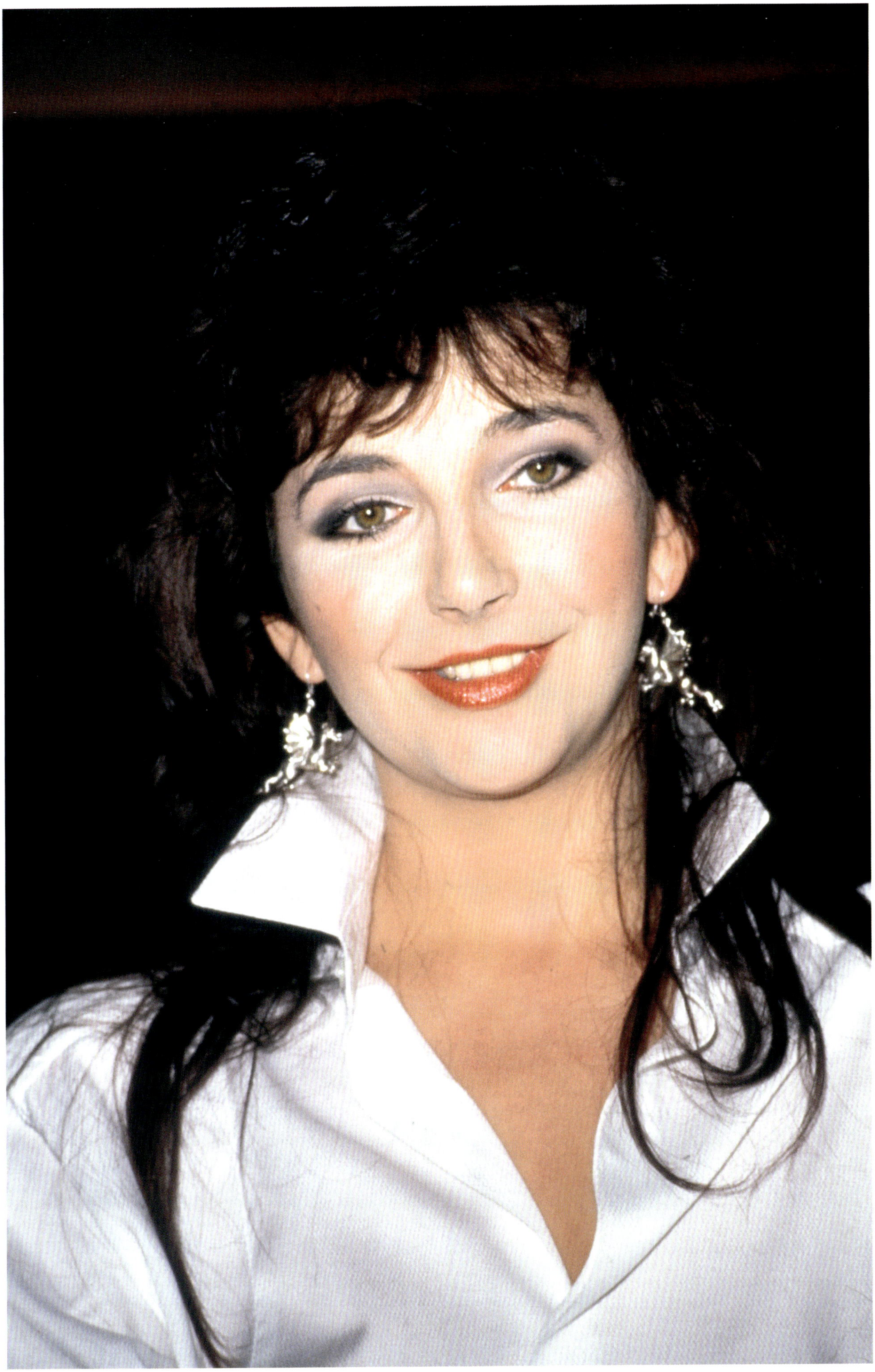

Lenny Henry, Kate Bush and Dawn French launching Comic Relief merchandise, 23rd October 1986.

135

Kate arriving at The British Phonographic Industry award ceremony at The Grosvenor House, London, 9th February 1987.

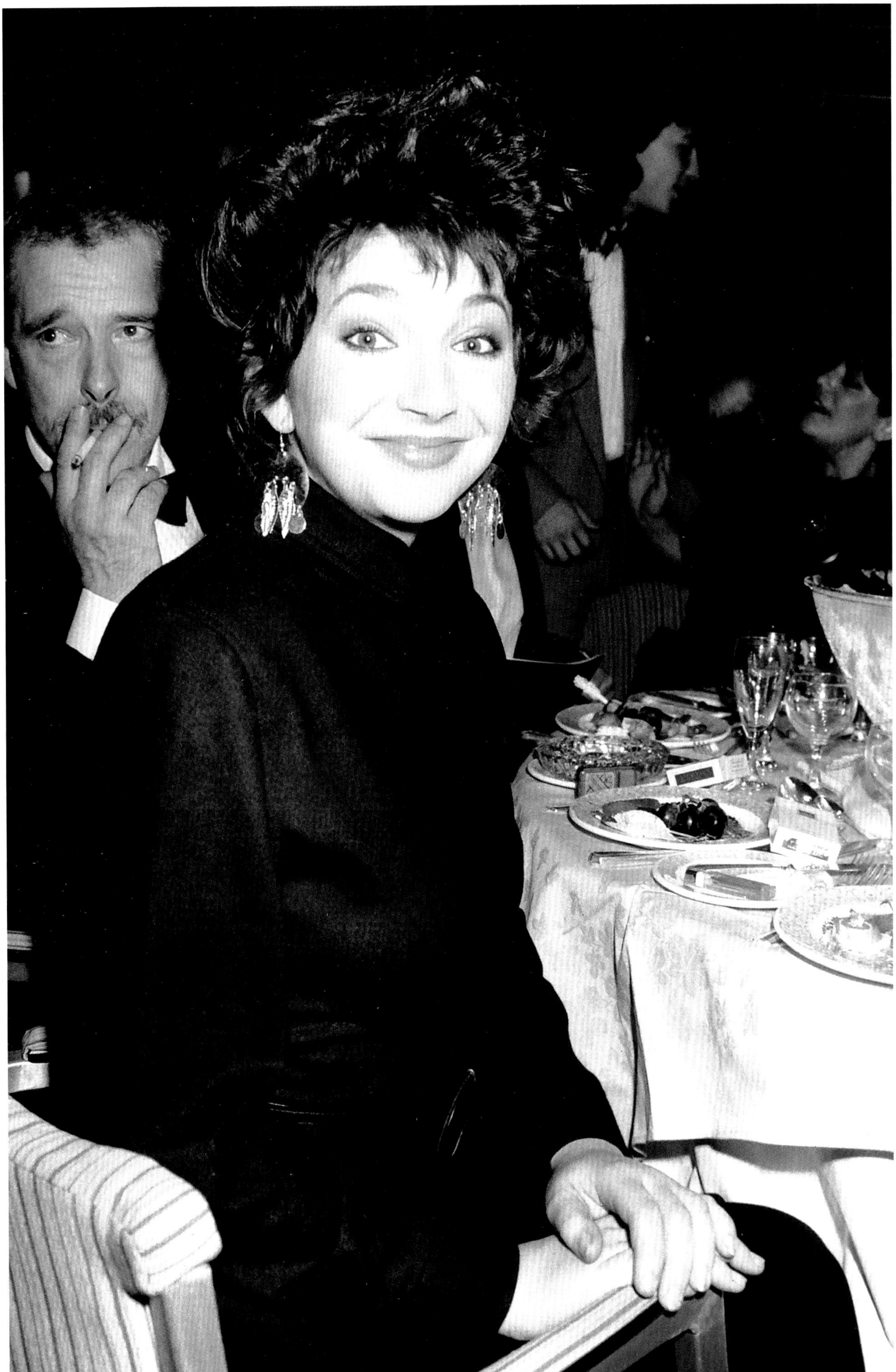

Kate with the other BPI award winners at The Grosvenor House, London, 9th February 1987.

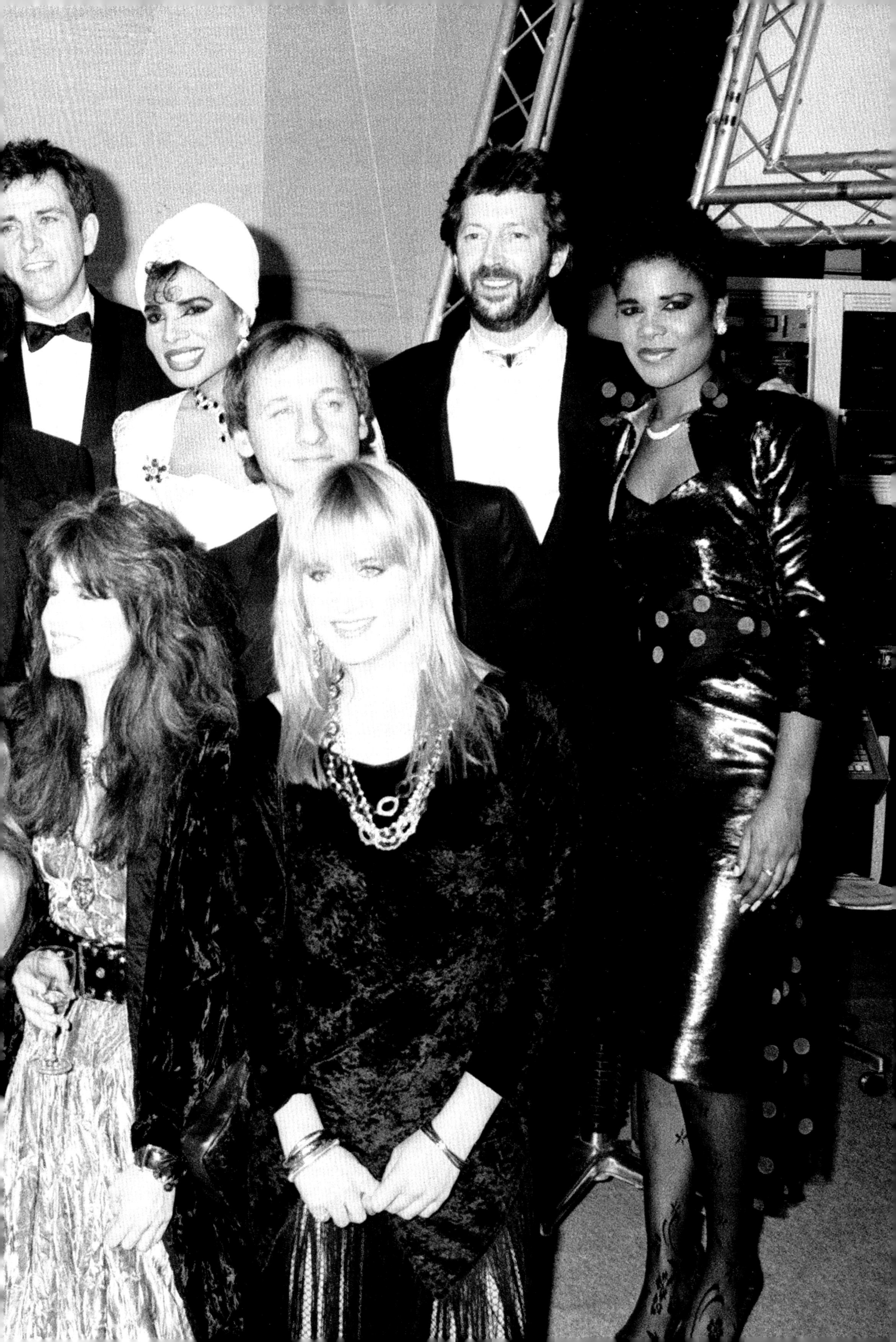

Kate cuts her 30th birthday cake at Blazers Boutique where she was participating in a chartity event called 'Shop Assistance' to benefit the Terrance Higgins Trust to help people living with HIV/AIDS.

Kate released *The Sensual World* in 1989. She once described it as "her most honest, personal album". The track, 'Heads We're Dancing', is characterised by Kate's quirky brand of black humour. It is about a woman who dances all night with a charming stranger, only to discover in the morning that he is Adolf Hitler. She said of the song at the time; "I wrote the song two years ago, and in lots of ways I wouldn't write a song like it now. I'd really hate it if people were offended by this... Hitler was very attractive to women because he was such a powerful figure, yet such an evil guy. I'd hate to feel I was glorifying the situation, but I do know that whereas in a piece of film it would be quite acceptable, in a song it's a little bit sensitive."

The Sensual World got to number two in the UK. It went on to become Kate's biggest-selling album in the US, where it was awarded an RIAA gold certification four years after its release for selling 500,000 copies.

The first single released from the album was the title track, which peaked at number twelve in the UK. Kate took inspiration for it from James Joyce's 1922 novel, *Ulysses*. The song is about the character, Molly Bloom, who steps out of the black and white, two-dimensional pages of the novel, and into the real world, and is immediately struck by the sensuality of it all. Kate's original idea was for the character's speech that features at the end of the novel to be set to music. Unable to secure the rights from the Joyce estate though, Kate had to alter her original idea (only in 2011 would the Joyce estate grant license to the material, upon which Kate rerecorded the song as 'Flower Of The Mountain', which features on her album, *Director's Cut*).

The music video made to accompany the single release of 'The Sensual World' features Kate dancing through an enchanted forest in a medieval dress. She co-directed it with Peter Richardson, whose career as a member of the comedy team, *The Comic Strip*, had been going strong throughout the decade.

The second single released from *The Sensual World* was 'This Woman's Work'. It got to number twenty-five in the UK. Prior to this, Kate's song was originally featured on the soundtrack to the John Hughes film, *She's Having A Baby* (1988). A slightly remixed version features on Kate's 1989 release of the song.

In early 1990, 'Love And Anger' was the third and final single to be released from *The Sensual World*. Featuring David Gilmour on guitar, it got to number thirty-eight in the UK. Also in that year, the boxset, *This Woman's Work: Anthology 1978–*

Promotional photo for *The Red Shoes* album, 1993.

1990, was released. Including all of Kate's albums with their original cover art, it also came with two discs of all her singles' B-sides that had been recorded from 1978 onwards.

Also in 1990, Kate starred in the black comedy film, *Les Dogs*, produced by *The Comic Strip*. She played the role of the bride, Angela.

In 1991, Kate released a cover of Elton John's 'Rocket Man'. It got to number twelve in the UK and to number two in Australia. She had recorded the song for her contribution to *Two Rooms: Celebrating The Songs Of Elton John & Bernie Taupin*. On the B-side of the single was another cover of an Elton John song, 'Candle In The Wind'.

November 1993 saw the release of Kate's seventh studio album, *The Red Shoes*. Providing her with her highest album chart position in the US, it got to number twenty-eight there. The only single from the album to chart there though was 'Rubberband Girl', which peaked at number eighty-eight in January 1994.

In the UK, *The Red Shoes* peaked at number two, whilst the singles from the album – 'Rubberband Girl', the title track, 'Moments Of Pleasure', and 'And So Is Love' all hit within the top thirty. It was during this period of her career that Kate directed and starred in the short film, *The Line, The Cross And The Curve*. It featured music from *The Red Shoes*, which itself was inspired by the 1948 film of the same name. Kate's film was released on VHS in the UK in 1994. Globally, it was also given a small number of cinema screenings.

Kate's initial plan had been to tour with *The Red Shoes* release but it didn't come to fruition in such way. For the album, she deliberately produced her tracks live, using less of the studio production methods that had typified her earlier albums (and would have been too difficult to re-create on stage). Due to this, *The Red Shoes* emerged to be a polarising album for much of her fan base, with many who had enjoyed the intricacy of her earlier compositions, disappointed in the new direction. On the other side of the fence, other fans enthused of how on *The Red Shoes*, they appreciated the complexities in the lyrics and the emotions expressed therein.

Kate told *Rolling Stone* in 1994; "Albums are like diaries. You go through phases, technically and emotionally, and they reflect the state that you're in at the time." And clearly, *The Red Shoes* is a very different piece of work to *The Kick Inside* or even, say, *Hounds Of Love*. It is understandable as to how many fans have their favourites, as well as the titles that they're perhaps not so keen on.

During the period surrounding *The Red Shoes*, Kate suffered

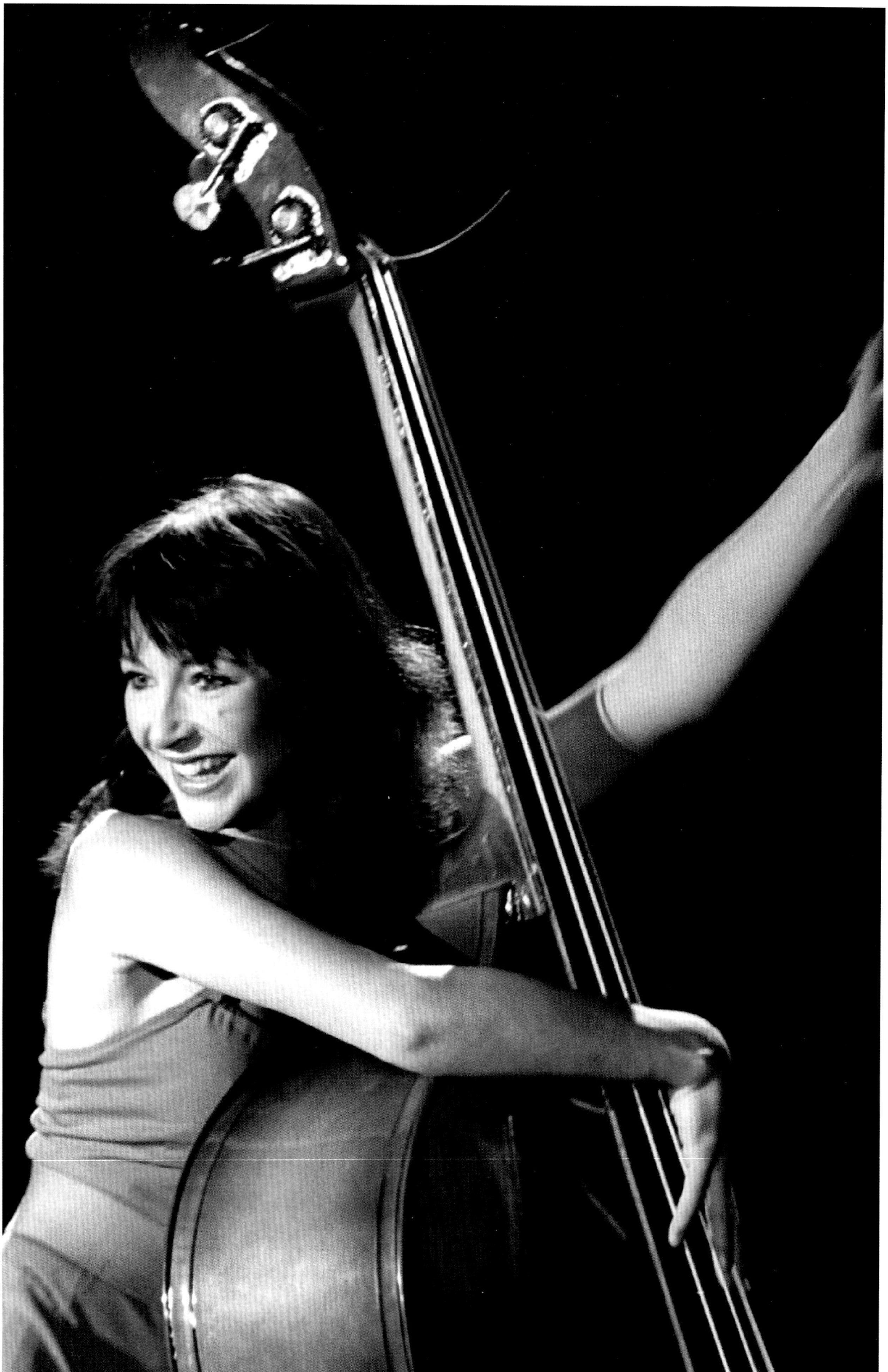

a number of bereavements, including the loss of guitarist Alan Murphy. He had started working with her for the 1979 tour. Also, Kate lost her mother Hannah, to whom she was close. In the ballad, 'Moments Of Pleasure', Kate pays tribute to those lost. It should be noted though that Hannah was still alive when the song was written and recorded: Kate recalled playing the song to her.

Although a hiatus was on the horizon, it would certainly be flawed to say that Kate had met all of her goals as an artist by this point in her career. She told *Q* magazine in 1993; "I don't think of myself as a musician. As a writer, I suppose. I only ever play the piano to accompany myself singing. I could never sit and read a piece of music. At best, I'm an accompanist. I suppose the worst thing is frustration at your own ability. Not being able to do what you want to do."

However, Kate had evidently reached the point of being able to reject projects where she didn't feel she would be a good match for them, as was the case with Erasure, where upon being invited to produce for them, she declined. Band member Vince Clarke recalled; "she didn't feel that that was her area."

Following the release of *The Red Shoes*, Kate dropped out of the public eye. Initially, she had only intended to take a year off. Although she would continue to work on new material, a total of twelve years would pass before her next album release.

Of course, she didn't go into hiding entirely, despite what some of the media may have had fans believe. In 1994, she covered George Gershwin's 'The Man I Love' for the tribute album, *The Glory Of Gershwin*. In 1996, she contributed a version of 'Mná Na hÉireann' (Irish for 'Women Of Ireland') for the Anglo-Irish folk-rock compilation project *Common Ground: Voices Of Modern Irish Music*. In having to sing the song in Irish, she learned to do so phonetically.

Also in 1990, Del Palmer had engineered and mixed a song that Kate had contributed vocals to, 'Wouldn't Change A Thing'. It was penned by Lionel Azulay, who had played drums with the original band (Company) that later became the KT Bush Band. The song wouldn't see an official release until 2008, when it came out online as part of Azulay's album, *Out Of The Ashes*. Azulay said; "The now legendary and hugely all round nice person Kate Bush kindly lent her unique and wonderful voice to one of my songs."

With many fans hungry for more, Kate's name occasionally cropped up in the media with rumours of a new album release. The press often referred to her as something of an eccentric recluse, so much so that one critic compared her to Miss

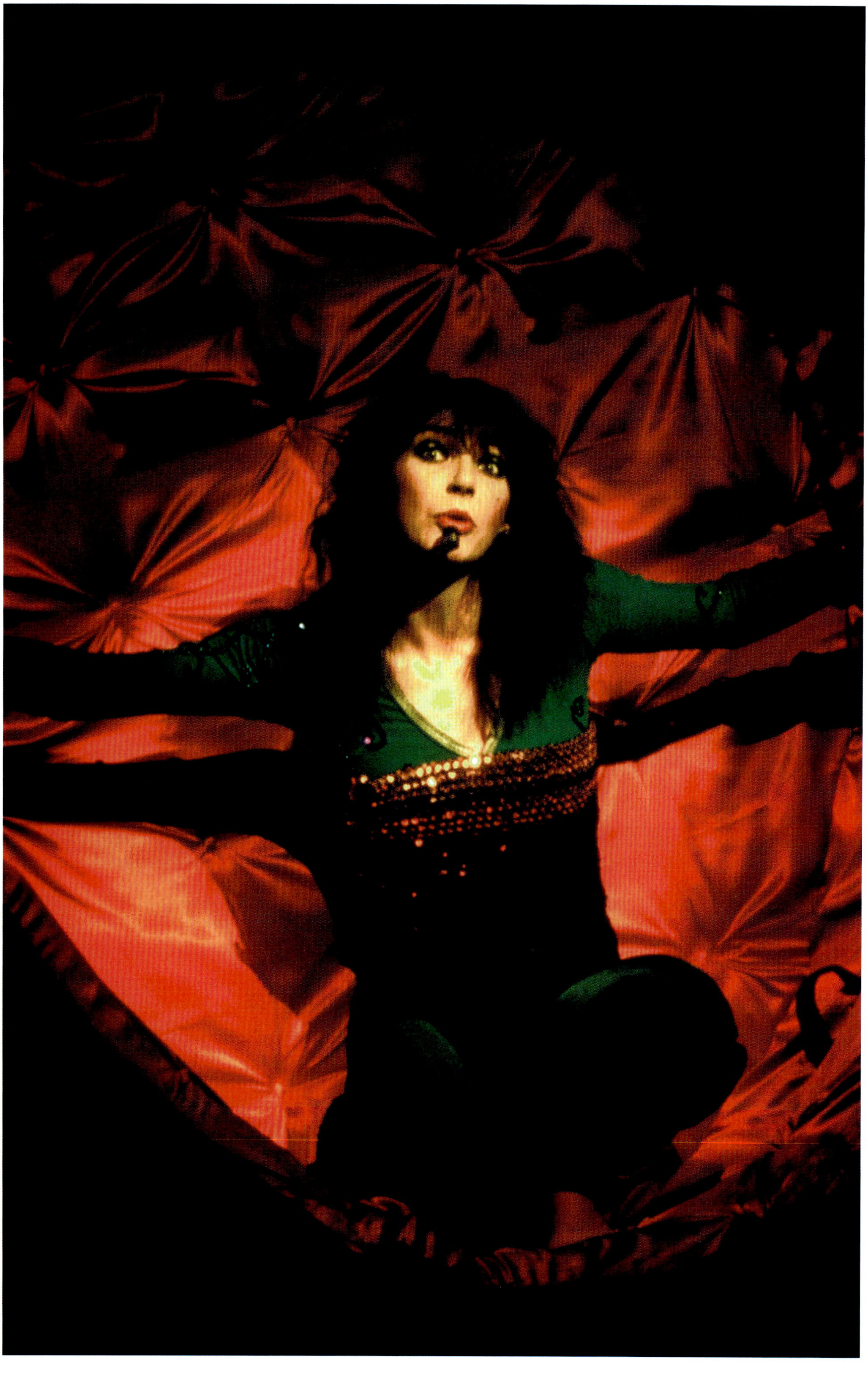

At Heathrow Airport, having just returned from Amsterdam, 10th March 1979.

Domestic goddess

Hem of anorak, hair of doormat... Kate Bush can't stop singing about her home. It's a delight to drop by, says Alexis Petridis

Kate Bush
Aerial
★★★★★

(EMI) £14.99

These days, record companies try to make every new album seem like a matter of unparalleled cultural import. The most inconsequential artists require confidentiality agreements to be faxed to journalists, the lowliest release must be delivered by hand. So it's hard not to be impressed by an album that carries a genuine sense of occasion. That's not to say EMI – which earlier this year transformed the ostensibly simple process of handing critics the Coldplay album into something resembling a particularly Byzantine episode of Spooks – haven't really pushed the boat out for Kate Bush's return after a 12-year absence. They employed a security man specifically for the purpose of staring at you while you listened to her new album. But even without his disconcerting presence, Aerial would seem like an event.

In the gap since 1993's so-so The Red Shoes, the Kate Bush myth that began cause a lot of door slamming and shouts of "oh-God-mum-you're-so-*embarrassing*" when Bertie reaches the less luvv-er-ly age of 15, but it's still delightful.

The second CD is devoted to a concept piece called A Sky of Honey in which virtually nothing happens, albeit very beautifully, with delicious string arrangements, hymnal piano chords, joyous choruses and bursts of flamenco guitar: the sun comes up, birds sing, Bush watches a pavement artist at work, it rains, Bush has a moonlight swim and watches the sun come up again. The pavement artist is played by Rolf Harris. This casting demonstrates Bush's admirable disregard for accepted notions of cool, but it's tough on anyone who grew up watching him daubing away on Rolf's Cartoon Club. "A little bit lighter there, maybe with some accents," he mutters. You keep expecting him to ask if you can guess what it is yet.

Domestic contentment even gets into the staple Bush topic of sex. Ever since her debut, The Kick Inside, with its lyrics about incest and "sticky love", Bush has given good filth: striking, often disturbing songs that, excitingly, suggest a wildly inventive approach to having it off. Here, on the lovely and moving piano ballad

Havisham from Charles Dickens' 1860 novel, *Great Expectations*. Ironic really, considering that so much of Kate's work had also taken inspiration from literature!

With more time and space to focus on her personal life whilst on a break from the public eye, in 1998 – with guitarist Dan McIntosh, who she had met in 1992 – Kate gave birth to a son, Albert (known as Bertie). Her achievements had certainly not been forgotten whilst she was on hiatus. In 2001, she was awarded a Q Award for Classic Songwriter, and in 2002, she was awarded an Ivor Novello Award for Outstanding Contribution to Music. When she performed 'Comfortably Numb' with David Gilmour at the Royal Festival Hall in London that year, it was her first professional public appearance in quite a while.

November 2005 saw the release of Kate's eighth studio album, *Aerial*. Owing to the popularity of both mediums at the time, it was released as a double CD and also on vinyl. The album's single, 'King Of The Mountain', had been premiered on BBC Radio Two, two months prior to that (which certainly succeeded to generate excitement for a new Kate Bush album – the single entered the UK Downloads Chart at number six, and would become Kate's third-highest-charting single ever in the UK, peaking at number four on the main chart). *Aerial* also did well, entering the UK albums chart at number three, and, in the US, at number forty-eight. It went platinum in Canada for 100,000 copies sold. *Aerial* earned Kate two nominations at the 2006 BRIT Awards; one for Best British Female Solo Artist and the other for Best British Album.

As with *Hounds Of Love*, *Aerial* is split into two sections, each with its own theme and mood. The first disc subtitled A Sea Of Honey, features an eclectic set of songs that are thematically unrelated. It includes 'King Of The Mountain', 'Bertie' (a Renaissance-style ode to Kate's son), and 'Joanni', which is based on the story of Joan of Arc. In the song 'π', Kate sings 117 digits of the number pi. The second disc, subtitled A Sky Of Honey, features one continuous piece of music that describes the experience of twenty-four hours as a passage of time.

On having been away from making albums for a while by that point, Kate said; "I wanted to give as much time as I could to my son. I love being with him, he's a lovely little boy and he won't be little for very long. I felt my work could wait, whereas his growing up couldn't."

Reviews were generally positive, with fans and critics alike glad to have some new Kate Bush songs to enjoy. For many, *Aerial* was a breath of fresh air, inspired by the life that

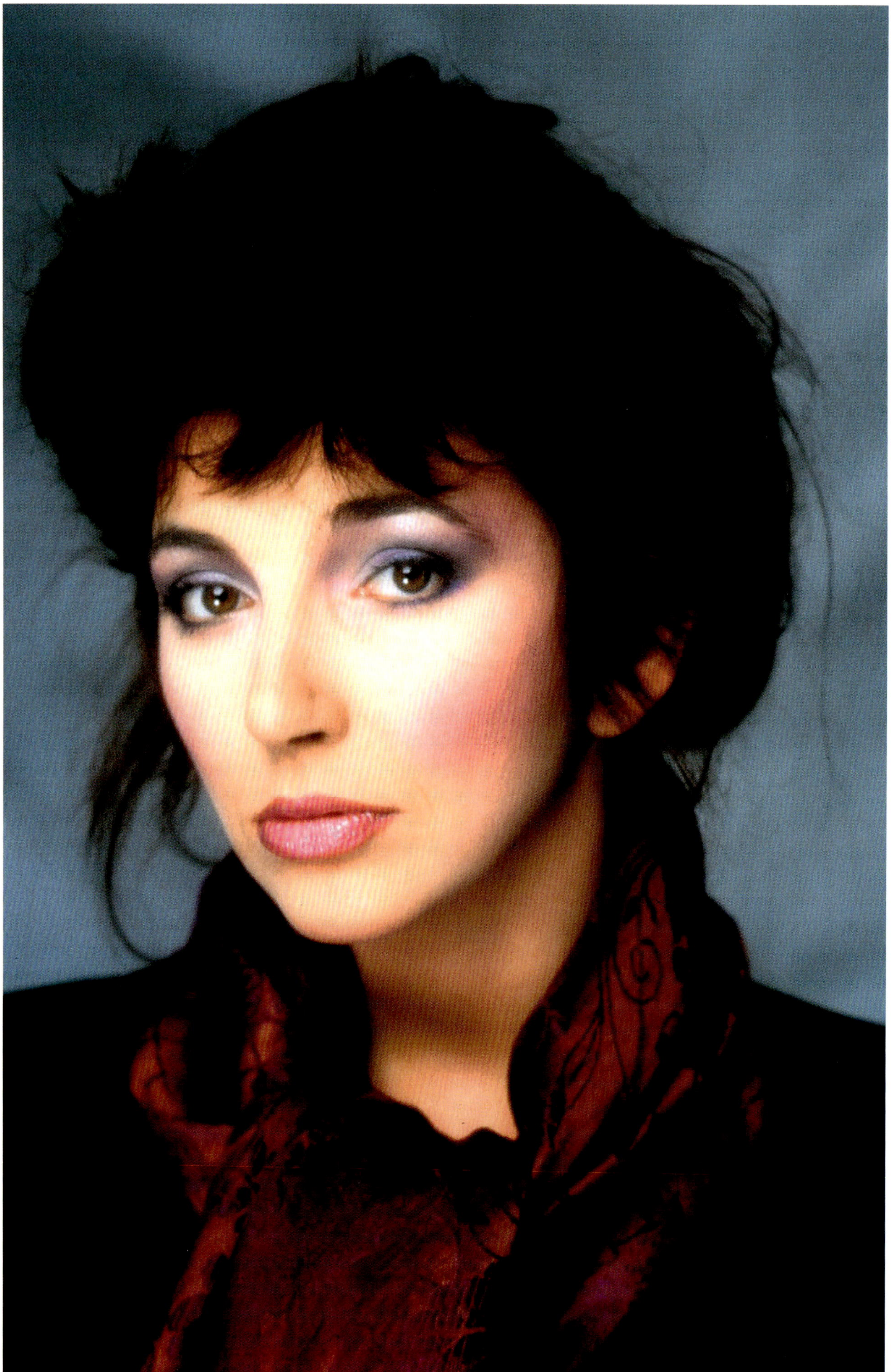

Kate had built for herself away from the limelight. As *Stylus Magazine* opined; "*Aerial* was a triumph, a towering dual masterpiece arriving like a huge galleon into the shallow pool of enforced worthiness and happiness which defined that era's pop. It sought to give new life to dead souls – whether Elvis or her own mother or even the number pi – and found that renewed life in young Bertie."

In 2007, Bush was invited to compose a song for *The Golden Compass* soundtrack in reference to the lead character, Lyra Belacqua. The resulting song, 'Lyra', which got to number 187 in the UK singles chart, was used in the closing credits of the film. The International Press Academy nominated 'Lyra' for a Satellite Award for best original song in a motion picture. According to Del Palmer, Bush had been asked to compose the song on such short notice that she completed the project in just ten days.

In May 2011, Kate released the album, *Director's Cut*, which debuted at number two in the UK. It consists of eleven reworked tracks from *The Sensual World* and *The Red Shoes* and was recorded via the use of analogue (rather than digital) equipment. Each of the tracks were given new lead vocals, drums, and instrumentation. As part of such process, some of them were transposed to a lower key to accommodate Kate's vocal range at the point of recording. Three of the songs, including 'This Woman's Work', were rerecorded entirely, with different lyrics to the original pieces often used in places. Kate described *Director's Cut* as a new project rather than as a collection of remixes. It was the first to be put out on her new label, Fish People, through EMI Records. As well as being released on a single CD format, *Director's Cut* was also released as part of a boxset containing other albums: *The Sensual World* and (the analogue re-mastered version of) *The Red Shoes*.

Kate's next studio album, *50 Words For Snow*, was released in November 2011. Featuring seven new songs "set against a backdrop of falling snow", the music is built around Bush's quietly jazzy piano and American session veteran Steve Gadd's drums, set to the use of both sung and spoken word vocals in what *Classic Rock* considered to be a "supple and experimental affair, with a contemporary chamber pop sound grounded in crisp piano, minimal percussion and light-touch electronics" with "billowing jazz-rock soundscapes, interwoven with fragmentary narratives delivered in a range of voices from shrill to Laurie Anderson-style cooing". Bassist Danny Thompson – who had previously played on *The Dreaming*, *Hounds Of Love* and *Director's Cut* – appears on the album, which also features a performance from actor, TV presenter and author Stephen

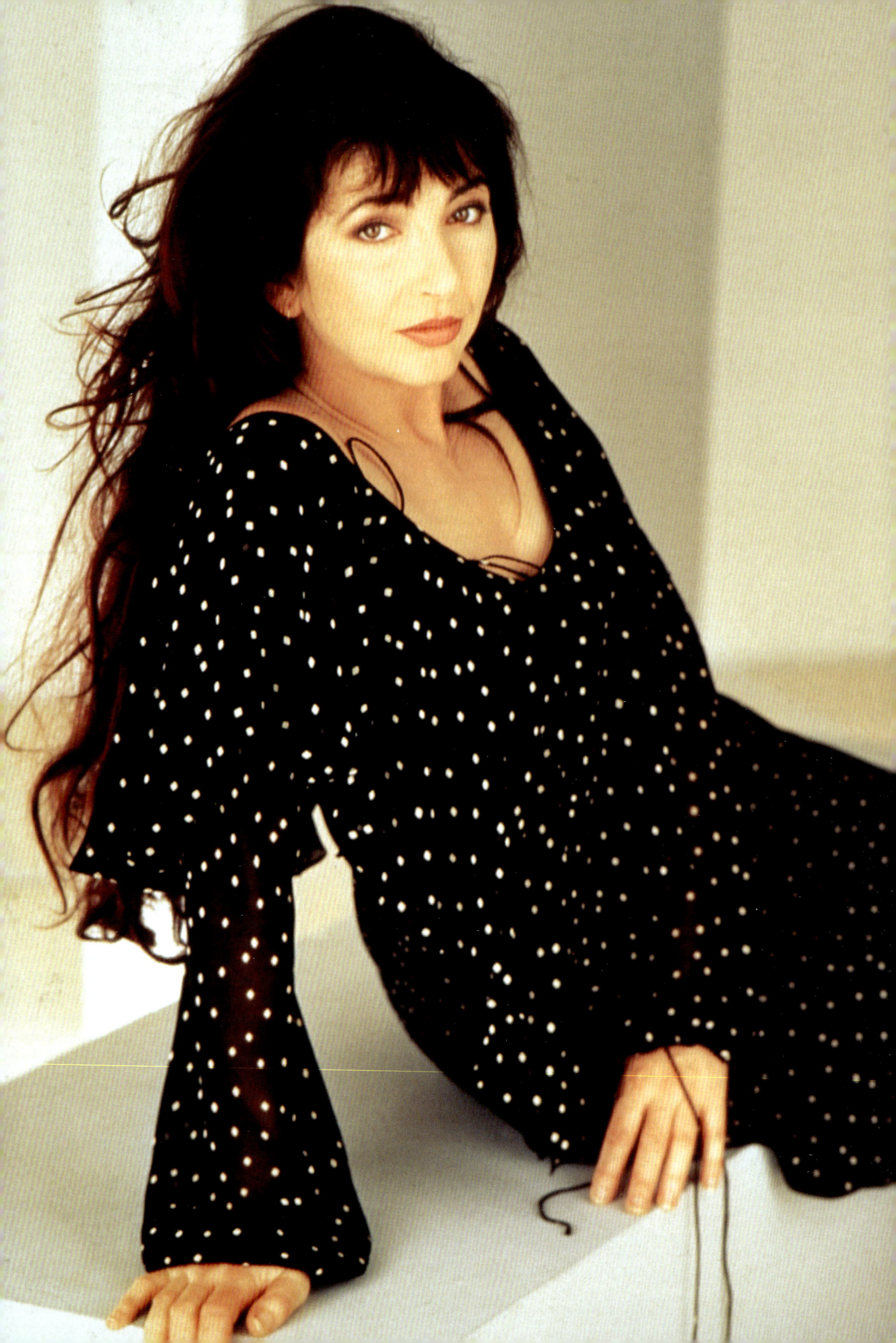

Fry reciting the fifty words for snow. It features a high-profile cameo appearance from Elton John on the duet, 'Snowed In At Wheeler Street'.

Kate said of the album; "I think it's really magical stuff. It's a very unusual, evocative substance and I had really great fun making this record because I love snow... It's not really a conceptual piece; it's more that the songs are loosely held together with this thread of snow... This has been quite an easy record to make actually and it's been quite a quick process. And it's been a lot of fun to make because the process was uninterrupted. What was really nice for me was I did it straight off the back of *Director's Cut*, which was a really intense record to make. When I finished it I went straight into making this so I was very much still in that focused space; still in that kind of studio mentality. And also there was a sense of elation that suddenly I was working from scratch and writing songs from scratch and the freedom that comes with that."

Generally, *50 Words For Snow* was welcomed positively by music critics. The album resulted in Kate's nomination for a BRIT Award for Best Female Artist. The album also won the 2012 Best Album at the South Bank Arts Awards, and received a nomination for Best Album at the Ivor Novello Awards.

In 2012, Kate turned down an invitation to perform at the Summer Olympics closing ceremony. Instead, a new remix of her 1985 single, 'Running Up That Hill', was played.

In March 2014, Kate announced the news that many had been waiting for decades to hear — that of a series of live concerts. Before The Dawn would be a twenty-two-night residency at London's Hammersmith Apollo, spanning 26th August to 1st October. Within just fifteen minutes of the announcement, all tickets had sold out.

News of Before The Dawn prompted a surge of interest in Kate Bush. As the story was covered by many music websites, radio stations and newspapers, Kate's own website crashed due to the high web traffic. The vocalist was said to be "completely overwhelmed by the response to the shows", and that she was "looking forward to seeing you all later this year". In the week leading up to the show's debut, *The New York Times* ran an article documenting the journey of some of Kate's fans who were travelling from around the world to be there.

Boosted by the publicity surrounding Before The Dawn, Kate became the first female performer to have eight albums in the UK top forty chart simultaneously. The only artists to have achieved something similar previously were Elvis Presley (who had twelve entries in the top forty following his passing in 1977) and the Beatles (who had eleven in 2009). Bearing

Kate arrives at the Park Lane Hotel, Mayfair, London, 29th October 2001 for the *Q Magazine* annual music awards.

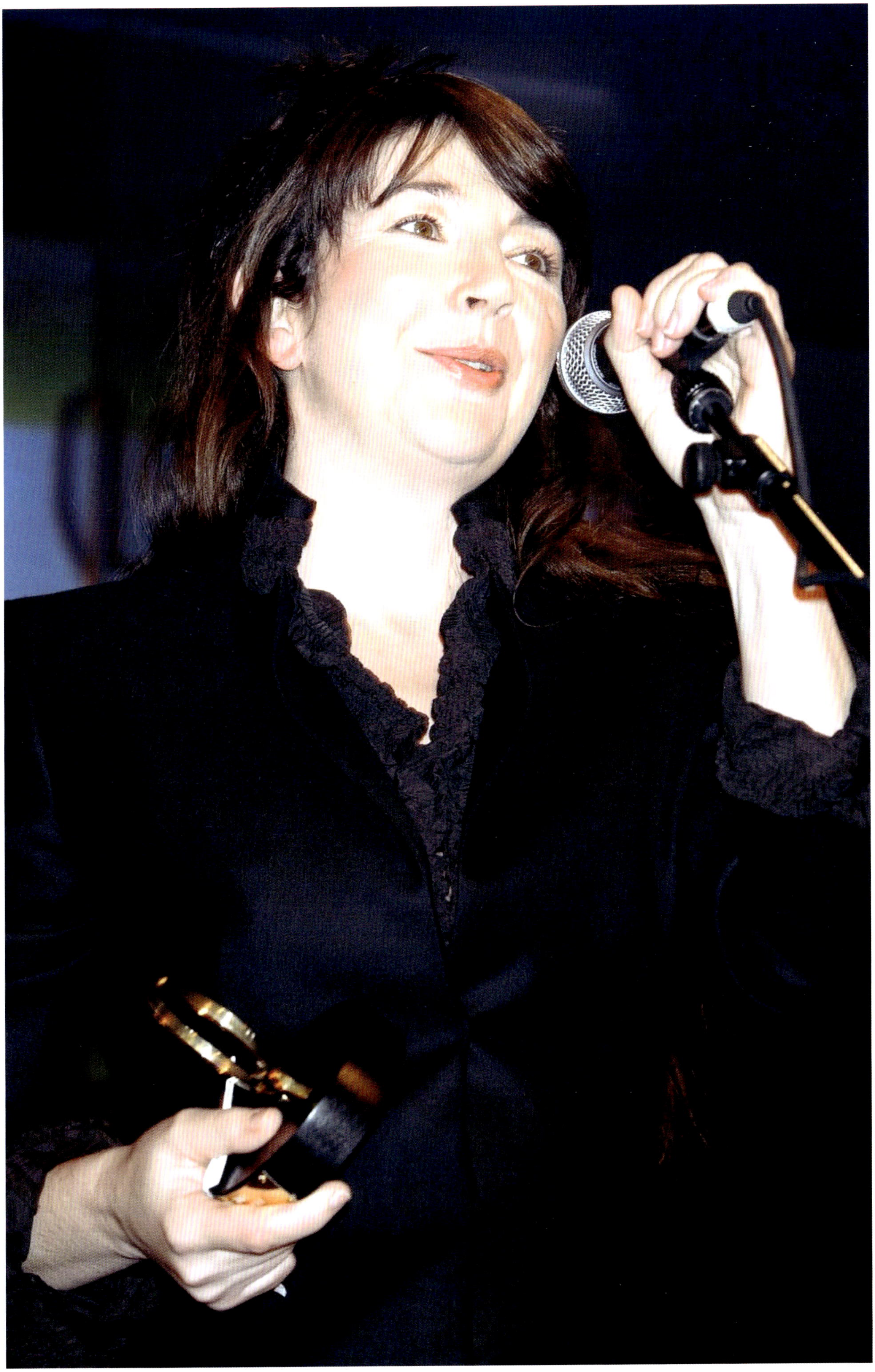

Royal Music Day Reception - Buckingham Palace,
1st March 2005.

the top fifty in mind, Kate had eleven albums in that at the time of her phenomenal success with the top forty. Notably, *The Whole Story* and *Hounds Of Love* were the highest charting during this period, at numbers six and nine respectively.

For the setlist, Before The Dawn consisted of most of the songs from *Hounds Of Love* (the entire The Ninth Wave suite was included), and songs from *Aerial* (including the entire A Sky Of Honey suite), two songs from *The Red Shoes*, and one from *50 Words For Snow*. Bush's first four albums – as well as *The Sensual World* – were noticeably excluded from the setlist (although a recording of 'Never Be Mine' – from earlier rehearsals – features on the CD and LP releases).

With the exception of 'Running Up That Hill', which Kate had previously performed live in 1987 with David Gilmour as part of The Secret Policeman's Third Ball, all of the songs were given their live debut.

THE ༄ FELLOWSHIP
presents

BEFORE THE DAWN
2014

AT LONDON'S EVENTIM APOLLO, HAMMERSMITH

AUGUST: TUESDAY, 26TH • WEDNESDAY, 27TH • FRIDAY, 29TH • SATURDAY, 30TH • **SEPTEMBER:** TUESDAY, 2ND • WEDNESDAY, 3RD • FRIDAY, 5TH • SATURDAY, 6TH • TUESDAY, 9TH • WEDNESDAY, 10TH • FRIDAY, 12TH • SATURDAY, 13TH • TUESDAY, 16TH • WEDNESDAY, 17TH • FRIDAY, 19TH • SATURDAY, 20TH • TUESDAY, 23RD • WEDNESDAY, 24TH • FRIDAY, 26TH • SATURDAY, 27TH • TUESDAY, 30TH • **OCTOBER:** WEDNESDAY, 1ST

Act One

Lily
Hounds Of Love
Joanni
Top Of The City
Running Up That Hill (A Deal With God) (extended)
King Of The Mountain (extended)
The Ninth Wave:
Video Interlude – Astronomer's Call (spoken monologue)
And Dream Of Sheep
Under Ice
Waking The Witch
Watching Them Without Her (dialogue)
Watching You Without Me
Little Light
Jig Of Life
Hello Earth
The Morning Fog

Act Two

A Sky Of Honey:
Prelude
Prologue (extended)
An Architect's Dream
The Painter's Link
Sunset
Aerial Tal
Somewhere In Between (extended)
Tawny Moon (performed by Albert McIntosh)
Nocturn (extended)
Aerial

Encore

Among Angels
Cloudbusting

FREE MUSIC FOR 60 DAYS!
Q
COMEBACKS OF THE YEAR
THREE SPECIAL COVERS!
APHEX TWIN
BACK AFTER 13 YEARS. EXCLUSIVE INTERVIEW!
U2 SPEAK
THAT ALBUM... THE INSIDE STORY
ALT-J
ART-ROCK'S NEW HEROES!
HER REMARKABLE TRIU
KATE BUSH
THEN AND NOW: A 22-PAGE CELEBRATION

FREE MUSIC FOR 60 DAYS!
Q
SPECIAL LIMITED EDITION
EXCLUSIVE TO TESCO
The Triumph Of
KATE BUSH
BEFORE THE DAWN: LIVE
A 22-PAGE CELEBRATION
Plus TWO SOUVENIR POSTERS
U2 SPEAK
PRINCE RETURNS
ALSO INSIDE THIS MAGAZINE
BECK ROCKS FESTIVAL No6
Plus! THE MOST INFLUENTIAL MAN IN MODERN MUSIC STEPS OUT OF THE SHADOWS...

Daily Mail
MONEY MAIL
STARTS PAGE 36
WEDNESDAY, AUGUST 27, 2014
www.dailymail.co.uk
60p
Kate Bush makes triumphant return – after 35 years
JAN MOIR'S VERDICT
PAGE THREE

As was the case with Kate's 1979 tour, Before The Dawn was presented as a multi-media performance. It included — as well as standard rock music performance — dancers, puppets, shadows, maskwork, conceptual staging, 3D animation, and an illusionist. Dialogue written by David Mitchell was also featured. To film the scenes that were played during the performance, Kate spent three days in a flotation tank. The video and projection design was by Jon Driscoll.

Also involved in the production were Adrian Noble (former artistic director and chief executive of the Royal Shakespeare Company), costume designer Brigitte Reiffenstuel, lighting designer Mark Henderson, and Italian Shadows Theatre company Controluce Teatro d'Ombre. The illusionist was Paul Kieve, the puppeteer Basil Twist, the movement director Sian Williams, and the designer Dick Bird.

Bush's son, Bertie, performed in the show as a backing vocalist and actor. He was also credited as creative advisor. Also participating, keyboard player Kevin McAlea had previously contributed to Kate's 1979 tour.

Parts of the show contained a narrative based on the song-suites, The Ninth Wave and A Sky Of Honey.

During The Ninth Wave, Kate's character is lost at sea after her ship, the Celtic Deep, sinks. Fading in and out of consciousness, sometimes underwater and sometimes above, she can only hope to be rescued. With only a flickering red light to make her visible in the darkness, she has an almost out-of-body experience, observing herself as though under ice. She sees her family without her, and imagines entering Earth's atmosphere until she is found. Surviving this gives her character a new-found appreciation of love and life. During A Sky Of Honey, Bush portrayed a bird-like woman, observing the actions of a nineteenth-century painter and a wooden puppet.

Describing the excitement surrounding the opening night, the *Los Angeles Times* considered; "Until Tuesday night, the English singer Kate Bush hadn't performed a concert in thirty-five years. To say that the Brits, and the world of Bush fans, were excited is an understatement. To read the pre-concert coverage, it's as though Bush had not merely decided to perform again after so long, but that she'd been resurrected to do so."

The Guardian gave the show five stars out of five, regarding it as "another remarkable achievement" and saying of Kate, "for someone who's spent the vast majority of her career shunning the stage, she's a hugely engaging live performer". Grateful for the performance, the reviewer elaborated; "Over the course of nearly three hours, Kate Bush's first gig for thirty-five years variously features dancers in lifejackets attacking the stage with axes and chainsaws; a giant machine that hovers above the auditorium, belching out dry ice and shining spotlights on the audience; giant paper aeroplanes; a surprisingly lengthy rumination on sausages, vast billowing sheets manipulated to represent waves, Bush's sixteen-year-old son Bertie – clad as a nineteenth-century artist – telling a wooden mannequin to 'piss off' and the singer herself being borne through the audience by dancers clad in costumes based on fish skeletons. The concert-goer who desires a stripped-down rock and roll experience, devoid of theatrical folderol, is thus advised that Before The Dawn is probably not the show for them, but it is perhaps worth noting that even before Bush takes the stage with her dancers and props, a curious sense of unreality hangs over the crowd. It's an atmosphere noticeably different than at any other concert, but then again, this is a gig unlike any other, and not merely because the very idea of Bush returning to live performance was pretty unimaginable twelve months ago."

The Evening Standard also awarded the opening show five stars out of five, referring to what was an "extraordinary mix of magical ideas, stunning visuals, attention to detail and remarkable music" and that it was "so obviously, so unambiguously brilliant" that it "made last night something to tell the grandchildren about".

The Independent opined that the performance was "just what everyone was hoping for" and "quite stunning, undoubtedly the most ambitious, and genuinely moving, piece of theatrical pop ever seen on a British stage". It also stated that "the long wait felt worth it", elaborating on the surreal nature of the performance of The Ninth Wave section; "Two seahorses then climb out of the audience – no, really – and abduct the real Kate, leaving her backing singers (now rescuers) assailing the stage with axes and chainsaws in an attempt to rescue her from beneath the "ice". When they pull her up, she's berated by a priest before sinking back."

The Daily Express considered of the eccentric nature of the show; "It would be easy to laugh just like it's always been easy to laugh: some of it is daft, some of it wilfully daft but that's what makes English eccentricity so cherished." It also applauded Kate for her brave choice of setlist in terms of how she chose to omit many fan favourites: "By the end, she has done not one single song from that last concert. That means no 'Wuthering Heights', no 'Man With The Child In His Eyes', no 'Wow'. Unbelievable! It takes a brave woman. The whole show takes a brave woman. Kate Bush is that woman. And then she flies."

Billboard described the joyous and supportive reaction from the audience; "The fifty-six-year-old British singer was met with a rapturous reception as she playfully marched on stage, dressed all in black, bare foot and leading a small procession of backing vocalists that included her teenage son Bertie. The standing ovation that followed opening song 'Lily', taken from her 1993 album *The Red Shoes*, would turn out to be the first of many throughout the show, which, in keeping with Bush's experimental back catalogue, was divided into three distinct parts, each one containing a mixture of the sublime, ridiculous and unique... Bush has long talked about her desire to stage The Ninth Wave in its entirety and its execution didn't disappoint. With the stage transformed into the remnants of a shipwreck, audiences were treated to an elaborate mix of music, puppetry, theatre, film, dance, mime, comedy and special effects that culminated in the singer being carried aloft into the crowd by a series of menacing-looking sea creatures. Remarkably, the entire audience appeared to obey Bush's earlier request not to take photos or use their phones throughout the show with a respectful, if slightly eerie silence filling the venue during the set's quieter, more intimate moments. On stage, Bush appeared to be enjoying herself hugely, displaying none of the nerves or apprehension you would expect of someone who hadn't performed live in over three decades. 'Thank you so much for such a warm and positive response,' she told the crowd after her umpteenth standing ovation of the night."

With the exception of a few negative ones (and some dissatisfied punters who wanted a greatest hits show), reviews of the performances were generally positive. An album of recordings from them was released in November 2016.

Kate wrote for the album's liner notes: "It was an extraordinary experience putting the show together. It was a huge amount of work, a lot of fun and an enormous privilege to work with such an incredibly talented team. This is the audio document. I hope that this can stand alone as a piece of music in its own right and that it can be enjoyed by people who knew nothing about the shows as well as those who were there. I never expected the overwhelming response of the audiences, every night filling the show with life and excitement. They are there in every beat of the recorded music. Even when you can't hear them, you can feel them. Nothing at all has been re-recorded or overdubbed on this live album, just two or three sound effects added to help with the atmosphere."

"On the first disc the track, 'Never Be Mine', is the only take that exists, and was recorded when the show was being filmed without an audience. It was cut because the show was too long but is now back in its original position. Everything else runs as was, with only a few edits to help the flow of the music. On stage, the main feature of The Ninth Wave was a woman lost at sea, floating in the water, projected onto a large oval screen – the idea being that this pre-recorded film was reality. The lead vocals for these sequences were sung live at the time of filming in a deep water tank at Pinewood. A lot of research went into how to mic this vocal. As far as we know it had never been done before. I hoped that the vocals would sound more realistic and emotive by being sung in this difficult environment. (You can see the boom mic in the photo on the back of the booklet. This had to be painted out of every shot in post-production although very little of the boom mic recording was used. The main mic was on the life jacket disguised as an inflator tube!) The rest of the lead vocals on this disc were sung live on stage as part of the dream sequences. The only way to make this story work as an audio piece was to present it more like a radio play and subdue the applause until the last track when the story is over and we are all back in the theatre again with the audience response."

"Unlike The Ninth Wave which was about the struggle to stay alive in a dark, terrifying ocean, A Sky Of Honey is about the passing of a summer's day. The original idea behind this piece was to explore the connection between birdsong and light, and why the light triggers the birds to sing. It begins with a lovely afternoon in golden sunlight, surrounded by birdsong. As night falls, the music slowly builds until the break of dawn. This show was one of the most exciting things I've ever been involved in. Thank you to everyone who made it happen and who embraced the process of allowing it to continually evolve."

In December 2018, Kate published her first book. Titled *How To Be Invisible*, it features a compilation of lyrics. In November 2018, she released two boxsets of remasters of her studio albums. Vocals that had originally been provided by Rolf Harris on the *Aerial* album, who was convicted of multiple sexual assault charges in 2014, were replaced by versions from Bertie. In March 2019, *The Other Sides* – a compilation of rare tracks, cover versions and remixes from the boxsets – was released. It includes the previously unreleased track 'Humming', which was recorded in 1975. September 2019 saw the release of – in France – 'Ne t'enfuis pas'/'Un baiser d'enfant' on vinyl as a limited-edition promotional single.

Throughout her phenomenal career, not only has Kate achieved an incredible amount through her solo projects, but she has also contributed to the works of many other artists.

She provided vocals for Peter Gabriel on the songs, 'Games

Without Frontiers', 'Don't Give Up' and 'No Self-Control' (when Gabriel appeared on Bush's 1979 television special, they sang a duet of Roy Harper's 'Another Day'). Kate sung on two Roy Harper tracks; 'You', which features on his 1980 album, *The Unknown Soldier*; and 'Once', the title track of his 1990 album. She has also sung on the title song of the 1986 Big Country album, *The Seer*; the Midge Ure song 'Sister And Brother' from his 1988 album, *Answers To Nothing*; Go West's 1987 single, 'The King Is Dead'; and several songs with Prince – 'Why Should I Love You?' (for her 1993 album *The Red Shoes*) and vocals on his 1996 album, *Emancipation*.

In 1987, Kate sang a verse on the Beatles cover charity single, 'Let It Be', by Ferry Aid. The single was released following the Zeebrugge Disaster whereby on 6th March, the ferry MS Herald of Free Enterprise capsized, killing 193 passengers and crew. All proceeds from sales of the single were donated to the charity set up in response to the disaster. The recording of the single was organised by *The Sun* newspaper (they had sold discounted tickets for the ferry).

Journalist Garry Bushell (then with *The Sun* newspaper) organised the recording of the song. He recruited popular producers of the time, Stock, Aitken and Waterman for the job. The trio then put out an invitation to the music industry for artists to contribute to the song. Although many stars were initially reluctant to join forces with the newspaper, eventually a cast including Boy George, Gary Moore, Mark Knopfler, and of course, Kate Bush, agreed to participate. Original writer, Paul McCartney, who also contributed to the song, opted to record his part individually. It later emerged that he had provided the original recording of his voice that features on the original 1970 Beatles song. The song for Ferry Aid was recorded over three days over 14th to 16th March. The single was released just days later on the 24th.

In 1989, Kate sang a line on the charity single, 'Spirit Of The Forest'. The single, written by Gentlemen Without Weapons, was released in June and launched by Richard Branson with the Earth Love Fund (ELF) Rainforest Appeal in conjunction with the United Nations Environment Programme. The single was a double A-side, with the big music names of the day performing on each. All proceeds from the record were donated to programmes dedicated to saving the rainforests of the world. Three recording sessions took place – in Los Angeles, London and New York. The aim was to get as many stars involved as possible. Kate participated in the London session, as did, among others, David Gilmour, Ringo Starr, Jon Anderson, XTC, Fish, Chris Rea and Kim Wilde.

As well as contributing vocals and keyboards, Kate produced a song for Alan Stivell. Titled 'Kimiad', it features on his 1993 album, *Again*. Stivell had appeared as a guest musician on *The Sensual World* on the tracks, 'The Fog' and 'Between A Man And A Woman'.

In late May 2022, 'Running Up That Hill' once again graced the UK and US charts (iTunes and Spotify) in response to it being featured on the Netflix series, *Stranger Things*. In June, it got to number one on the main UK chart and in doing so, resulted in Kate breaking three records: 1) it overtook Wham!'s 'Last Christmas' for reaching the number one spot after the longest time following its original release, 2) it beat its previous chart position and 3) it saw Kate, at sixty-three years old, become the oldest woman to reach number one with a solo hit (the previous record-holder was Cher, who was fifty-two when she had a hit with 'Believe').

A star in her own right and having worked with many icons – Elton John, Eric Clapton, Jeff Beck, David Gilmour, Nigel Kennedy, Gary Brooker, Danny Thompson, and Prince, to name just a few – Kate Bush ranks right up there as one of the most relevant and influential artists of the twentieth century and indeed, beyond. With her unique, ethereal and endearing sound, it would be an easy bet to say that her music will remain strong in the public consciousness – and indeed her many fans – for a long time to come.

****

billboard
GLOBAL 200

	SONG	ARTIST
1	Running Up That Hill (A Deal With God)	Kate Bush
2	As It Was	Harry Styles
3	Me Porto Bonito	Bad Bunny & Chencho Corleone
4	Tití Me Preguntó	Bad Bunny
5	Ojitos Lindos	Bad Bunny & Bomba Estéreo
6	About Damn Time	Lizzo
7	I Like You (A Happier Song)	Post Malone ft. Doja Cat
8	Moscow Mule	Bad Bunny
9	Provenza	Karol G
10	First Class	Jack Harlow

Discography

Studio Albums

The Kick Inside (1978)
Lionheart (1978)
Never For Ever (1980)
The Dreaming (1982)
Hounds Of Love (1985)
The Sensual World (1989)
The Red Shoes (1993)
Aerial (2005)
Director's Cut (2011)
50 Words For Snow (2011)

Live Albums

Live at Hammersmith Odeon (1994)
Before The Dawn (2016)

Compilation Albums

The Whole Story (1986)
The Other Sides (2019)

168

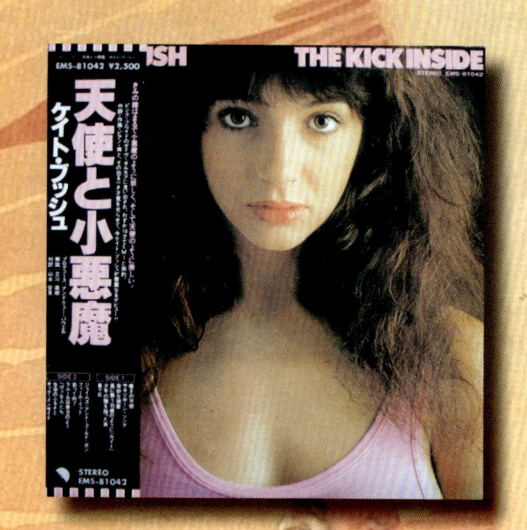

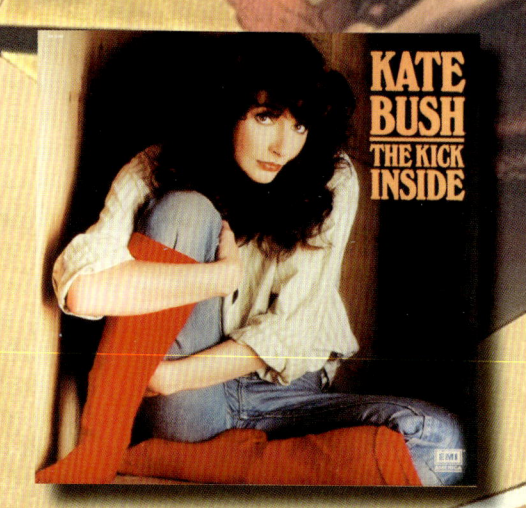

The Kick Inside

Side One
1. Moving (3:01)
2. The Saxophone Song (3:51)
3. Strange Phenomena (2:57)
4. Kite (2:56)
5. The Man With The Child In His Eyes (2:39)
6. Wuthering Heights (4:28)

Side Two
7. James And The Cold Gun (3:34)
8. Feel It (3:02)
9. Oh To Be In Love (3:18)
10. L'Amour Looks Something Like You (2:27)
11. Them Heavy People (3:04)
12. Room For The Life (4:03)
13. The Kick Inside (3:30)

Debenham's rock

KATE BUSH
'Lionheart'
(EMI EMA 787)**

HO HUM ho hum, so I'm in the same cell as purdy Ms. Bush this week. She won't speak to me. SOLITUDE. She sits astride the gawdy cover nothingness and stares at me expressionless. I love her and I hate her and you all feel exactly the same way, only you're too unreal to confess the terrible crime. Oh, but she's really awful, she's dire, she's inadvisable. She's uncool. Impasse and out.

Don't feel guilty 'cos I'm the same and that's why it's torture sitting here opposite her latest jumpy jittery delivery. Who's the father? Who cares. It's probably us all and therefore I think we should all take the new-born arms and limbs of credit and blame as BELONGING TO US. It's that simple, Mildred.

You have to take her seriously in spite of all the flying sneers and jeers. The songs on 'Lionheart' are constructed stiffly, but, I suppose, well, for all that. Tinkle, tinkle, bzzzz. 'Symphony In Blue' opens the gallery doors and we step ahead with furrowed brows and much biting of nails. The song sets a pattern of early 70's Regular Rock Music. Artists against the piss-artists with bells on. *"The more I think about sex/The better it gets,"* our lady hisses. *"Here we have a purpose in life,"* she assures us with an admirable lack of conviction. She's not Connie Francis yet, you know! Sickly Hampstead Garden Suburb shallowness. I live in Hampstead Garden Suburb. The cell. The cell. She coos 'Peter In Search Of Peter Pan' at me. Charmingly insipid, Jesus, it's a pity you couldn't wash yourself clean of your hot-house forced background, Ms. Bush. I'll help you if you like. Me and Joe Strummer. Maybe not. Sorry I suggested it.

'Wow' is a magnificent song and easily the best thing she's ever done. *"Wow wow wow wow..."* floats the chorus, a chorus so staggeringly strong and uplifting that even the gauche lyrics are for once totally swept to the corridors of your attention. She's young (they tell me, she could be 62 for all I know) and she'll doubtless stop writing songs that begin merrily with lines like *"We're all alone on the stage tonight."* She better! 'Wow' will be a No 1 hit single.

'Don't Push Your Foot On The Heartbrake', not as bad as the title suggests, features probably the most, ah, together sets of lines on the opus, lines reading, as in the singalong bit, *"Her heart is there but they've greased the road/Her heart is out there but she's no control."* Stick at it, young woman. There is hope. 'Oh England My Lionheart' is civilised 'Hurry Up Jeremy, Let's Go Down The Club' sweetness and petiteness. All tarted up with nowhere to sing about. Nowhere that's real at any rate. I have NEVER seen *"umbrellas flapping in the rain"*, nor have I been within farting distance of *"Shepherds who'll bring me home."* Shortcomings Inc. humbly apologise to all concerned.

By the second side you know what's going on. The songs themselves aren't individually strong at all. It's more the aura she creates. A series of hills of soft cushy warm melodies that are winning and dreadfully insidious. 'Fullhouse' and 'Hammer Horror' for example aren't yet in the Abba (swoon) class but they're nudging in that direction which is excellent news. Trouble is, songs such as 'In The Warm Room' and 'Coffee Homeground' seem to rely upon the Bushesque mystique which simply isn't there. She's wholesome, boys and don't you forget it! It's Shirley Temple on mandies and emotional mystique which will always get the chair and whip treatment in those circumstances.

Tawibly tawibly URBANE music that trickles around Debenham's on chilly Saturday afternoons. I know. She's looking at me again. But this is an album to be played at low volume. As a precaution. Or an admission. The purdy lady understands....

DAVE McCULLOUGH

Lionheart

Side One
1. Symphony In Blue (3:35)
2. In Search Of Peter Pan (3:46)
3. Wow (3:58)
4. Don't Push Your Foot On The Heartbrake (3:12)
5. Oh England My Lionheart (3:10)

Side Two
6. Fullhouse (3:14)
7. In The Warm Room (3:35)
8. Kashka From Baghdad (3:55)
9. Coffee Homeground (3:38)
10. Hammer Horror (4:39)

Never For Ever

Side One
1. Babooshka (3:20)
2. Delius (Song Of Summer) (2:51)
3. Blow Away (For Bill) (3:33)
4. All We Ever Look For (3:47)
5. Egypt (4:10)

Side Two
6. The Wedding List (4:15)
7. Violin (3:15)
8. The Infant Kiss (2:50)
9. Night Scented Stock (0:51)
10. Army Dreamers (2:55)
11. Breathing (5:29)

The Dreaming

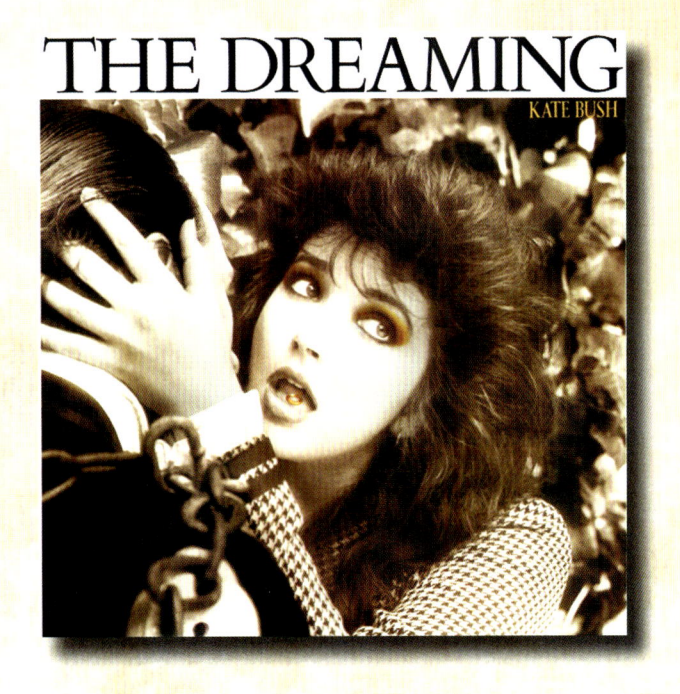

Side One
1. Sat In Your Lap (3:29)
2. There Goes A Tenner (3:24)
3. Pull Out The Pin (5:26)
4. Suspended In Gaffa (3:54)
5. Leave It Open (3:20)

Side Two
6. The Dreaming (4:41)
7. Night Of The Swallow (5:22)
8. All The Love (4:29)
9. Houdini (3:48)
10. Get Out Of My House (5:25)

174

Girl with stars in her eyes

KATE BUSH

HOUNDS OF LOVE
EMI

CRITICS, interviewers, cricket commentators, Russian spies and even, I suspect, a large proportion of her fiercely devoted following, seem consistently unable to explain the elusive appeal of Kate Bush. How can someone so charming and giggly and apparently straightforward get to write a song as complex and mystical as "The Dreaming"; or as blatantly sexual as "Breathing"; or as evocatively surreal as "Babooshka"?

The question is: is she ten years ahead of her time, or ten years behind it? Whatever... she's way out of sync with anything else that's going down right now — and that's probably not a bad thing. It's just a shame that because she's so eminently marketable her often radical experiments with percussive rhythms, startling melody lines, ambiguous lyrics and eccentric vocals haven't earned the credit they've deserved. Eurythmics for one have surely come under her influence.

This is her fifth album and, we are told, the second side of it — sub-titled "The Ninth Wave" — is a *concept*. I can hear the shudders from here. But then virtually everything Kate has ever done has seemed like a mini concept album... all those dramatic atmospherics and cinematic lyrics. She has as much in common with opera as she does with conventional pop music.

This said, I don't much care for "The Ninth Wave" as an idea. Full of hippy talk and religious theory, it purports to tell the story of someone skating on thin ice who promptly gets trapped beneath that ice with all the panic and psychological trauma such an experience would entail. But, of course, it's actually about much *more* than that as the tracks flow into a blurred metaphysical overview of the meaning of life, bringing in themes of magic, death, spiritual existence and — ultimately, on the jaunty closing track "The Morning Fog" — reincarnation.

However, it does include one brilliantly compelling extract, "Jig Of Life", which gives full, inspiring vent to her interest in traditional themes and her Irish background (with John Sheahan playing some blazing, earthy fiddle), and driven along by the magnificent uillean piper, Liam O'Flynn). But she makes huge demands on her listener and the theme is too confused and the execution too laborious and stilted to carry real weight us a complete entity.

Some of the central obsessions of "The Ninth Wave" also crop up on the other "non-concept" side. A deal with God, for example, is struck on "Running Up That Hill", the hit single which seems even more stirring as the opening track here. It's the most telling line on the album — *everyone* has made a deal with God sometime — and its exotic nature makes it instantly more arresting than the disconcerting admission of fear and faint hearts on "Hounds Of Love" or the faintly irritating whimsical meandering of "The Big Sky".

"Hounds Of Love" is, though, far and away the best track on the album... rich and colourful, it successfully overcomes the disco rhythms that otherwise tend to overbalance the album, and inspires Kate to a truly astonishing vocal performance. The biggest plus of the album is, in fact, her singing: she squawked and shrieked her way through "The Kick Inside" and "Lionheart" and even on "Never For Ever" (surely her greatest work) there were moments when hysteria got the better of her.

Here she has learned you can have control without sacrificing passion and it's the heavyweight rhythm department aided and abetted by some overly fussy arrangements that get the better of her. And a pox on the concept album.

COLIN IRWIN

Hounds Of Love

Hounds Of Love

Side One: Hounds Of Love
1. Running Up That Hill (A Deal With God) (5:03)
2. Hounds Of Love (3:02)
3. The Big Sky (4:41)
4. Mother Stands For Comfort (3:07)
5. Cloudbusting (5:10)

Side Two: The Ninth Wave
6. And Dream Of Sheep (2:45)
7. Under Ice (2:21)
8. Waking The Witch (4:18)
9. Watching You Without Me (4:06)
10. Jig Of Life (4:04)
11. Hello Earth (6:13)
12. The Morning Fog (2:34)

(Note: the original 1985 cassette release included the 12inch single version of 'Running Up That Hill (A Deal With God)' at the end of side one.)

The Whole Story

Side One
1. Wuthering Heights (New Vocal) (4:57)
2. Cloudbusting (5:09)
3. The Man With The Child In His Eyes (2:38)
4. Breathing (5:28)
5. Wow (3:46)
6. Hounds Of Love (3:02)

Side Two
7. Running Up That Hill (5:00)
8. Army Dreamers (3:13)
9. Sat In Your Lap (3:29)
10. Experiment IV (previously unreleased) (4:21)
11. The Dreaming (4:14)
12. Babooshka (3:29)

The Sensual World

Side One
1. The Sensual World (3:57)
2. Love And Anger (4:42)
3. The Fog (5:04)
4. Reaching Out (3:11)
5. Heads We're Dancing (5:17)

Side Two
6. Deeper Understanding (4:46)
7. Between A Man And A Woman (3:29)
8. Never Be Mine (3:43)
9. Rocket's Tail (4:06)
10. This Woman's Work (3:32)

The Red Shoes

Side One
1. Rubberband Girl (4:42)
2. And So Is Love (4:16)
3. Eat The Music (5:08)
4. Moments Of Pleasure (5:16)
5. The Song Of Solomon (4:27)
6. Lily (3:51)

Side Two
7. The Red Shoes (4:00)
8. Top Of The City (4:14)
9. Constellation Of The Heart (4:46)
10. Big Stripey Lie (3:32)
11. Why Should I Love You? (5:00)
12. You're The One (5:52)

Live At Hammersmith Odeon

1. Moving (3:32)
2. Them Heavy People (4:02)
3. Violin (3:33)
4. Strange Phenomena (3:26)
5. Hammer Horror (4:26)
6. Don't Push Your Foot On The Heartbrake (4:00)
7. Wow (4:00)
8. Feel It (3:14)
9. Kite (6:12)
10. James And The Cold Gun (8:44)
11. Oh England My Lionheart (3:23)
12. Wuthering Heights (4:50)

Aerial

Disc One: A Sea Of Honey
1. King Of The Mountain (4:53)
2. π (6:09)
3. Bertie (4:18)
4. Mrs. Bartolozzi (5:58)
5. How To Be Invisible (5:32)
6. Joanni (4:56)
7. A Coral Room (6:12)

Disc Two: A Sky Of Honey
8. Prelude (1:26)
9. Prologue (5:42)
10. An Architect's Dream (4:50)
11. The Painter's Link (1:35)
12. Sunset (5:58)
13. Aerial Tal (1:01)
14. Somewhere In Between (5:00)
15. Nocturn (8:34)
16. Aerial (7:52)

Director's Cut

1. Flower Of The Mountain (5:15)
2. Song Of Solomon (4:45)
3. Lily (4:05)
4. Deeper Understanding (6:33)
5. The Red Shoes (4:58)
6. This Woman's Work (6:30)
7. Moments Of Pleasure (6:32)
8. Never Be Mine (5:05)
9. Top Of The City (4:24)
10. And So Is Love (4:21)
11. Rubberband Girl (4:37)

50 Words For Snow

1. Snowflake (9:52)
2. Lake Tahoe (11:08)
3. Misty (13:32)
4. Wild Man (7:17)
5. Snowed In At Wheeler Street (8:05)
6. 50 Words For Snow (8:31)
7. Among Angels (6:49)

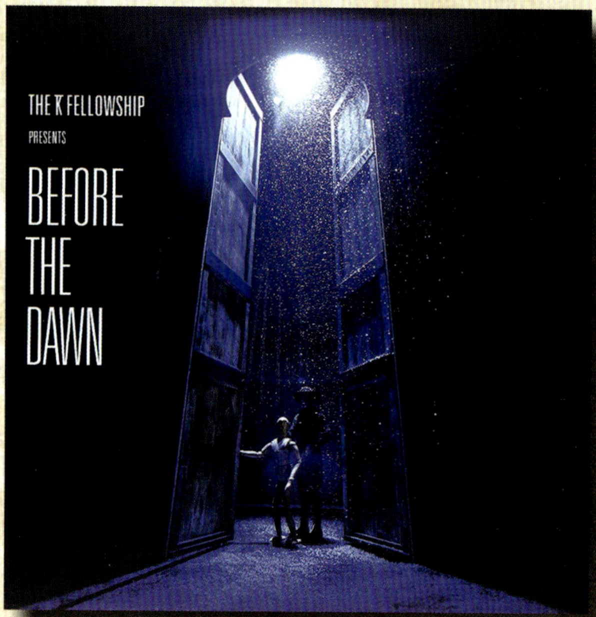
THE KT FELLOWSHIP
PRESENTS
BEFORE
THE
DAWN

Before The Dawn

Disc One: Act One
1. Lily (4:50)
2. Hounds Of Love (3:29)
3. Joanni (6:09)
4. Top Of The City (5:13)
5. Never Be Mine (5:57)
6. Running Up That Hill (A Deal With God) (5:39)
7. King Of The Mountain (8:08)

Disc Two: Act Two
8. Astronomer's Call (2:38)
(spoken monologue; writers: Kate Bush and David Mitchell)
9. And Dream Of Sheep (3:35)
10. Under Ice (2:59)
11. Waking The Witch (6:42)
12. Watching Them Without Her (2:01)
(dialogue; writers: Kate Bush and David Mitchell)
13. Watching You Without Me (4:25)
14. Little Light (2:04)
15. Jig Of Life (4:09) (performed and written by Kate Bush and John Carder Bush)
16. Hello Earth (8:00)
17. The Morning Fog (5:19)

Disc Three: Act Three
18. Prelude (1:53)
19. Prologue (10:12)
20. An Architect's Dream (5:19)
21. The Painter's Link (1:33)
22. Sunset (7:59)
23. Aerial Tal (1:29)
24. Somewhere In Between (7:01)
25. Tawny Moon (performed by Albert McIntosh) (6:10)
26. Nocturn (8:48)
27. Aerial (9:45)
28. Among Angels (5:50)
29. Cloudbusting (7:16)

Kate Bush
The Other Sides

The Other Sides

Disc One: 12" Mixes
  1. Running Up That Hill (A Deal With God) (5:49)
  2. The Big Sky (Meteorological Mix) (7:46)
  3. Cloudbusting (The Orgonon Mix) (6:33)
  4. Hounds Of Love (Alternative Mix) (3:49)
  5. Experiment IV (Extended Mix) (6:43)

Disc Two: The Other Side One
  1. Walk Straight Down The Middle (3:49)
  2. You Want Alchemy (4:21)
  3. Be Kind To My Mistakes (3:02)
  4. Lyra (3:18)
  5. Under The Ivy (2:10)
  6. Experiment IV (Video Mix) (4:49)
  7. Ne t'enfuis pas (2:34)
  8. Un baiser d'enfant (3:02)
  9. Burning Bridge (4:12)
  10. Running Up That Hill (A Deal With God) (2012 Remix) (5:34)

Disc Three: The Other Side Two
  1. Home For Christmas (1:47)
  2. One Last Look Around The House Before We Go (1:04)
  3. I'm Still Waiting (4:28)
  4. Warm And Soothing (2:44)
  5. Show A Little Devotion (4:18)
  6. Passing Through Air (2:04)
  7. Humming (recorded 1975, previously unreleased) (3:16)
  8. Ran Tan Waltz (2:47)
  9. December Will Be Magic Again (4:52)
  10. Wuthering Heights (New Vocal) (5:03)

Disc Four: In Others' Words
  1. Rocket Man (by Elton John and Bernie Taupin) (5:01)
  2. Sexual Healing (by Marvin Gaye and Odell Brown (5:55)
  3. Mna Na Heireann (traditional) (2:57)
  4. My Lagan Love (traditional) (2:30)
  5. The Man I Love (by George Gershwin and Ira Gershwin) (3:18)
  6. Brazil (Sam Lowry's First Dream) by (Ary Barroso and Bob Russell) (2:15)
  7. The Handsome Cabin Boy (traditional) (3:14)
  8. Lord Of The Reedy River (by Donovan) (2:42)
  9. Candle In The Wind (by Elton John and Bernie Taupin) (4:30)

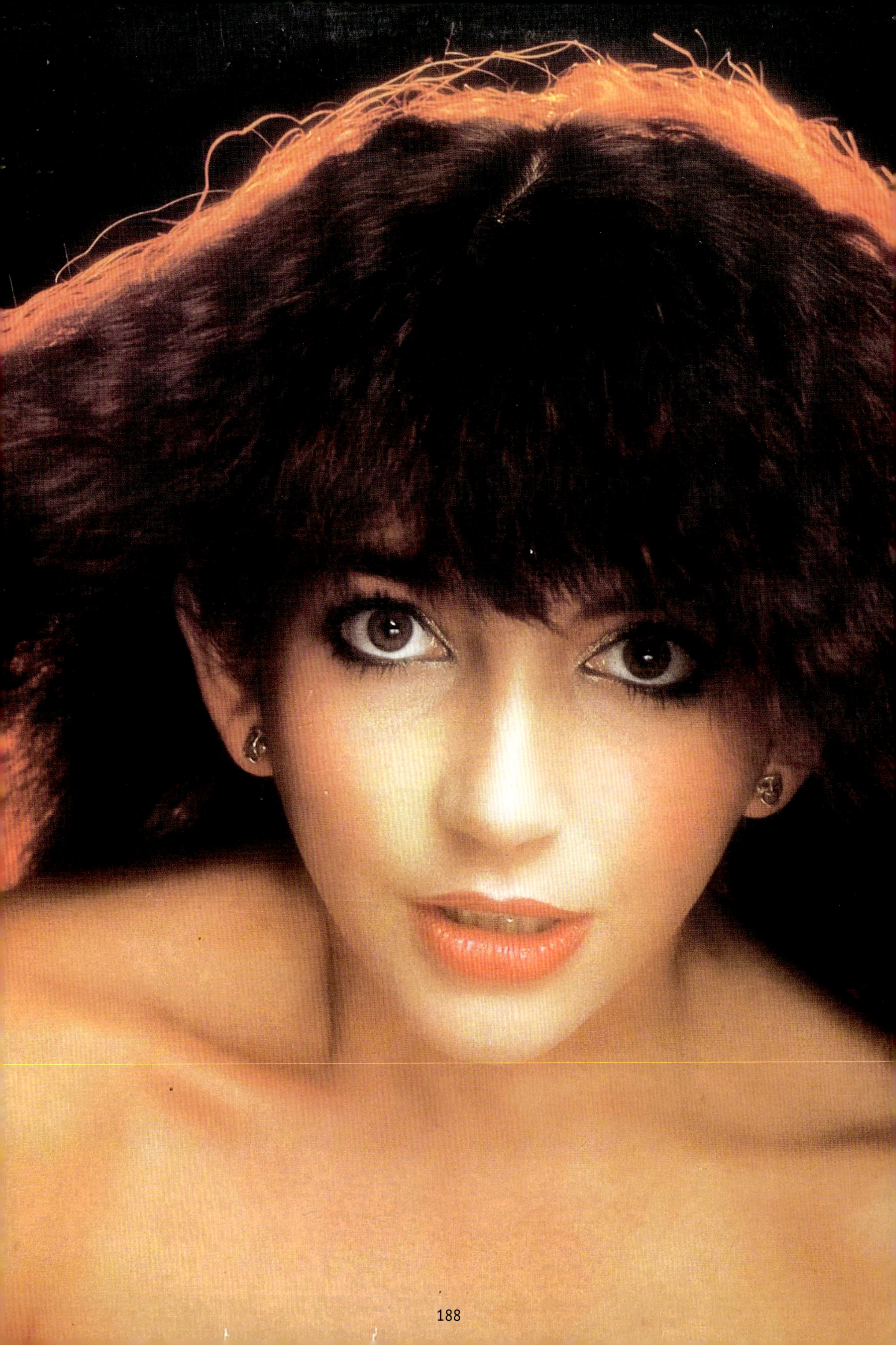

Other Contributions

Peter Gabriel (Peter Gabriel, Charisma, 1980) – 'Games Without Frontiers' and 'No Self Control' (backing vocals)

The Seer (Big Country, Mercury, 1986) – 'The Seer'

So (Peter Gabriel, Charisma, 1986) – 'Don't Give Up' (co-lead vocals)

Castaway (EMI, 1986) – 'Be Kind To My Mistakes'

Ferry Aid - 'Let It Be' (1987, CBS) (charity single)

'The King Is Dead' (Go West, Chrysalis, 1987) – (backing vocals)

The Secret Policeman's Third Ball – *The Music* (Virgin Records, 1987)
(charity concert for Amnesty International: 'Running Up That Hill' performed with David Gilmour; comedy song 'Do Bears...?' performed in duet with Rowan Atkinson)

Answers To Nothing (1988, Chrysalis) – 'Sister And Brother' (co-lead vocals with Midge Ure)

She's Having A Baby (I.R.S., 1988) – 'This Woman's Work'

The Comic Strip Presents...: 'GLC: The Carnage Continues...' (1990) – 'Ken', 'The Confrontation' and 'One Last Look Around The House Before We Go...'

Two Rooms: Celebrating The Songs Of Elton John & Bernie Taupin (Polydor, 1991) – 'Rocket Man (I Think It's Going To Be A Long Long Time)'

Brazil (Milan, 1992) – 'Sam Lowry's 1st Dream/Brazil'
(vocals with Michael Kamen and The National Philharmonic Orchestra of London)

Again (Sony Music, 1993) – 'Kimiad'
(keyboards and backing vocals with Alan Stivell)

The Glory Of Gershwin (1994, Mercury) – 'The Man I Love'
(vocals, with Larry Adler on harmonica)

Common Ground – Voices Of Modern Irish Music (EMI, 1996) – 'Mná Na hÉireann'

Emancipation (Prince, NPG/EMI, 1996) – 'My Computer' (backing vocals)

The Golden Compass (New Line, 2007) – 'Lyra'

A Symphony Of British Music (Decca, 2012) – 'Running Up That Hill (A Deal With God Remix)'

Tour Dates

1979

Monday 2nd April	Arts Centre, Poole (warm-up concert)
Tuesday 3rd April	Empire Theatre, Liverpool (opening night)
Wednesday 4th April	Hippodrome, Birmingham
Thursday 5th April	Hippodrome, Birmingham
Friday 6th April	New Theatre, Oxford
Saturday 7th April	Gaumont Theatre, Southampton
Monday 9th April	Hippodrome, Bristol
Tuesday 10th April	Apollo, Manchester
Wednesday 11th April	Apollo, Manchester
Thursday 12th April	Empire Theatre, Sunderland
Friday 13th April	Usher Hall, Edinburgh
Monday 16th April	Palladium, London
Tuesday 17th April	Palladium, London
Wednesday 18th April	Palladium, London
Thursday 19th April	Palladium, London
Friday 20th April	Palladium, London
Tuesday 24th April	Konserthuset, Stockholm, Sweden
Thursday 26th April	Falkoner Theatre, Copenhagen, Denmark
Saturday 28th April	Congress Centre, Hamburg, Germany
Sunday 29th April	Carré Theatre, Amsterdam, Netherlands
Wednesday 2nd May	Kongresszentrum Liederhalle, Stuttgart, Germany
Thursday 3rd May	Circus Krone, Munich, Germany
Friday 4th May	Gürzenich, Cologne, Germany
Sunday 6th May	Théâtre des Champs-Élysées, Paris, France
Tuesday 8th May	Mannheimer Rosengarten, Mannheim, Germany
Thursday 10th May	Jahrhunderthalle, Frankfurt, Germany
Saturday 12th May	Hammersmith Odeon, London (benefit concert with altered setlist)
Sunday 13th May	Hammersmith Odeon, London
Friday 14th May	Hammersmith Odeon, London

2014

Tuesday 26th August	Eventim Apollo, Hammersmith, London
Wednesday 27th August	Eventim Apollo, Hammersmith, London
Friday 29th August	Eventim Apollo, Hammersmith, London
Saturday 30th August	Eventim Apollo, Hammersmith, London
Tuesday 2nd September	Eventim Apollo, Hammersmith, London
Wednesday 3rd September	Eventim Apollo, Hammersmith, London
Friday 5th September	Eventim Apollo, Hammersmith, London
Saturday 6th September	Eventim Apollo, Hammersmith, London
Tuesday 9th September	Eventim Apollo, Hammersmith, London
Wednesday 10th September	Eventim Apollo, Hammersmith, London
Friday 12th September	Eventim Apollo, Hammersmith, London
Saturday 13th September	Eventim Apollo, Hammersmith, London
Tuesday 16th September	Eventim Apollo, Hammersmith, London
Wednesday 17th September	Eventim Apollo, Hammersmith, London
Friday 19th September	Eventim Apollo, Hammersmith, London
Saturday 20th September	Eventim Apollo, Hammersmith, London
Tuesday 23rd September	Eventim Apollo, Hammersmith, London
Wednesday 24th September	Eventim Apollo, Hammersmith, London
Friday 26th September	Eventim Apollo, Hammersmith, London
Saturday 27th September	Eventim Apollo, Hammersmith, London
Tuesday 30th September	Eventim Apollo, Hammersmith, London
Wednesday 1st October	Eventim Apollo, Hammersmith, London

About The Author

Laura Shenton MA LLCM DipRSL has been thinking about music since she first heard it, possibly whilst still in the womb. She has a Master's degree in 'Music Since 1900' from Liverpool Hope University. Her hobbies and interests include writing, playing the piano, staying up into the small hours wondering about life whilst eating crisps and obsessing about music, hamsters and dogs.